CALCUTTA UNDER FIRE

David Lockwood is an Associate Professor in modern history and a Visiting Research Fellow at the University of Adelaide. He is a specialist in the modern history and politics of India and in Soviet history. He is especially interested in the role of the bourgeoisie in historical development and in the concept of hegemony in the historical process. He combines this with work in the broad areas of the role of the state in economic development; the transition from state-controlled to market economies; and the effects of globalization on national states.

He has published a monograph on the bourgeois revolution in Russia and another on the evolution of the bourgeoisie in India, concentrating on its relationship with the state. His most recent book was on the role of the Communist Party of India in the Indian Emergency under Indira Gandhi.

CALCUTTA UNDER FIRE
The Second World War Years

David Lockwood

RUPA

Published by
Rupa Publications India Pvt. Ltd 2019
7/16, Ansari Road, Daryaganj
New Delhi 110002

Sales centres:
Allahabad Bengaluru Chennai
Hyderabad Jaipur Kathmandu
Kolkata Mumbai

Copyright © David Lockwood, 2019

The views and opinions expressed in this book are the author's own and the facts are as reported by him which have been verified to the extent possible, and the publishers are not in any way liable for the same.

All rights reserved.

No part of this publication may be reproduced, transmitted, or stored in a retrieval system, in any form or by any means, electronic, mechanical, photocopying, recording or otherwise, without the prior permission of the publisher.

ISBN: 978–93–5333–328–7

First impression 2019

10 9 8 7 6 5 4 3 2 1

Printed by Parksons Graphics Pvt., Ltd. Mumbai

This book is sold subject to the condition that it shall not, by way of trade or otherwise, be lent, resold, hired out, or otherwise circulated, without the publisher's prior consent, in any form of binding or cover other than that in which it is published.

CONTENTS

Introduction	vii
1. Well Done Calcutta!	1
2. Hegemony and Counter-Hegemony	28
3. 1942	56
4. The British	80
5. Congress and the War	118
6. The Foundations of Quit India	152
7. Quit India!	181
8. War on the Air	215
9. State Decay	251
Conclusion: Howrah Bridge	280
Further Reading	286
Index	288

INTRODUCTION

This book is about political strategy and warfare, mostly in Bengal and mostly in 1942. It concentrates on the Indian National Congress and the British colonial state. Their political strategies at this time were worked out under the shadow of what appeared to be an imminent invasion by the forces of Japan. This account will assess how those strategies evolved and what impact each had on the other. How would the British react to an invasion of Bengal and the surrounding areas? What would the Congress do in the face of possible British retreat and Japanese occupation?

In 1942, the citizens of Bengal expected a Japanese invasion of India, starting in their own province or perhaps in Assam or Orissa. The Japanese, after all, gave no indication of halting their victorious march through Southeast Asia at the Burmese border. On the other hand, they gave some indication that the territorial aspirations of the Great East Asia Co-Prosperity Sphere stretched to include northern India. By the middle of the year, the British colonial authorities believed that an invasion was likely. Given the recent debacle in Malaya, Singapore and Burma, they were distinctly pessimistic about the prospects of resisting it.

No such invasion took place. As we now know, the full-scale version was never really contemplated by the Japanese. But a study of official (public and private) discussions, military analyses, political statements and the general atmosphere in 1942 confirms that it was regarded as a very real—possibly inevitable and possibly unstoppable—threat.

The British relationship with India had become an increasingly knotty problem since the end of the Great War. Having taken some steps towards constitutional reform, the British attempted to freeze this process in place (indeed, in some ways, to reverse it) with the outbreak of hostilities in 1939. Discovering that this was not possible, since the nationalist movement considered the march to independence far more important than the march to war, they had to resort to repression in order to hold the line and mount a significant war effort. The threat of a Japanese invasion made that effort all the more vital. The basic British dilemma was this: successful resistance to the Japanese necessitated a mobilisation of the Indian population in favour of the war—but such a mobilisation required real steps towards India's freedom, which the British were not willing to take. The result was Indian apathy towards the war, leaving the British to contemplate, alone, the gloomy choice of fight or flight.

The Indian National Congress had followed a strategy of 'counter-hegemonic' advance since the 1920s (described in detail in Chapter Two). This moved between spectacular mass movements of civil disobedience and a quieter, subversive undermining of the British state. The strategy seemed to have reached its highpoint in the elections of Congress Provincial governments in 1937—but in fact, that experience produced as many problems as it did successes. When the Congress ministers resigned in 1939, the organization entered a somewhat directionless period. From then until 1942 Congress spent much of its time deciding on its policy towards the war and then adjusting that policy to accommodate the possibility of invasion. It seemed to be confronted with an impossible choice: either support British imperialism against the Japanese or oppose the war and prepare for new Japanese overlords. Opposition to Britain's war was strong but it tended to encourage an attitude of apathy towards the threatened Japanese aggression. During the first half of 1942, Gandhi broke out of the 'Britain or Japan?' dichotomy, advancing instead a strategy that continued to recognise Britain as the main enemy—and an enemy that could not defend India against Japan and would not let Indians take on the job. It undermined the colonial state by putting forward Congress as the real and only defender of India.

The book looks at political strategy through two prisms; that of the threatened Japanese invasion—and therefore the year 1942, in which fear of that invasion was at its height—and that of the province of Bengal, as a frontline province in Britain's war with Japan. It tries to show what various political actors in Bengal—the British authorities, the Congress, ordinary Indians and British civilians—believed they would do should a Japanese invasion occur. Naturally, accounts of this kind cannot (and should not) be too strictly delineated either chronologically or geographically. This one stretches backwards and forwards from 1942 and inside and outside the borders of Bengal. An understanding of Congress policy, for example, cannot start in 1942. An understanding of the previous two decades is necessary to comprehend what Congress' problem was in 1942 and the continuity between the Congress strategy and Gandhi's solution to that problem. At the same time, much British policy was all-India policy. While attempting to concentrate on how it affected frontline Bengal, it has also been necessary to follow its formulation in London and New Delhi and to consider its effects elsewhere in India.

There are clear absences in the account. I have not covered the Bengal famine, partly because it has been adequately dealt with by others and partly because it is generally reckoned to have gripped the province from 1943, the year following the bulk of this study. Readers will be able to detect signs of its approach, particularly in the effects of Britain's 'denial' policy in Bengal and the seriousness with which the alternative governments approached the problem of food supply during the Quit India campaign. I have also not devoted significant attention to communalism—except to illustrate that the Congress underestimated the seriousness of the problem (Gandhi, for example, believed that the problem would burn itself out in short order once the British withdrew). Undoubtedly, the Congress should have taken stock of the communal situation after the Quit India campaign, particularly the extent to which the British were profiting by it—but from their gaols this was difficult. Lastly, I have only considered the activities of Subhas Chandra Bose up to the end of 1942 and of the Indian National Army in its first version (that is, before Bose arrived in Southeast Asia). To move beyond this, to Bose in Singapore and Burma and to the INA Mark II, would have necessitated a lengthy diversion in both time and place.

1

WELL DONE CALCUTTA!

> The following morning we went off with the twins to Calcutta to see what damage was caused by the bombing. On our way we were met by the astonishing sight of a great exodus from Calcutta. Men, women and children, cars and lorries of all descriptions, donkeys, goats tethered to carts, parrots in cages on top of lorries, one solid mass of humanity were moving along the trunk road, all terrified out of their wits trying to reach a place of safety anywhere away from Calcutta. We continued on our way but apart from a small hole in the road in front of the Great Eastern hotel there was nothing much to see.
>
> —Eugenie Fraser, A Home by the Hooghly.[1]

December 20, 1942, was a Sunday. On that day, Calcutta's 'Oldest Nationalist Daily' (according to the masthead), the *Amrita Bazar Patrika*, reported that in Burma there was a possibility of 'the end of defensive warfare on this frontier [by the Allies] and the beginning of a war of attack.' Meanwhile, in the Don-Volga area, 'the Soviet ring is drawing tighter around the enemy.' Despite this optimistic note, the paper reflected evidence of wartime stringencies. The Imperial Tobacco Company appealed to its customers to accept cigarettes without packets in order to alleviate the paper shortage. The Government denied a shortage of rice. Women were told that they were 'the Inner Wall of Defence' and as such they should join the Women's Auxiliary Corps (India). Indian political problems were also evident in the shape of the continuing Quit India campaign. An attack on a police station, bombs in Baroda and acid attacks on the police were reported.

The Calcutta races, however, went ahead as normal and were graced by the presence of the Marchioness of Linlithgow, His Excellency the Governor of Bengal, and Lady Mary Herbert. There was cricket on Saturday and Sunday and a tennis carnival to look forward to on Thursday. Cinemas catering to English-speakers were featuring Chaplin in *Goldrush*, Robert Taylor in *Her Cardboard Lover* and Abbott and Costello in *Pardon My Sarong*. The paper reported an increase in the production of Indian films for 'the surging crowds during yuletide hungry for entertainment.'[2]

That night Calcutta was bombed by the Japanese air force. The structural damage was minimal, but the panic that ensued was widespread. Large numbers of Calcutta residents fled. Fear was exacerbated by indications that neither the Government of India nor the Government of Bengal nor the Calcutta municipality were prepared for the defence of the city.[3]

The air raid took place in a context of overwhelming Japanese military success and territorial expansion. The British—the assumed defenders of India—had been pushed out of Malaya, Singapore, Hong Kong and Burma. In late 1942, it was widely expected, in India and beyond, that a Japanese move into northern India was inevitable, imminent—and perhaps unstoppable.

Calcutta served as an industrial centre, a port and a transit point for troops moving up to fight the Japanese in Malaya and then in Burma. It was a city of considerable strategic importance to the Allies. Once Burma fell, Calcutta was the mainstay of the Allies' Asian front. Consequently, it was a Japanese target. As Prasad points out, 'Their air force was also well poised...to inflict continuous and heavy raids on Calcutta and the industrial area in the eastern regions.'[4]

The official reaction to these first raids on the city was very much along the 'we can take it' and 'business as usual' line, modelled no doubt on the (officially) stoic British reaction to the Blitz. The Governor of Bengal, Sir John Herbert, telegrammed the Viceroy after the first raid that despite two deaths and fourteen injuries, there had been 'No noticeable effect on morale.' Later the Chief Secretary related that 'A.R.P. Services are in general reported to have done excellent work,' demonstrated by the fact that 'defections were very few.'[5] The Viceroy was moved to tell Calcutta's citizens:

> Yours is the first capital city in India to suffer in this war a baptism of fire and her citizens have provided an admirable example of steadiness and fortitude. Well done Calcutta.[6]

The English press was, if anything, even more relaxed. The European-owned *Statesman* declared that the first raid was 'a small affair and, if the city has to be raided, it can be described as a very suitable introduction.'[7] Even the *Amrita Bazar Patrika* reported that 'Little damage was done and no nervousness was shown by the townspeople.'[8]

Down amongst the townspeople, however, things were not quite so sanguine. After the first raid, 'nervousness' broke out on a wide scale. According to Joydeep Sircar, the raid was a 'devastating blow to the morale of the inhabitants.' Sircar suggests that 'one-and-a-half million people' fled, causing a breakdown in 'the civil services.'[9] There was a widespread feeling that 'The Government had not prepared for the eventuality and seemed overwhelmed by developments in Southeast Asia.'[10]

In the ensuing days and weeks, some signs of defence began to appear: a number of Hurricane aircraft were moved to Calcutta; emergency airfields were constructed, including one in the centre of the city between Chowringhee and the Maidan; slit trenches were dug in the same area. But following the December 1942 raids, many of Calcutta's citizens were not concerned with defence. They were more interested in flight.

On December 23, Governor Herbert reported to the Viceroy that there had been a 'considerable exodus of people from Calcutta though not yet amounting to a panic rush.' Workers had 'wholly disappeared from the dock area' and morale was deteriorating—though 'nothing like a landslide'.[11] The post-bombing exodus took up the full capacity of the railways. Special trains were laid on to cope with the numbers attempting to leave the city.[12] On December 27, 'measures were taken to clear crowds of refugees collected at railway stations along the evacuation routes.' The British authorities estimated that some 2,50,000 people left the city by road and another 1,00,000 by rail.[13] Katyun Randhawa, a Calcutta schoolgirl, remembered the exodus and the railway stations 'packed with people trying to get out'—some permanently. 'Some of our street hawkers also disappeared,' she relates, '—we never saw our bread delivery man again.'[14]

Not unnaturally, those who felt the most vulnerable—from working-class suburbs, industrial establishments and around the docks—were those most inclined to leave. The Bengal Government Labour Commissioner put a brave face on the situation on the Monday morning after the first raid: 'there was full attendance this morning in mills and in engineering firms. In fact, some engineering firms reported better attendance than on normal Monday mornings.'[15] The docks presented a different picture. The Chief Secretary reported that boatmen, port employees and contract labour (including coal coolies) all evacuated. Workers from outside Calcutta 'left in large numbers on foot both by way of the Grand Trunk Road and the Orissa Trunk Road.' He estimated their number at 2–3,00,000.[16] Severe labour shortages ensued. The workers that remained took the opportunity of pressing their demands on the employers. There was an increase in strikes in Calcutta after the raids.[17] The

Australian war correspondent, Wilfred Burchett, was present in the Calcutta Port Commissioner's office after one of the December raids, when the latter was confronted by a deputation of wharf labourers. They told him:

> We don't mind staying and working, even if they do bomb us, but we want food in our bellies and decent shelters. At present we've got neither.[18]

The Scavengers' Union demanded wage increases and free accommodation as 'a large number of sweepers had already left the city and many would go away in the near future.'[19] The wharf labourers' demand for shelters reflected, again, the feeling in the city and in the province—and perhaps across India as a whole—that the Government had not prepared well enough for the possibility of war and was not doing enough about it now that it had arrived. In the aftermath of the raids, Sudata Debchaudhury argues, '[t]he Government had practically collapsed.'[20] This may be overstating the case, but at the time the *Amrita Bazar Patrika* was complaining that the Government of Bengal had done nothing to organize an orderly evacuation, or to provide the evacuees with alternative means of livelihood, shelter and conveyance.[21] Confidence in the authorities could not have been strengthened by the fact that during the December raids about 10 per cent of 'the lower ranks of the Calcutta Police' themselves abandoned their posts and fled.[22]

Widespread fear of air raids and even invasion had taken hold in India well before December 1942, and this laid the basis for the civilian exodus from Calcutta. In the early part of the year, the example of Burma was there for all to contemplate. The Government should have known what to expect. On the basis of Burma's experience of attack from the air, the Government of India's Civil Defence Department sent out a circular, *Lessons learned during air raids*, to all Provincial Governments in August 1942. It discussed the effects of the Japanese tactic of 'pattern bombing'—dropping bombs on a set area (that is, not dive bombing).

> ...after one such experience the slightest rumour of its repetition is sufficient to dissolve an entire town to a mere empty shell within a few hours. Once in this frame of mind...practically no inducement can be found to keep the lower orders of the community at their posts. The loss of employment, pay, pension and gratuities, the shame of criticism and ridicule, even fear of imprisonment are not strong enough reasons at such a period as this to prevent a wholesale exodus of a complete community, not excluding servants of the State.[23]

The Intelligence Service was reporting 'large-scale evacuation' from Calcutta in January 1942.[24] According to Chaudhuri's reminiscences, 'The panic began on 9 December [1941]'— that is, the day after Japan attacked Malaya, Hong Kong and the Philippines—'There was a stampede to flee Calcutta and to go as far away as possible.'[25]

The jitters reached the highest levels. The Viceroy, Lord Linlithgow, reported to the Secretary of State, Leo Amery, on the first night of a tour of Calcutta:

> I was turned out of bed unceremoniously at 12.30 a.m. and despatched to Barakpore [sic] 14 miles away, in view of a signal suggestion that a Japanese air division might be expected to land in Calcutta at 5.30 the next morning![26]

Elsewhere in India there had been similar scares, but these were sometimes brought on by actual air raids. Chittagong, in eastern Bengal, was bombed in May, October and December 1942, with scores killed and injured.[27] There followed 'a wholesale exodus from the town, and labour became unobtainable in the docks and at the aerodrome.'[28] The province of Assam was also bombed with similar results.[29] The Chief Secretary, reporting on Imphal, lamented:

> *Prima facie* it appears likely that the number of persons who stuck to their posts after the second raid was in most departments exiguous, and the accounts of eye-witnesses show that a large and motley stream of labourers probably accompanied by demoralized subordinate officials has been passing down the road.[30]

Meanwhile, *The Statesman* reported that the Commissioner of Delhi ('the least likely area to be invaded,' the paper commented) had told the civilian population to evacuate 'as soon as the city comes within effective bombing range of the enemy.'[31]

Following actual Japanese bombing raids on Ceylon in April 1942, an exodus from Bombay commenced.[32] A government report noted that mill hands had started leaving in April. 'The total number of absentees in the day shift of all the mills in the City has now increased to about 50,000.'[33] People returned to their ancestral homes having buried their valuables—sometimes frightened by air raid practice rather than a raid itself.[34] In the United Provinces, people moved from east to west to avoid air attack. The population of Kanpur increased; the populations of Allahabad and Benares were depleted. From Bihar it was reported: 'The exodus from Jamshedpur continues and shopkeepers are reported to be closing off their stocks. Something like 46,000 people have gone away and probably there are not more than 100,000 [left].'[35]

It was not only bombs, or the threat of them, that made people leave the urban centres. Various other dangers were perceived to have arisen from the war situation. One of these was the fear of civil disorder were the Japanese to invade India—and even before that, the social dislocation that the war was producing.[36] Another was the increased visibility of a war-time regime. The arrival of troops in a previously non-militarised area was likely to cause apprehension, if not flight.[37] The presence of troops meant the presence of war. In Jamshedpur, the Bihar authorities noted that this 'led to the fear that the town will soon be in the front line. The persistent impression is that following the "scorched earth" policy, the Jamshedpur [steel] works will be blown up... The exodus from the town still continues.'[38] In Mandar (also in Bihar), when the military showed some interest in a water tank, the local villagers promptly drained it 'for fear that troops might camp in the locality and harass the villagers.'[39] And in Cawnpore:

> Cawnpore labour has recently been considerably upset by rumours that [in] order to ensure that they will not run away when the town is bombed they are to be chained to their machines. This has led to considerable absenteeism.[40]

As has been noted, the extensive movement of people before, during and after the first Japanese air raids on India indicated a lack of confidence on the part of Indian civilians in the Government's preparations for war and in its ability to defend people where they lived. In fact, in early 1942 the Government of Bengal's strategy in Calcutta was not to restore confidence by preparation and defence—it was to move more people out. The Governor reported:

> Although some 700,000 persons have already left, it is essential to remove more <u>now</u> so that advantage can be taken of present conditions for an orderly withdrawal. It is expected that few will be able to leave by boat or train, and that only 140,000 people a day can leave by road. I fear that panic leading to disorder may develop if the population of Calcutta is caught in a raid, unable to get out and terrified by bombing. If the numbers can quietly be reduced, the remainder will be more easily controlled, and less liable to panic.[41]

The raids of December 1942 were not the last that Calcutta was to endure. In mid-January 1943, there were raids on industrial establishments along the Hooghly River (including the Dunlop factory at Sahaganj). The Bengal Chamber of Commerce reported another exodus of workers, 'tho[ugh] on a much smaller scale than at Christmas.'[42] There were also raids at this time on Chittagong, Noakhali, Cox's Bazaar and Tripura.[43] After the mid-January raid, Calcutta itself was spared further Japanese attention for eleven months. But on December 5, 1943, in the first daylight raid, Calcutta was bombed by 'a comparatively large force of Japanese bombers with fighter support.'[44] The raid was especially directed at the Kidderpore docks. The damage was considerable and the casualty rate high.

In this context, it is worth noting that the government seemed just as concerned to manage the news on air raids as to defend the city against them. The Joint Secretary of the Government of Bengal told all District Officers and District Magistrates in May 1943:

> Where it is necessary to publish any mention of casualties the general terms "slight", "moderate" and "heavy", or synonyms of these terms will be used. These terms will have no relation to any specific numbers of casualties.[45]

Given the secrecy over casualty figures in previous raids, the seriousness of the December 5 raid moved the *Amrita Bazar Patrika* to report:

> It is considered to be in the public interest on this occasion to reveal the extent to which civilians...suffered in this last raid...reports now available confirm some 500 civilian casualties of which over a third were fatal... No panic has been caused by the raid and the normal life of the city is unaffected. The morale of workshop labour is excellent and attendance is normal.[46]

But once again, the excellent morale and normal attendance were not on display among dock workers. Early reports indicated 'nervousness' among these workers. After a further air raid alarm on December 6, the Commissioner of Police reported that 'Coolies in the dock area...were panicking and about 3000 to 4000 left on foot towards the North.' Another 2,000 'were seen proceeding along Grand Trunk Road.' The ARP Controller of the Bengal-Nagpur Railway reported that 'At one time a crowd assembled at the launch and ferry jetties and attempted to force their way out, some with a view to crossing the Shalimar...the launch and ferry services were shut down until the crowd dispersed.' Labour attendance was, however, restored shortly after that, which indicates that, in the demonstrated absence of further raids, workers were willing to return.[47]

Morale among the dock workers was probably not raised by the general flight from the docks at the time of the raid by soldiers, seizing any kind of transport that came to hand on their way. 'The services of this area,' complained the Port ARP Report form, 'were seriously disorganized by interference of military B.O.R.s [British Other Ranks] who removed stretchers, vehicles and ambulances.' One man was reported run over by soldiers fleeing the docks in a jeep. British, American and Indian soldiers were apparently equally at fault. A Bengal government official wrote to the British and US military suggesting that soldiers working in the docks should take cover there. 'We want the coolies to do this but they certainly will not as long as men in uniform rush for the gates immediately they hear the sirens.'[48]

December 1943 was the last major raid that Calcutta suffered. By the beginning of 1944, much of the Japanese air force in Burma (whence the raids came) had been transferred elsewhere, taking the aerial threat to Calcutta with it.

The lack of Indian confidence in British defence, which had led to flight, was partly due to the Indian attitude to the war. From the British point of view, especially before the entry of Japan, this left much to be desired—and seemed, if anything, to be steadily deteriorating. Perhaps because of India's involuntary participation in the conflict, the authorities were hard put to arouse the interest of the population, let alone its enthusiasm. 'There has been little in the course of the war to arouse particular interest,' reported the Chief Secretary of Bengal in early 1940, followed by 'little on which to comment in the public attitude to the war' a month later.[49] This tended to produce a complementary reaction from the British that nothing could be done to change the situation: 'the question has been raised whether propaganda is either necessary or useful amongst them'—Indians in general, but in this case the villagers of the Dacca Division.[50] What reaction there was to the war was confined to 'uneasiness' (but again, not 'panic') or demands for reform: 'the claim that Bengalis shall receive military training or that one or more Bengali battalions shall be recruited' was raised.[51]

Once Japan entered the war, the mood shifted, though not in a direction necessarily pleasing to the colonial authorities. *Amrita Bazar Patrika* reported the attacks on Pearl Harbour, Hong Kong and Malaya and editorialised:

> So war has actually come to the very door of India. Assam, a message states, is to be considered within the war zone... It is no time for nervousness but calm thinking and steady action for the protection of the individual and the community.

But the newspaper's message to the British at this stage was essentially a political one. It enjoined the Government of India to make 'a genuine gesture' to the national movement—to break the political deadlock and thus 'galvanise the whole Indian nation into activity'.[52]

The British, for their part, now detected 'widespread alarm and some despondency'.

> As the war draws nearer to Bengal the lethargy and apathy which have been so often commented upon in these reports tend to be exchanged not for an attitude of determination but for panic and despair.[53]

The continuing military success of the Japanese gave sustenance to the prevailing mood of gloom. Together with their substantial territorial gains, their interest in India seemed to be becoming more marked. After the raid on Colombo in April 1942, *Amrita Bazar Patrika* noted 'It is not unlikely that at this juncture one should be assailed by a strong feeling of panic'—'the one thing that should be avoided,' it hastened to add.[54] There followed reports of the Japanese navy steaming freely around the Bay of Bengal, raids on Cocanada and Vizagapatam and an explosion off the Cuttack coast (giving rise to rumours of a landing).

Fear of a Japanese invasion was accompanied by the impression (marching steadily through Malaya, Singapore and Burma) that the British were on the run.

> There is now a widespread conviction...that Britain cannot win the war and that the conquest of India by Japan is, in effect, inevitable... [There exists] a belief that resistance to the enemy is bound to be profitless and that acquiescence is probably the policy likely to involve individuals in the least hardship and distress.[55]

Shyama Prasad Mookerjee, a minister in the Bengal government, submitting his resignation to the Governor in 1942, expressed the hope that Bengal (and India) could be successfully defended. But if an invasion came, he said, 'you and others...will, like your friends similarly situated in Burma, desert this province, [leaving] we remaining here, unarmed, unprepared and emasculated.'[56] Worse than that, the British felt that Indians might actually welcome the invaders. According to the Inspector-General of Police in Calcutta, 'the populace was ready to welcome the Japanese with open arms should they walk into the city.'[57] Furthermore, according to General William Slim, 'The Non-Congress Government of Bengal, a coalition of Indian politicians, would on the first signs of Japanese invasion have collapsed.'[58]

The mood in British society before the first Calcutta raids reflected official stoicism. Eugenie Fraser (the wife, as she put it, of 'a Jute wallah') wrote that 'Overall, Calcutta got off lightly.

We suffered no hardships compared to other theatres of war. The tea and mah-jong parties continued with a variety of home-baked cakes gracing the table.'[59] Burchett, the war correspondent, commented:

> Dinner jackets and evening dresses; clubs and shining cars; hotel orchestras and cocktail parties; conversations centring around shortage of whisky and gin; more rigid distinction between various grades of European society than the Hindus with their caste system... Such was Calcutta at the end of the Burma campaign, with the Japs likely to launch an attack on India at any moment. Calcutta, 1942: front-line city.[60]

The continuing and deliberate display of British imperial normality was the preferred policy of the Government of India. Lord Linlithgow wrote:

> I think there is probably a good deal of importance in retaining, even in times of stress such as these, a sufficient degree of public appearance to indicate that we have not retired into our shell and sunk into the depths of depression.[61]

The *Statesman* described this as a 'laboured continuance, apparently for reasons of prestige, of opulences that seemed unrelished.'[62] The Calcutta races have already been mentioned. They and other sporting events had become an important feature of keeping up appearances. At the 1941 meeting, the *Amrita Bazar Patrika* reported 'A large attendance including His Excellency the Commander-in-Chief General Sir Archibald Wavell, His Excellency the Governor of Bengal and the Lady Mary Herbert' together with the Aga Khan.[63] This, it should be noted, was on December 5, 1941—a year before the Calcutta raid, but only two days before the attack on Pearl Harbour and Japan's entry into the war. On December 6, 'Before a distinguished gathering including H.E. The Governor of Bengal and the Lady Mary Herbert the seventh annual Head of the Lake Regatta came off on Sunday evening in fine rowing weather at the Lake Club course.'[64]

This display of pleasure-as-usual occasioned a question for the Secretary of State in the British parliament on April 15, 1942, regarding:

> ...what steps he is taking to impress on the Government of India the necessity for the European community in India to set an example and to put themselves on a war basis as regards limited amusements, restricted food, petrol, luxuries and living in general without further delay.

Amery wrote to the Viceroy, 'it would be helpful here if some early opportunity could be found by you and [the] Governors to enjoin greater austerity of living on wealthier class Indian and European as definite contribution to the war effort.'[65]

Some steps were taken to put Bengal on a more serious war footing after Japan entered the conflict. The Calcutta Commissioner of Police broadcast on All-India Radio on December 8, 1941, 'this war is the concern of every citizen of Calcutta. It is a matter purely of self-preservation. Every man and every woman in Calcutta to-day should be asking himself or herself, "What can I do to help?"'[66] All the Japanese in the city (about thirty) were taken into custody, except for the Consul-General, and a guard was put on the consular offices in the Nipon Club.[67] A director of the European Group corporation suggested to the Governor that Calcutta should be placed under martial law. This was not taken up—but his further suggestion that the Bengal Government should leave the city preceded three months' active discussion (March-May 1942) about moving the Legislative Council and Assembly, along with their offices, to Suri or Berhampore or to a district in North Bengal.[68] Test blackouts were conducted in Calcutta and Darjeeling in March 1941.[69]

But official resilience on the part of the British and the war measures taken were continually vitiated by a general sense of inaction and unpreparedness. 'I cannot help feeling,' reported the

Governor in May 1941, 'that in general the problem of organizing passive defence is not being tackled by the Government of India with sufficient speed or resolution.'[70] In early 1942, Calcutta, India's frontline industrial city, possessed 150 anti-aircraft guns (it was estimated that 1,500 were needed) and eight 'serviceable fighter planes.'[71] The *Amrita Bazar Patrika* had editorially pleaded back in March 1940 'that measures for land and coastal defence should be organized not only as an [emergency] measure but on a permanent basis without any further delay.'[72] Meanwhile, confidence was not inspired by statements like that of the Madras government in 1943, that it was not practicable 'to give warning to the public before bombs are actually dropped'—let alone stop them. The public 'should seek shelter as soon as they hear the sound of bombs falling.'[73]

To unpreparedness was added an element of confusion. In early February 1942, the Governor of Bengal seemed convinced that:

> ...the most important problem affecting the Calcutta area is whether the policy is to be one of gradual evacuation or of maintaining war production until the last possible moment... there can be no half measures regarding the defence of Calcutta... I am convinced that a definite decision to hold eastern India is essential if we are to maintain the military prestige necessary to hold Central India.[74]

But a month later his resolve had weakened and he was suggesting the organization of a form of flight in advance (see note 47 above). But such a plan, which could encompass partial civilian evacuation combined with 'scorched earth' measures, might trigger an even greater panic than bombing raids. In November the Viceroy complained to Amery that Governor Herbert was 'pressing for the issue of a communique in Calcutta warning the population of the possibility of further attacks [after the raids on Ceylon and elsewhere] and urging them to evacuate.' This was not the

Government of India's preferred course of action. The Viceroy told Amery that he, his advisers and the Commander-in-Chief were all 'entirely opposed to it and think that something of this nature would be calculated merely to start a panic... Herbert must be told that he cannot publish his communique.'[75]

Measures to organize evacuation were almost certainly guaranteed to generate a flight mentality. A state of emergency was declared in Calcutta on December 24, 1941. British women and children were being encouraged to leave even before the fall of Rangoon in March 1942. The Government ordered the closure of all schools and began requisitioning buildings, houses and boats.[76] In neighbouring Orissa, Government employees were granted advances to enable them to remove their families from the coastal towns. The provincial government decided to shift the staff and records from Cuttack to Sambalpur (265 kilometres inland).[77] Back in Calcutta, the authorities informed the University that if the city 'became exposed to the risk of heavy and intensive bombing from the air, compulsory evacuation may be necessary.' Reporting this, the *Amrita Bazar Patrika* asked, not unreasonably, if this applied to the University, should it not apply to the city as a whole?[78] The flight mentality was evident in the case of George Smith, an ARP Training Instructor working in Calcutta, applying for a job as a Forest Assistance officer further inland. 'I want to join at once,' he wrote, 'as the Japs may be here at any time...please wire by [Traffic Management Order] my Inter-Class fare etc.'[79]

Madras provides us with an outstanding example of the combined effect of official evacuation measures, bombs and faulty intelligence. 'Pre-evacuation' measures had been taken in Madras. Business houses shifted their premises to places like Salem and Bangalore; the library of Madras University was moved inland; and potentially dangerous animals in the zoo were shot.[80]

In mid-February 1942 the Madras Chief Secretary reported 'it is estimated that about 1/3rd of the population have left Madras by road and rail.'[81] The provincial government maintained 'the

Japanese activities have caused very considerable fear in the minds of many of the inhabitants of South India, but it would not be justifiable yet to call it by the strong word panic.'[82] Nevertheless, 'It is estimated that about 20 to 30 per cent of the population of Madras have left the City but the exodus is mainly confined to women and children.'[83]

The Madras exodus was probably exacerbated by the Government announcement in February that, while there was no necessity for anyone to leave the city, 'those who had no business to keep them in the city and wished to leave later might do so as soon as they could, in order to avoid rush and confusion.'[84]

After the Japanese bombed the ports of Colombo in Ceylon, Cocanada and Vizagapatam (both several hundred kilometres to the north of Madras) in April 1942, the exodus from Madras intensified. In Vizagapatam, after the bombs fell on April 6:

> The railways were practically paralysed and all the subordinate staff and labour fled from the place. All provision shops were closed and practically everyone deserted the town; the Port labour fled and so did the coolies employed on the construction of the new aerodrome.[85]

On April 9, 1942, the Government of Madras told the District Magistrates:

> Government would strongly advise all Government servants who can do so to send their families away <u>at once</u> to places outside the coastal belt... It is Government's intention that their officers should not fall into the hands of the enemy if this can be avoided.[86]

It was estimated that between 9 and 14 April, some 2,00,000 more people left Madras. With tens of thousands on the move, the *Amrita Bazar Patrika* noted that 'Owing to the heavy traffic the trains are leaving slightly later than the scheduled timings.'[87] The Congress newspaper *The National Herald* reported that 'The rush of [railway] passengers is considerably increased following the Government notification advising non-essential people to leave Madras.'[88] By then the Madras Police Commissioner had issued an order forbidding those involved in water supply and transport from leaving the city without his permission.[89]

On April 10 or 11, military command informed the Government 'that a large Japanese force was on its way to South India and that the spearhead might be expected to arrive any day after the 15th.' They advised evacuation, especially of the Secretariat. The Governor, Arthur Hope, reported later:

> Although I knew that moving the Government offices would add to the panic, I could not run the risk of having the whole Government, High Court, etc., captured if there was a successful landing...to have the whole administration involved in possible street fighting was unthinkable.

Consequently, half the Secretariat was sent to Ootacamund and half to Chittoor. The Governor, with his advisers and secretaries, remained behind.[90]

The invasion did not occur. Hope wrote somewhat ruefully later, 'I hope that the invasion alarm was founded on accurate information, because another alarm like it would finish morale altogether. They are very jittery people in South India.' He singled out the Europeans for comment: 'the Europeans have not been as good as they should have been in certain areas and have set a bad example... I am sorry to say that some of the Europeans, even in the hills, gave way to sheer terror and were demanding to be evacuated from Ootacamund of all places.'[91]

The flash and crash of Calcutta's Christmas air raids threw a number of questions about India in 1942 into sharp relief.

Firstly, they brought the war with Japan home to Bengal and to other vulnerable areas of eastern and southern India. They raised the prospect and the problem of further, more extensive raids— and ultimately of a Japanese invasion. Was such an invasion—if not of India as a whole then of its exposed parts—possible? Was it likely? In 1942, the working assumption of almost all our players, Indian and British alike, was that it was. The further that the Japanese advanced through Burma, the firmer that assumption became. The movements of people and governments that we have noted were clearly based on the expectation of invasion.

Secondly, the possibility of invasion raised questions of defence. Was Britain capable of defending Bengal? Dunkirk, the Blitz, Malaya, Singapore, Hong Kong and Burma did not contribute to a vision of radiant confidence. When the bombs fell on Calcutta, as they had in other Ceylonese and Indian port cities, there seemed little to stop them. Calcutta's defences, the lack of which had been pointed out in the preceding months, appeared manifestly inadequate for a 'light' air raid, let alone a full-scale invasion by land and/or sea.

Thirdly, given the obvious doubts on this score, the question then arose: in the event of invasion, for both Indians and the British, was it the intention of the British to defend Bengal and its surrounding areas or to retreat? Or, perhaps more realistically in light of recent events, would they attempt to defend it, fail and then flee? Tens of thousands of Indians voted with their feet on this one, leaving the areas under (or vulnerable to) attack for safe inland locations. Others made clear their intention not to resist the Japanese (and even to welcome them) as the British authorities frequently noted in their reports.

The British answer was (perhaps necessarily) ambiguous. For it was clearly not impossible that British forces would be pushed back by the Japanese—and that, therefore, evacuation would be necessary. To initiate that evacuation a moment too soon would unleash panic; a moment too late would risk a repeat of Burma where the Japanese were able to help themselves to crucial resources left behind by the retreating British.

All of this speculation (which will be unpacked in detail in the following chapters) leaves out the question of what independent role Indians, despite being under foreign rule, would play in the potential defence of their country. I have not as yet addressed the political aspect of these events: the crucial question in a time of crisis—who was in charge? Was it a clearly weakened British state, on the run in Europe and defeated in its Asian colonies outside India? Was this state weakened enough to be under serious challenge from its main opponent in India, the Indian National Congress? In fact, even as the war with Japan commenced, India was locked in a political stalemate. The British had nothing further to offer India and had to concentrate on exploiting the country's resources for its war effort. The Congress, having declared itself against the war and resigned from the provincial ministries, had to find new ways to challenge British rule.

We will examine the two sides of the stalemate in due course. First, it is necessary to set the political struggle in a wider theoretical framework: that of British hegemony and Congress counter-hegemony—and Congress' strategy to build the latter into a challenge for the former.

Notes

1 Eugenie Fraser, *A Home by the Hooghly: A Jute Wallah's Wife* (Edinburgh: Mainstream Publishing Company, 1989), 104.
2 *Amrita Bazar Patrika* (henceforward ABP), 20 December 1942, 1–12.
3 For reports of the first bombing on 20 December 1942, see ABP, 24 December 1942, 1. There were further raids up to and including 24 December.
4 Bisheshwar Prasad, *Official History of the Indian Armed Forces in the Second World War, 1939–45: Volume Twelve, Defence of India—Policy and Plans* (Kanpur: Combined Inter-Services Historical Section (India and Pakistan), 1963), 193–4.
5 Viceroy to Governor of Bengal Telegram, 21 December 1942. British Library, India Office Records (henceforward IOR): Viceroy's Correspondence with Provincial Governors, Mss Eur F125/41: 1942; Chief Secretary Bengal Report, second half December 1942. IOR: Fortnightly Reports of Governors, Chief Commissioners and Chief

Secretaries (1937–1948) L/PJ/5/149.
6   ABP, 24 December 1942, 1.
7   *Statesman*, 22 December 1942. Accessed at http://gypsyscholar.com/31618historiceventsjapbombst.html.
8   By the time of the fourth raid however, the newspaper was reporting 'Bombs Dropped Indiscriminately'; 'Some Casualties and Damage Done' (ABP, 24 December 1942, 1; 27 December 1942, 1).
9   Joydeep Sircar, 'In the Skies of Calcutta: A Tribute to Maurice Pring,' *Bharat Rakshak: Indian Air Force* (www.bharat-rakshak.com). See also Janam Mukherjee, *Hungry Bengal: War, Famine, Riots and the End of Empire* (Noida: Harper Collins, 2015), 85.
10 Sudata Debchaudhury, *Japanese Imperialism and the Indian Nationalist Movement: A Study of the Political and Psychological Impact of Possible Invasion and Actual Occupation, 1939–1945* (Ph.D. Dissertation, University of Illinois-Urbana, 1992), 132.
11 Governor of Bengal to Viceroy Telegram, 23 December 1942. IOR: Mss Eur F125/42:1942).
12 WBSA W–954/42 Evacuation.
13 Governor of Bengal to Viceroy Telegram, 27 December 1942. IOR: Mss Eur F125/42:1942; Chief Secretary Bengal Report 2nd half December 1942. IOR: Fortnightly Reports of Governors, Chief Commissioners and Chief Secretaries (1937–1948). L/PJ/5/149. Estimates of the number leaving vary from 'thousands' (Debchaudhury, Japanese Imperialism, 132) to 6–7,00,000 (Bengal Chamber of Commerce in Mukherjee, Hungry Bengal, 82).
14 Katyun Randhawa at www.bbc.co.uk/ww2peopleswar/stories/50/a5756150.shtml.
15 ABP, 24 December 1942, 1.
16 Chief Secretary Bengal Report 2nd half December 1942. IOR: Fortnightly Reports of Governors, Chief Commissioners and Chief Secretaries (1937–1948). L/PJ/5/149.
17 Suranjan Das, 'Nationalism and Popular Consciousness: Bengal 1942,' *Social Scientist* 23 (4/6) April-June 1995: 62. Calcutta was seething with industrial discontent for much of 1942, particularly among transport workers. Their union was demanding major improvements in pay and conditions. Major strikes occurred in May and July. The disputes were partially resolved when the Calcutta Tramway Company made concessions in the wake of the Japanese bombing (Siddhartha Guha Ray, 'Protest and Politics: Story of Calcutta Tram Workers 1940–47,' in *Calcutta: The Stormy Decades*, ed. Tanika Sarkar and Sekhar

Bandyopadhyay (New Delhi: Social Science Press, 2015), 155–161.
18 Wilfred G. Burchett, *Bombs over Burma* (Melbourne: F.W. Cheshire Pty Ltd, 1944), 237.
19 'Calcutta feared a Japanese attack, says Netaji file.' *The Hindu*, 25 September 2015.
20 Debchaudhury, Japanese Imperialism, 133.
21 ABP Editorial, 29 December 1942, 2.
22 Chief Secretary Bengal Report 2nd half December 1942. IOR: Fortnightly Reports of Governors, Chief Commissioners and Chief Secretaries (1937–1948). L/PJ/5/149.
23 WBSA W 732/42.
24 Intelligence Summary, 10 January 1942. IOR: L/WS/1/317.
25 Nirad C. Chaudhuri, *Thy Hand, Great Anarch! India: 1921–1952* (London: The Hogarth Press, 1990), 53.
26 Gowher Rizvi, 'The Congress Revolt of 1942: A Historical Revision,' *Indo-British Review* XI (1) December 1984: 34.
27 See ABP, 10 May 1942, 5; S. Woodburn Kirby et al, *The War against Japan, Volume II: India's Most Dangerous Hour* (London, HMSO 1958), 259.
28 Chief Secretary Bengal Report 2nd half December 1942. IOR: Fortnightly Reports of Governors, Chief Commissioners and Chief Secretaries (1937–1948). L/PJ/5/149.
29 Fortnightly Report Assam 1st half February 1942 in Bipan Chandra and Salil Misra (eds.), *Towards Freedom: Documents on the Movement for Independence in India, 1942* (New Delhi: Oxford University Press, 2016), 735; Fortnightly Report Assam 1st half May 1942 in Rizvi, Congress Revolt, 33.
30 Chief Secretary to Government of Assam, May 1942 in Francis G. Hutchins, *Spontaneous Revolution: The Quit India Movement* (Delhi: Manohar Book Service, 1971), 233.
31 *Statesman*, 18 April 1942 in Rizvi, Congress Revolt, 34.
32 For the attacks on Colombo see ABP, 5 April 1942, 5.
33 Fortnightly Report Bombay 1st half April 1942 in Chandra & Misra, Towards Freedom 1942, 739.
34 David Hardiman. 'The Quit India Movement in Gujarat,' in *The Indian Nation in 1942*, ed. Gyanendra Pandey (Calcutta: K.P. Bagchi & Company, 1988), 81.
35 Fortnightly Report Bihar 1st half February 1942 in Chandra & Misra,Towards Freedom 1942, 707.
36 See Fortnightly Report Delhi 1st half April 1942 in Chandra & Misra,

Towards Freedom 1942, 755; Fortnightly Report Madras 1st half February 1942 in Chandra & Misra, Towards Freedom 1942, 703.
37 See Fortnightly Report Orissa 2nd half February 1942 in Chandra & Misra, Towards Freedom 1942, 715.
38 Fortnightly Report Bihar 1st half March 1942 in Chandra & Misra, Towards Freedom 1942, 723.
39 Hutchins, Spontaneous Revolution, 234.
40 Fortnightly Report United Provinces 1st half February 1942 in Chandra & Misra, Towards Freedom 1942, 707.
41 Governor's Report 2nd half March 1942. IOR: Fortnightly Reports of Governors, Chief Commissioners and Chief Secretaries (1937–1948) L/PJ/5/149. The same report mentions that the Government was attempting to make ready 250 camps for evacuees within a radius of one hundred miles of Calcutta. The Governor wrote in October: 'we cannot guarantee to control a mass exodus from Calcutta, if it is bombed, unless some of our ineffectives are persuaded to move out now.' (Governor's Report 2nd half October 1942. IOR: Fortnightly Reports of Governors, Chief Commissioners and Chief Secretaries (1937–1948) L/PJ/5/149.)
42 WBSA W–30/43 (I) 6th Raid. This time however it included 'the desertion of a number of warders in Dum Dum and Presidency Jails.' (CS Bengal Report 1st half January 1943. IOR: Fortnightly Reports of Governors, Chief Commissioners and Chief Secretaries (1937–1948). L/PJ/5/150).
43 Chief Secretary Bengal Report 2nd half January 1943; 2nd half March 1943; 1st half April 1943. IOR: Fortnightly Reports of Governors, Chief Commissioners and Chief Secretaries (1937–1948) L/PJ/5/150.
44 Chief Secretary Bengal Report 1st half December 1943. (IOR: Fortnightly Reports of Governors, Chief Commissioners and Chief Secretaries (1937–1948) L/PJ/5/150) By this stage, the expectation of continuing air attack was such that a printed report form had evolved for the police to complete. It demanded:
'(a) Estimate of the general morale as a result of the raid.
(b) Extent of panic.
(c) Whether any exodus of the population and, if so, extent, direction, classes and number involved.
(d) Crime during raid, especially looting.'
(WBSA W–30/43 III Air Raids in Calcutta Area 1943 8th Raid).
45 WBSA W 296/43 Reporting of Air Raids memo 18 May 1943.
46 ABP, 7 December 1943, 1–2. The official figures were 187 killed and 435 injured (WBSA W–30/43 III Air Raids in Calcutta Area 1943 8th

Raid).
47 WBSA W-30/43 III Air Raids in Calcutta Area 1943 8th Raid.
48 WBSA W-30/43 III Air Raids in Calcutta Area 1943 8th Raid.
49 Chief Secretary Bengal Report 1st half January and 1st half February, 1940. IOR: Fortnightly Reports of Governors, Chief Commissioners and Chief Secretaries (1937–1948) L/PJ/5/146.
50 Chief Secretary Bengal Report 2nd half February 1941. IOR: Fortnightly Reports of Governors, Chief Commissioners and Chief Secretaries (1937–1948) L/PJ/5/148.
51 Chief Secretary Bengal Report 1st half January 1942 IOR: Fortnightly Reports of Governors, Chief Commissioners and Chief Secretaries (1937–1948) L/PJ/5/149; 2nd half January 1940 L/PJ/5/146. As to the latter, S.P. Mookerjee, a minister in the Bengal government, demanded the formation of a Bengal National Army. As a leading light of the Hindu Mahasabha however, the government believed his requests 'have as their sole objective Hindu domination.' (Governor Bengal's Report 1st half March 1942. IOR: Fortnightly Reports of Governors, Chief Commissioners and Chief Secretaries (1937–1948) L/PJ/5/149).
52 ABP, 8 December 1941, 1 & 7; 9 December 1941, 1–7.
53 Chief Secretary Bengal Report 2nd half February 1942; 2nd half March 1942. This attitude was being carried into the villages by 'persons leaving the industrial areas' (Chief Secretary Bengal Report 2nd half June 1942). The Chief Secretary was able to note 'a marked increase in confidence' in early June, which he ascribed to the fact that Bengal had not been invaded (Chief Secretary Bengal Report 1st half June 1942). IOR: Fortnightly Reports of Governors, Chief Commissioners and Chief Secretaries (1937–1948) L/PJ/5/149.
54 ABP, 6 April 1942, 4.
55 Chief Secretary Bengal Report 1st half April 1942. IOR: Fortnightly Reports of Governors, Chief Commissioners and Chief Secretaries (1937–1948) L/PJ/5/149.
56 Resignation letter of S.P. Mookherjee (see note 56) to the Governor of Bengal, 16 November 1942, in 'Free India', *India Ravaged: Being an account of atrocities committed under British Aegis over the whole subcontinent of India in the latter part of 1942* (No place or publisher: 1943), 120.
57 Cited in Gyanendra Pandey, 'The Revolt of August 1942 in Eastern UP and Bihar,' in *The Indian Nation in 1942*, ed. Gyanendra Pandey (Calcutta: K.P. Bagchi & Company, 1988), 155. A District Officer in Bihar reported that the followers of Subhas Chandra Bose's Forward

Bloc 'are looking forward to para-troops from Japan dropping arms to the people who would go over to the Bose group.' (Fortnightly Report Bihar 1st half March 1942 in Chandra & Misra, *Towards Freedom 1942*, 723.)

58 William Slim, *Defeat into Victory* (London: Cassell and Company Ltd., 1956), 128.
59 Fraser, Home by the Hooghly, 111. Huntley and Palmer declared in the *Amrita Bazar Patrika* in December 1941 that they had 'kept the flag flying and will continue to do so for British quality in biscuits.' (ABP, 8 December 1941, 1.)
60 Burchett, Bombs, 216–217. Nevertheless, John Masters, then in Quetta, wrote later: 'The war against Japan began and Singapore fell. General Auchinleck...ordered that officers must put away their mess kits and dinner jackets for the duration, and wear uniform all the time. The war had reached India.' (John Masters, *The Road Past Mandalay: a personal narrative* (London: Michael Joseph Ltd., 1961), 85.
61 Cited in Philip Mason, *A Shaft of Sunlight: Memories of a Varied Life* (London: Andre Deutsch, 1978), 151.
62 Cited in Philip Woodruff [Philip Mason], *The Men Who Ruled India. Volume II: The Guardians* (London: Jonathan Cape, 1965), 307. Burchett also remarked that 'it seems that the atmosphere in Calcutta was the same as in Singapore and Rangoon—and in Honolulu—before the bombs fell. Dressing for dinner, races, bridge, cocktail parties—all the hooh-ha without which life becomes unbearable for conscientious "bearers of the white man's burden". (Burchett, Bombs, 178)
63 ABP, 7 December 1941, 11; Christopher Bayly & Tim Harper, *Forgotten Armies: Britain's Asian Empire and the War with Japan* (London: Penguin, 2005), 80.
64 ABP, 8 December 1941, 3.
65 Secretary of State to Viceroy, 1 April 1942. Question in Parliament, 15 April in Nicholas Mansergh (ed.), *The Transfer of Power 1942–7. Volume 1: The Cripps Mission, January-April 1942* (London: Her Majesty's Stationery Office, 1970), 605. Linlithgow's reply is at 765.
66 ABP, 9 December 1941, 5.
67 ABP, 8 December 1941, 1.
68 Plans and Proposals for defence of East Bengal and Calcutta: question of maintenance of civil administration. IOR: R/3/2/27; WBSA W488/42 (A) Removal.
69 Chief Secretary Bengal Report 1st half March 1941. IOR: Fortnightly Reports of Governors, Chief Commissioners and Chief Secretaries

(1937–48) L/PJ/5/148.
70 Governor Bengal Report 2nd half April 1941. IOR: Fortnightly Reports of Governors, Chief Commissioners and Chief Secretaries (1937–48) L/PJ/5/148.
71 Milan Hauner, *India in Axis Strategy: Germany, Japan and Indian Nationalists in the Second World War* (Stuttgart: Klett-Cotta, 1981), 444.
72 ABP, 28 March 1940, 2.
73 A. Srivathsan, 'And Then Madras was Bombed,' *The Hindu*, 5 October 2012.
74 Governor Bengal Report 2nd half February 1942. IOR: Fortnightly Reports of Governors, Chief Commissioners and Chief Secretaries (1937–49). L/PJ/5/149.
75 Viceroy to Secretary of State, 9 November 1942 in Nicholas Mansergh (ed.), *The Transfer of Power 1942–7. Volume 3: Reassertion of Authority, 21 September 1942–12 June 1943* (London: Her Majesty's Stationery Office, 1971), 227.
76 Bhupen Qanungo, 'The Quit India Movement, 1942,' in *A Centenary History of the Indian National Congress. Volume Three: 1935–1947* ed. M.N. Das (New Delhi: All-India Congress Committee (I), 1985) 475–6.
77 Fortnightly Report Orissa 2nd half March 1942 in Chandra & Misra, Towards Freedom 1942, 727.
78 ABP, 9 April 1942, 4.
79 WBSA W–647/42 George Smith. His letter was passed from military censorship to military intelligence with the comment 'If A.R.P. workers are being trained by men of this calibre, one cannot [expect] the best results.'
80 Indivar Kamtekar, 'The Shiver of 1942,' *Studies in History* XVIII (1) 2002: 88.
81 Chief Secretary Madras Report 1st half February 1942. IOR: Fortnightly Reports of Governors, Chief Commissioners and Chief Secretaries (1937–1948). Madras L/PJ/205.
82 Chief Secretary Madras Report 6 January 1942. IOR: Fortnightly Reports of Governors, Chief Commissioners and Chief Secretaries (1937–1948). Madras L/PJ/205. The same report noted that the well-to-do were renting houses outside Madras. The author, R.K. Narayan, had some experience of this. He was living at the time in Mysore. His landlord wanted to repossess the house so as to be at a safe distance from possible Japanese attacks on the city of Bangalore: 'he began to drop in frequently from Bangalore to suggest that we vacate the house..."we

don't feel that Bangalore is going to be safe anymore with the Japanese planes coming up to Madras."' Narayan points out that Mysore was 150 kilometres from Bangalore. (R.K. Narayan, *My Days* (London: Chatto & Windus, 1975), 156–7.)

83   Chief Secretary Madras Report 1st half January 1942. IOR: Fortnightly Reports of Governors, Chief Commissioners and Chief Secretaries (1937–1948). Madras L/PJ/205.
84   Chief Secretary Madras Report 2nd half February 1942. IOR: Fortnightly Reports of Governors, Chief Commissioners and Chief Secretaries (1937–1948). Madras L/PJ/205.
85   Fortnightly Report Madras 1st half April 1942 in Chandra & Misra, Towards Freedom 1942, 738.
86   IOR: Administration of the Province L/PJ/177/42.
87   ABP, 9 April 1942, 5.
88   *National Herald*, 14 April 1942 in Chandra & Misra, Towards Freedom 1942, 738. See also A. Srivathsan, 'When 5 lakh fled the city in two weeks', *The Hindu* 3 October 2012.
89   A. Srivathsan, 'When Madras ran out of milk and food', *The Hindu* 4 October 2012.
90   Governor Report Madras, 3 of 1942, 18 April 1942. IOR: Fortnightly Reports of Governors, Chief Commissioners and Chief Secretaries (1937–1948). Madras L/PJ/205. See also Fortnightly Report Madras 1st half April 1942 in Chandra & Misra, Towards Freedom 1942, 737. In Orissa at this time the Secretariat was moved from Cuttack to Sambalpur. According to Biswamoy Pati: 'The news of this spread like lightning. It not only implied a "breakdown" of colonial authority, but was also looked upon as a signal for rebellion.' (Biswamoy Pati, 'The Climax of Popular Protest: The Quit India Movement in Orissa', *Indian Economic and Social History Review* 29 (1) 1992: 12.
91   Governor Report Madras, 3 of 1942, 18 April 1942. IOR: Fortnightly Reports of Governors, Chief Commissioners and Chief Secretaries (1937–1948). Madras L/PJ/205.

2

HEGEMONY AND COUNTER-HEGEMONY

> But always after one of these arguments—or, rather, disputes—
> with his fellow workmen, he almost relapsed into hopelessness
> and despondency, for then he realised how vast and how strong
> are the fortifications that surround the present system; the great
> barriers and ramparts of invincible ignorance, apathy and self-
> contempt, which will have to be broken down before the system
> of society of which they are the defences, can be swept away.
>
> —Robert Tressell, The Ragged-Trousered Philanthropists.[1]

This book will proceed on the assumption that the British colonial state in India was a semi-hegemonic state and that the Indian National Congress adopted a counter-hegemonic strategy against it. This necessitates some explanation.

The foremost Marxist theoretician of hegemony and counter-hegemony was the Italian Antonio Gramsci. As we shall see, he was somewhat preceded by Karl Kautsky from the German Social Democracy, but it was Gramsci who undoubtedly gave the concept its most thorough working over. Gramsci argued that for ruling classes there were two possible methods of maintaining their rule:

coercion and consent. Joseph V. Femia explains:

> Gramsci states that the supremacy of a social group or class manifests itself in two different ways; "domination" (*dominio*) or coercion, and "intellectual and moral leadership" (*direzione intelletuale e morale*).[2]

Despite the fact that ruling classes can generally call on the state and its coercive forces, they also rule 'by acquiring the consent of the subaltern classes through leadership and persuasion —that is, through hegemony.'[3] The exercise of hegemony—non-coercive rule—by a ruling class indicates the support that the class enjoys amongst those it rules. Thus for Gramsci:

> The "normal" exercise of hegemony on the now classical terrain of the parliamentary regime is characterised by the combination of force and consent, which balance each other reciprocally, without force predominating excessively over consent. Indeed, the attempt is always made to ensure that force will appear to be based on the consent of the majority.[4]

At their extremes, the two methods of rule produce coercive regimes, like political dictatorships (where force outweighs consent) at one end, and parliamentary or representative ones (where consent tends to dominate) at the other. But it should be understood that the extremes lie, as ever, along a continuum and co-exist around its centre. Green argues 'hegemony is protected by coercion and coercion is protected by hegemony, and they both protect the dominant group's political and economic positions.'[5]

The two methods of rule determine two different (though, at times, complementary—the continuum again) strategies to bring about their overthrow. Karl Kautsky raised this in 1910, pointing out that 'modern military strategy distinguishes two types of strategy, the *strategy of annihilation* and the *strategy of attrition*.'[6] In the same article, he continued:

> The strategy of attrition differs from the strategy of annihilation only in the fact that it does not aim at the decisive battle directly, but prepares it long in advance and is only inclined to engage such a battle when it considers the enemy to have been sufficiently weakened.

Gramsci examined how that weakening might take place. Drawing on military experience in his turn—this time that of the First World War—he rechristened the concepts as the war of manoeuvre or movement (Kautsky's 'annihilation') and the war of position ('attrition').[7] The former was the insurrectionist scenario at that time, being prosecuted by the Communist International. The latter was a long-term strategy in which the forces aiming at overthrow worked to undermine, subvert and replace the hegemony established by the ruling class with a 'counter-hegemony' of their own. In the war of position, subaltern groups 'promote a new set of values in an attempt to take control of and promote a new conception of civil society. The war of position...is the struggle for hegemony.'[8] Gramsci insists that in this strategy the counter-hegemony of the subaltern groups has to be established before any ultimate struggle for power:

> A social group can, and indeed must, already exercise "leadership" before winning governmental power (this indeed is one of the principal conditions for the winning of such power).[9]

As Femia puts it, 'In the absence of a prior "revolution of the spirit", a seizure of state power would prove transitory if not disastrous.'[10]

But under what circumstances was it appropriate to prosecute a war of manoeuvre—a frontal assault on the state—and when was it necessary to undertake a drawn-out war of position? Gramsci wrote in the long shadow of the Soviet revolution and of the post-revolutionary wave that accompanied and followed it. But the revolutionary tide was on the ebb—the victory of fascism in Italy, for example, did not suggest a radiant future for the European working class. Despite this, the war of manoeuvre (insurrectionism) remained all the rage for most communists and this was reflected in the strategy of the Communist International. Gramsci, while not abandoning revolution, strongly suggested that as societies develop the war of position becomes a less appropriate revolutionary strategy and the war of manoeuvre a more appropriate one:

> ...in the case of the most advanced States..."civil society" has become a very complex structure and one which is resistant to the catastrophic "incursions" of the immediate economic element (crises, depressions, etc.). The superstructures of civil society are like the trench-systems of modern warfare.

Thus they are capable of withstanding 'a fierce artillery attack'.[11] In this sense, the war of position is appropriate to the developed capitalist societies.[12] In fact, for Gramsci, 'war of movement increasingly becomes war of position.' As the 'massive structures of the modern democracies' advance, they 'render merely "partial" the element of movement which before used to be "the whole" of war, etc.'[13] This would seem to imply that capitalism was entering a period in which only the war of position was appropriate as revolutionary strategy: 'a culminating phase in the political-historical situation' in which 'the "war of position", once won, is decisive definitively.'[14] Kautsky would certainly have agreed with this, describing (in 1910) his 'war of attrition' as 'the entirety of the practice pursued by the Social Democratic proletariat since the 1860s.'[15] The connection between the war of position and capitalist development for Gramsci can also be seen when he contrasts revolutionary strategy in 'the East' (Russia in 1917) with that in 'the West' (Europe in the 1920s).[16]

However, it would be unwise to bind Gramsci's position on revolutionary strategy too tightly to stages of social development. Writing on late nineteenth century Italy, he suggested that the war of position ('long ideological and political preparation') was necessary at the time, but that its point was 'to reawaken popular passions and enable them to be concentrated and brought simultaneously to detonation point.' There might be, he muses, 'an entire historical period' in which the war of position dominates— but only 'until...the war of position once again becomes a war of manoeuvre.'[17]

How then is the war of position to be fought? A substantial factor in this was the establishment of a counter hegemony on the part of the subaltern forces: 'A social group can, indeed must, already exercise "leadership" before winning governmental power.'[18] Gramsci was under no illusions as to how arduous such a strategy would be. Comparing it to a siege, he described it as 'concentrated, difficult, demanding exceptional qualities of patience and invention.'[19] Fundamentally, it required undermining the authority of the existing state and pushing that authority aside in ever-expanding areas. In this process, the authority of subaltern groups is built up as it is exercised. Kautsky described this with regard to working class struggle:

> This practice begins with the assumption that the war against the present state and the present society must be waged in such a way as to constantly strengthen the proletariat and weaken its enemies, without allowing the decisive battle to be provoked as long as we are the weaker. We are served by anything that disorganizes our enemies and undermines their authority and combativity, just as anything that contributes to organizing the proletariat, that widens its horizons and combativity, increases the confidence of the popular masses in their organizations.[20]

In Gramsci's terms, the object of the struggle is to undermine and then subsume the institutions and agencies of civil society.[21] Bhagwan Josh adds that 'the struggle for hegemony involves gain [by the subaltern groups] or loss [by the existing state] of prestige, respect, honour, influence and above all, authority over the various sections of the population.' This necessarily includes winning over sections of the population under the influence of the established authorities.[22] Josh adds an extra element to the counter-hegemony strategy which becomes important in the Indian context (as we shall see in the next section). He argues that the war of manoeuvre (which he refers to as the 'paradigm of insurgency') and the war of position (the 'paradigm of mass movements') are *mutually exclusive*. The former is a strategy of violence which may include moments of non-violence. The latter is a strategy of non-violence—though there may be moments of violence. But 'unlike the "paradigm of insurgency" these instances will not figure as interconnected moments in the inevitably rising crescendo towards violent insurrection.' In fact, the war of position is characterised by mass movements which rise, subside or [are] suppressed, only to rise again...as successive waves undermining the hegemony of the state.[23]

Gramsci argued that counter-hegemony would cohere around a particular group or class (his preoccupation being the Italian proletariat). But that group would create 'not only a unison of economic and political aims, but also intellectual and moral unity...thus creating the hegemony of a fundamental social group over a series of subordinate groups.' True, a state dominated by that group would be 'destined to create favourable conditions for the latter's maximum expansion. But the development and expansion of the particular group are conceived of, and presented, as being the motor force of a universal expansion, of a development of all the "national" energies.'[24] Gramsci points out that 'hegemony presupposes that account be taken of the interests and the tendencies of the groups over which hegemony is to be exercised'—thus, 'the leading group should make sacrifices of an economic-corporate kind.'[25]

INDIA

Turning our attention back to India, we will not be surprised that Gramsci wrote little about the sub-continent. He did not extend the reach of his theory of hegemony much beyond European societies. In fact, given his identification of the war of position with the advanced countries, he was inclined to rule out its application elsewhere.

> This question [the war of position] is posed for the modern States, but not for backward countries or for colonies, where forms which elsewhere have been suspended and have become anachronistic are still in vigour.[26]

In a later passage however he did briefly consider the national movement in India and wrote that it combined three forms of 'war': movement, position and underground warfare. He continued: 'Gandhi's passive resistance is a war of position, which at certain moments becomes a war of movement, and at others underground warfare.' He cautioned that if the movement were to become an insurrectionary one, 'then it would suit [the British] to *provoke* a premature outbreak of the Indian fighting forces, in order to identify them and decapitate the general movement.'[27]

There are historians of India who have tried to apply Gramsci's theory to colonial India in a more comprehensive manner. Bipan Chandra, for example, characterises the British colonial state in India as 'semi-hegemonic, semi-authoritarian in character.'[28] Sujeta Mahajan elaborates:

> A reliable social base for the state had to be secured on the one hand; and strategies had to be devised to limit the social reach and the clout of the anti-imperialist forces on the other. Active co-operation...was gained by a variety of techniques, extending from the handing out of jobs, favours and positions of some authority to the granting

of concessions to the "legitimate" political demands of the loyalist liberal sections.[29]

Some measure of consent from significant sections of Indian society was required in order to contain 'any dramatic explosions of conflict'. This, according to Shashi Joshi, 'dictated the introduction of colonial constitutionalism by the British.' Bhagwan Josh adds that from the end of the nineteenth century onwards the British built their hegemony on consent 'while still combining it with old forms of loyalty and obedience'. As the system became more elaborate, discontent was (the British hoped) 'to be neutralised by confining it within the constitutional arena in the Assemblies and Councils created by the political reforms.'[30] This kind of hegemonic set up was all the more important given the size of India's population relative to the numbers of British officials and soldiers in the country. Chandra also points to the external pressures on the Government of India to exercise consent rather than repression: its responsibility to the British electorate (exercised through the pressure of the latter on the British Government); and 'the sensitivities of the British colonial bureaucrats, who were socialised in public schools' (in liberal humanist values).[31]

The semi-hegemonic nature of the colonial state did not mean that it was not repressive. 'It only means,' writes Josh, 'that it carried on repression in a form and within limits which were imposed and circumscribed by the need for legitimation.' Repression 'could only be a partial and short-term tactic,' says Chandra. The British had to develop 'non-suppressive forms...or else give up the semi-hegemonic character of their rule and abandon the terrain of hegemonic struggle.' Thus, Mahajan concludes, 'repression was never immanent and pervasive, except in 1942'—an important exception, as we shall see.[32]

[The British colonial state] was also based on the creation of certain civil institutions and the rule of law, a certain amount of civil liberties, and a certain toleration of and civil behaviour towards its opponents.[33]

As evidence of this, Josh cites the free(ish) press, tolerance of mass meetings, an expanding (though still limited) franchise and the freedom (from 1926) to form trade unions.[34] Joshi is somewhat dismissive of these measures, describing them as 'a semblance of civil liberty in specious imitation of its democratic practice at home.' But she acknowledges that 'the peasant satyagrahas that were launched against the colonial government could have been operative only in a regime which allowed some scope for the expression of popular feeling.'[35]

On this analysis, Josh maintains:

> This colonial state in India, with its rule of law, distorted and limited civil liberties and an evolving constitutional framework was entirely different from the absolutist feudal state in Russia.[36]

For that reason, Gramsci's characterisation of India as a backward country, which was therefore ill-suited to a war of position, was wrong. It was precisely because the colonial state's hegemonic (not despotic) rule nevertheless produced 'passive acquiescence, resignation and unquestioned obedience to the state apparatus'—a 'defeatist, slave mentality' —that a 'psychological transformation' of the subaltern groups had to be brought about.[37] For that, counter-hegemonic strategies were vital.

One prominent Indian scholar, Ranajit Guha, agrees with Gramsci's original characterisation of the colonial state.[38] He contends that 'the colonial state was non-hegemonic with persuasion outweighed by coercion in its structure of dominance.'[39] It was 'based entirely on the so-called "right of conquest"' with 'fear as the fundamental governing principle of colonialism.' In short, 'It was an autocracy...a dominance without hegemony, as we have defined it.'[40] As a result, 'the colonial state was structured like a despotism, with no mediating depths, no space provided for transactions between the will of the rulers and that of the ruled.'[41]

In my view, this is not an accurate description of British rule in India.[42] Clearly the balance between coercion and persuasion was a fluid one, never set in concrete. The British did make efforts to extend the hegemonic aspects of their rule, as they had to do given the balance of (human) forces in India. Guha himself admits that the British had to rely 'to a certain extent on the collaboration of those over whom it rule[d].'[43] There were restricted forms of representation. Guha is quick to note the limited extension of the franchise between 1919 and 1935 and declares that the 1935 Act was 'the devolution of power...to its highest permissible degree.'[44] Perhaps that would have been the limit. But this was not a structure 'with no mediating depths, no space provided for transactions.'

Guha's characterisation of the colonial state has, I would argue, more to do with the conclusions he wishes to draw about the freedom struggle than with the state itself. His contention is that, since the British were despotic, counter-hegemonic strategies against their rule were at best mistaken and at worst a form of collaboration and appeasement. Armed struggle would have been more appropriate.[45] Independence in 1947 did 'nothing to replace or substantially alter the main apparatus of colonial domination—that is, the state.'[46] These failures he ascribes to 'the failure of the Indian bourgeoisie to speak for the nation.'[47]

In the following chapters of this book, I will examine whether the Congress' counter-hegemonic strategy was successful or not. I will also look at the considerable effect those strategies had on wearing down and transforming British state institutions, particularly the bureaucracy and the armed forces. In doing so, I hope to demonstrate that Guha's premise on the lack of hegemony in the colonial state and his conclusions about the national movement are deeply askew.[48]

CONGRESS AND HEGEMONY

Gandhi and the Congress leadership did not study Gramsci's writings. However, the Congress strategy to bring about Indian freedom was unconsciously imbued with his theories of hegemony and counter-hegemony. Chandra contends that the Indian struggle is 'the only historical example of a semi-democratic or democratic-type state structure being replaced or transformed[;] of the broadly Gramscian theoretical perspective of a war of position being successfully practised. In that long-drawn out hegemonic struggle...state power is not seized in a single historic moment of revolution but through a prolonged political process.'[49]

This was due not simply to the wisdom of the Congress leadership, but also to the circumstances in which they found themselves. Josh points out 'the nature of the state could not but have a determining influence on the form and substance of any anti-state politics.'[50] According to Joshi, Congress strategy aimed at taking advantage of the state's semi-hegemonic nature: 'to take hold of the proclaimed liberality of the colonial state and, bit by bit, expose its hollowness.' This would enlarge the political space occupied by Indians (through their national organization) and build up a national counter-hegemony. It 'turned every so-called and apparent act of cooperation or "collaboration" in working the system into its opposite...converting negotiations and compromises into channels of further erosion of state authority.'[51] Chandra points out that the reforms and structures won by the national movement were 'the ground that colonialism was forced to yield under national pressure, a measure of the continuing changing balance of forces.' Once opened up, the ground had to be occupied: 'though in a creative, uncharted way. The reforms had to be worked...evolving and following an alternative method that would upset imperialist calculations and advance the national cause.'[52] As a writer in Gandhi's paper, *Harijan*, put it in 1942:

The purpose of our politics is to get control of these key positions in the country so as to serve the needs of the masses better and help them to develop themselves to the utmost capacity they have been endowed with.[53]

Negotiations and 'working the system' were balanced with mass movements of civil disobedience. The aim was twofold: to 'achieve political effectiveness without succumbing to constitutional blandishments within the colonial framework, on the one hand, and without becoming sitting ducks in the range of imperialist fire, on the other.'[54] The mass movements of the Congress, therefore, had to be democratic and non-violent. The non-violent aspect was intimately bound up with Gandhi's philosophical beliefs, which are beyond the purview of this book.[55] But it was also based on a recognition—both of the physical power of the British state and of the nature of armed rebellion. On the latter Gandhi wrote:

> I hold that the world is sick of armed rebellions. I hold too that whatever may be true of other countries, a bloody revolution will not succeed in India. The masses will not respond. A movement in which [the] masses have no active part can do no good to them. A successful bloody revolution can only mean further misery for the masses. For it would still be foreign rule for them.[56]

A further aspect of Congress' hegemonic strategy was the constructive programme—a programme of work aimed especially at the villages (but applicable in urban areas as well) which sought to build up the confidence, self-reliance and political capacity of the people.

It was designed to bring about a psychological transformation—'to reconquer India from the British.'[57] It included programmes to forge communal unity, against untouchability, for prohibition, to encourage khadi and other village industries, to spread and strengthen education and to raise the status of women. These programmes were a means of promoting the Congress as the real representatives of India—those who genuinely had the interests of the Indian people at heart. 'Trust,' wrote Gandhi, 'begotten in the pursuit of constructive work becomes a tremendous asset at the critical moment.' Joshi points out 'The colonial bureaucracy, unlike many critics of Gandhi, was fully aware of the significance of Gandhi's programme of constructive work and felt extremely threatened by it.'[58] Work in these areas was also particularly important between civil disobedience campaigns—maintaining contact with the masses and occupying the energies of the Congress cadre: 'thus solving a basic problem that a mass movement faces, i.e. how to sustain a sense of activism in the non-mass movement phases of the struggle?'[59]

Gandhi was inclined to believe that the constructive programme was more important than civil disobedience campaigns. He declared that 'Civil disobedience without the backing of constructive effort is neither civil nor non-violent.' But he also regarded the latter as preparation for the former: 'The more the progress of the constructive programme, the greater is there a chance for civil disobedience.'[60] The three elements—counter-hegemony, non-violence and mass civil disobedience—were closely linked:

> Constructive work, therefore, is for a non-violent army what drilling etc., is for an army designed for bloody warfare.[61]

Congress strategy was a struggle for power. But it was not so much about destroying the power of its opponent (though this was certainly one of its effects) as establishing and demonstrating a *counter*-power based on mass support for a different system. 'You do not take power,' wrote Gandhi in 1942, 'It may descend to you being given by the people.'[62] Congress had to show, at least in part, what that alternative system would look like. As Gandhi told Rajkot Congress activists in 1939:

The question that you must seriously set yourself to answer is: "What shall we do with *swaraj*, supposing we got it today?"'[63]

An example of this approach could be seen in the Congress campaign against the British government's monopoly on salt in 1930. This began with a declaration of sovereignty and self-rule on January 26.[64] Armed with this, the campaign was aimed at abolishing the British monopoly. One approach to this may have been demonstrations, petitions and deputations demanding that the monopoly end. But instead, Gandhi marched his followers from his ashram near Ahmedabad to the coast at Dandi (about 390 kilometres). By the time they reached their destination, the original force had grown into a massive mobilisation of Congress supporters. At the beach, salt was made—an illegal act of mass proportions. The movement spread from the coast to the urban centres where the illegal salt was sold, accompanied by demonstrations and mass meetings. This campaign did not ask the British for anything—it simply demonstrated to them that, in this respect, their writ no longer ran.

When the movement reached the villages, it was organized by 'satyagraha centres' and 'Gandhi ashrams'. These bodies set about establishing their own authority by demanding the resignation of village officials who would not support the movement. The perceptive Collector in Surat told his superiors in the Home Department that the purpose of these organizations was 'to establish a progressive form of parallel government, educating the masses to disregard law and authority with a view to ultimately overthrow the present established order and administration.'[65] Sanyal relates that in some areas of Bengal, the movement became 'a part of the popular culture among peasants in these areas; in the 1930s this led to the development of something like a parallel authority to colonial rule.'[66]

Despite Gandhi's arrest, the salt campaign continued through 1930 and into early 1931 when Gandhi was released in order to hold talks with the British. These resulted in the celebrated 'pact' between Gandhi (representing the Congress) and the Viceroy Lord Irwin on March 5, 1931. This brought an end to the salt campaign, the lifting of bans on Congress, the release of many Congress prisoners and Congress participation in the next Round Table Conference. Not for the first time, the Congress left was disappointed by Gandhi's preparedness to settle. For them, the pact was a defeat. In it, however, Gandhi had achieved something on behalf of Congress which was perhaps not altogether obvious at the time. Gandhi and the Viceroy negotiated as equal representatives of opposing forces—which would increasingly be seen as alternatives to each other. This was not lost on the British. Winston Churchill's well-known denunciation of the Gandhi-Irwin talks was not aimed at Gandhi's career choice ('a seditious Middle Temple lawyer'), nor at his dress sense ('striding half naked up the steps of the Vice-regal palace')—but at the fact that he was able 'to parley on equal terms with the representative of the King-Emperor.'[67] The new Viceroy (from April 1931) Lord Willingdon told the Secretary of State that the negotiations meant that Gandhi was perceived by Indians as 'one who was practically the head of a parallel Government.'[68]

From the heights of the Salt campaign, Congress turned back to the constructive programme. While the government could hardly complain about these activities, it was aware of their subversive nature. In 1934 the Home Department considered them 'a very subtle and astute attempt to work up...a civil disobedience campaign,' on a much larger scale and with much wider support.[69]

So it was to be. But not before Congress' counter-hegemonic strategy reached a greater height—which revealed greater problems.

THE CONGRESS MINISTRIES

On the basis of the Round Table Conferences, the British Government issued a White Paper in 1933 setting out proposals for constitutional reform, which culminated in the 1935 Government of India Act. The proposals envisaged, in the first instance, a transfer of power at the provincial level (provincial governments responsible to provincial Legislative Assemblies). The Viceroy would continue to 'direct and control' defence and external affairs. At a later stage, power would be transferred to an Indian Federation of the provinces of British India together with the Princely States.[70]

After much debate, Congress decided to enter into the 1935 scheme—to contest the elections for provincial governments (in February 1937) and, if elected, to take office. This was, in one sense, a huge extension of counter-hegemony. But so great were the problems inherent in the structure the British had set up, it was, in another sense, a step too far. Congress provincial governments took 'power' in the provinces, while power was denied to the Congress at the centre—and even in the provinces that power could be taken away. But it was important that Congress should not refuse the opportunity to demonstrate 'its ability to govern and the capacity to rule.'[71]

The British had given away as little 'rule' as possible. Nehru wrote later:

> The whole complicated structure of government remained as it was, from the Governor down to the petty official and policeman; only somewhere in the middle a few ministers, responsible to a popularly elected legislature, were thrust in to carry on as best they could.

Conflict, he added, was inevitable: 'conflict with the representatives of British interests—the Viceroy, the Governor, the superior services; conflict also with vested interests in land and industry over agrarian questions and workers' conditions.'[72] The structures into which Congress entered were simultaneously political spaces to be occupied and instruments of co-option.[73] Nehru said that the decision to participate 'was itself by no means final and the possibility of change was kept in view'. He admitted however that as the provincial governments 'became entangled in the numerous problems that urgently demanded solution', opting out became increasingly difficult.[74]

Attempts were made to prevent a division between Congress' provincial governments and its mass base. As Congress president, Nehru wrote to Congress members in July 1937 that work outside the legislatures should remain the major task: 'the masses should be kept in touch with whatever we do and consulted about it. The initiative must come from the masses.'[75] Biswanath Das, Congress premier of Orissa, was reported as saying in April 1939:

> The purpose of the acceptance of office by the Congress is to utilise what little power we have in the constitution and remove the obstacles that stand in the way of getting full powers. The power lay with the masses to remove those obstacles and that could be done by strengthening the Congress. Let every man enrol himself as a member of the Congress ...'[76]

Once in office, there was considerable optimism about what could be achieved on the Congress side. Gandhi told a representative of the Hearst newspapers in March 1939:

> The outsiders may not realize the fact that the majority of the provinces of British India...are now administered by Nationalists, by Ministers of the Congress Party. That roughly shows that the National movement is already in the seats of power in this country.[77]

Rather more brashly, Morarji Desai, the newly-elected premier of Bombay, told the Governor, 'Yours is a disappearing Government, ours is an incoming one.'[78] Overly confident, perhaps, but there is little doubt that the Congress governments had a significant psychological effect on the national movement and its supporters. As Vengaswamy put it at the time:

> Everything has changed or is changing: the nation has grown alive to its greatness. Indians have shed their inferiority complex and are ready to play their part in the evolution of a new world of freedom and peace.[79]

Nehru drew attention to the competing hegemonies under the Congress ministries.

> There was vitality there, a bubbling life, a sense of tension, a desire to get things done, all of which contrasted strangely with the apathy and conservatism of the British ruling class and its supporters.[80]

In office, according to Chandra, the Congress 'did try to introduce some reforms, take some ameliorative measures, and make some improvement in the condition of the people—to give the people a glimpse of the future *Swaraj*.'[81] The Congress ministries released political prisoners and lifted censorship; removed bans on Congress propaganda; imposed prohibition; attempted educational reform; wrestled with language problems; and established law and order. They had less success, wrote Vengaswamy, in tackling communalism.[82] The salaries of Congress ministers were restricted to ₹500 per month.[83] Nehru wrote that one reason for taking office was 'the agrarian question' which 'especially demanded immediate attention.'[84] Chandra argues that within the constraints laid down and with more success in some provinces than others 'the agrarian policy of the Congress Ministries went a long way towards promoting the interests of the peasantry.' Likewise, 'The Congress Ministries adopted, in general, a pro-labour stance.'[85]

Congress counter-hegemony was certainly advanced by some aspects of the ministerial experience. Reginald Coupland, studying India on behalf of the Secretary of State and Stafford Cripps, complained that after the 1937 elections, 'all the committees of primary [Congress] party members, great and small, became quasi-official organizations overnight'—and started issuing instructions to the administration.[86] Mahajan confirms that the local Congress organizations became 'a locus of authority—parallel to the official administration—with the Congressmen directing that rents should be paid to them, deciding agrarian disputes and setting up the Congress *panchayat*.'[87] Tomlinson concludes that Congress managed to seize the initiative in the provinces at this time and that this 'disturbed and alarmed the British bureaucrats in India.'[88]

Yet the experience was not without its problems. Chief among these were the use of repression by provincial governments and corruption within the Congress ministries. Congress governments clashed with some popular movements, particularly among the peasants—with whom the need for solutions to their problems was the greatest, but also the most difficult, at the provincial level. In Bihar, from March 1937 to September 1939, peasant agitation was directed at the Congress government: 'the Congress provincial ministry reacted strongly, drawing on all the machinery of repression bequeathed to it by the Raj.' Max Harcourt continues, 'As tension mounted, the stage seemed set for a major conflagration in the countryside accompanied by an irretrievable split within the Bihari Congress party.'[89] This was only prevented by the resignation of the Congress ministries in the early stages of the Second World War. Repression was not confined to Bihar. In Bombay, the Congress government realised 'the loyalty and efficiency of the Police...[is] an asset which we would be most ill-advised to throw away.'[90] Gandhi was acutely aware of the effect that the use of repressive measures would have on the ministries and on future mass movements. He wrote in *Harijan* in April 1939:

> ...do they [the Congress ministries] not realize that it [the 1935 scheme] is likely to break down if Congress ministers cannot carry on without the aid of the Police and the Military, i.e. without British guns? If the partial autonomy was won by non-violent means, it must be held also by such means and no other...[91]

Gandhi linked this to corruption in the Congress. 'The Congress corruption is a sure sign of violence,' he said.[92] Nehru admitted that there were 'careerists' in the Congress ranks.[93] Access to the levers of power also gave access to money-making opportunities, to which some Congress officials were not averse. One reason for this may have been the contrast between the lifestyle which Congress officials had recently left (semi-poverty and periods of gaol) and the one with which they were now rubbing shoulders. 'They are adapting themselves too much to the old order and trying to justify it,' wrote Nehru to Gandhi in April 1938. As a result, 'We are sinking to the level of ordinary politicians who have no principles to stand by and whose work is governed by a day to day opportunism.'[94] With his characteristic optimism for the scheme, Vengaswamy declared:

> The Congress Premier drawing five hundred rupees only and travelling third class on railway must indeed force the fat salaried civil servants both European and Indian to search their conscience.[95]

But it could just have likely caused the premier and those around him to search their wallets—and wonder why they were not full. In some despair at the effect that ministerial office was having on the Congress, Gandhi concluded in April 1939: 'The purging of corruption is the first indispensable condition to the smooth running of the Congress. Once the corruption is banished the Congress will carry on its great work.'[96]

But could it be banished while Congress remained in the provincial ministries?

The ministerial experience can be seen as a high point in Congress' counter-hegemonic strategy before the war. But it can also be seen as a deviation from it—a step too far into the enemy camp without firm enough foundations in the mass base. It contained within it the seeds of its own decay. Gandhi blamed the ministerial period for a decline in the quality of the Congress which was not easily corrected. As late as 1942, he wrote 'I see clearly that the Congress is going downward each day. Selfishness, infighting, untruth and violence have crept into the Congress and are on the increase. I fear we are destroying ourselves because of our inner failures.'[97] Membership of the organization declined from about four and a half million in 1938–9 to one and a half million in 1940–41.[98] Gandhi told workers of the Gandhi Seva Sangh in May 1939, 'we cannot carry on by controlling just a handful of Congressmen. It had ever been our boast that the whole country was with us. Today we are not able to control more than a handful of people.' The Congress, he told its 53rd session in Ramgarh the following year, was 'full of bogus members' who had joined 'because they know that getting into the Congress means getting to power.'[99]

There was, therefore, an urgent need to purge Congress ranks.[100] If this was not effective, Gandhi urged even more radical measures: 'I should not hesitate to bury the organization if the corruption cannot be removed,' he told the Gandhi Seva Sangh.[101] Asked to comment on communal rioting in Allahabad, he declared:

> I would scrap the existing Congress machinery. It is a burden today... If all Congressmen whose names are on the Congress register today were worth their salt, they would offer themselves to be cut to pieces before the communal trouble proceeds any further.[102]

In these circumstances—despite pressure from the left, especially once the war began and the Congress ministers resigned—Gandhi rejected the call for an immediate mass civil disobedience campaign.

> I smell violence in the air I breathe... The widening gulf between Hindus and Mussalmans points to the same thing... My impression is that [corruption in the Congress] is on the increase... In these circumstances, I see no atmosphere

for non-violent mass action... I have the firm belief that the Congress, as it is today, cannot deliver the goods, cannot offer civil disobedience worth the name.[103]

The Congress ministries resigned in October 1939 as part of the evolving Congress position on the Second World War. Gandhi (and other Congress leaders) recognised the resignations not only as a protest against India's unwilling involvement in the imperialist war, but a much-needed opportunity to cleanse the Congress organization, re-establish contact with its mass base and prepare for the next round of struggle.

Whatever the problems associated with this phase of Congress' counter-hegemonic strategy, it established Congress, albeit temporarily and imperfectly, as the alternative to the colonial state.[104] Congress would now enter a period in which its strategy was put to a severe test by war and the question of the defence of India. That test produced deeper and more mass-based attempts at counter-hegemony.

Notes

1   Robert Tressell, *The Ragged Trousered Philanthropists* (London: Lawrence & Wishart, 1978 [1914]), 396.
2   Joseph V. Femia, *Gramsci's Political Thought: Hegemony, Consciousness and the Revolutionary Process* (Oxford: Clarendon Press, 1987), 24. See also Shashi Joshi, *Struggle for Hegemony in India 1920–1947: The Colonial State, the Left and the National Movement. Volume I: 1920–34* (New Delhi: Sage Publications, 1992), 13.
3   Noaman G. Ali, 'Reading Gramsci through Fanon: Hegemony before Dominance in Revolutionary Theory,' *Rethinking Marxism* 27 (2) 2015: 242.
4   Antonio Gramsci, *Selections from the Prison Notebooks of Antonio Gramsci*. Ed. & trans. Quintin Hoare & Geoffrey Nowell Smith (New York: International Publishers, 1975)—henceforward SPN—80. See also Ranajit Guha, 'Gramsci in India,' *Journal of Modern Italian Studies* 16 (2) 2011: 292.
5   Marcus Green, 'Gramsci Cannot Speak: Presentations and Interpretations

of Gramsci's Concept of the Subaltern,' *Rethinking Marxism* 14 (3) Fall 2002: 7.

6   Karl Kautsky, 'Was nun?' (1910) in Massimo Salvadori, *Karl Kautsky and the Socialist Revolution, 1880–1938* (London: Verso, 1990), 140. Kautsky derived these terms from the German military historian Hans Delbrück in his *History of the Art of War in the Framework of Political History* (1900)—see Donald Abenheim, 'Hans Delbrück (1848–1929),' in *The Oxford Companion to Military History* eds. Richard Holmes, Charles Singleton and Spencer Jones (Oxford: Oxford University Press, 2004) (online version).

7   Gramsci, SPN 234. Whether Kautsky or Gramsci had accurately described contemporary military strategy and a permanent feature of it (see for example Daniel Egan, *The Dialectic of Position and Maneuver* (Leiden: Brill, 2016) 29–45) is not particularly relevant to the political/strategic argument. Gramsci warned against over-reliance on the military analogy, pointing out that the political sphere was 'enormously more complex' than war between nations (Joseph V. Femia, *Gramsci's Political Thought: Hegemony, Consciousness and the Revolutionary Process* (Oxford: Clarendon Press, 1987), 51).

8   Green, Gramsci Cannot Speak, 21. See also Ali, who equates Gramsci's war of position with 'hegemony before dominance' (Noaman G. Ali, 'Reading Gramsci through Fanon: Hegemony before Dominance in Revolutionary Theory,' *Rethinking Marxism* 27 (2) 2015: 246).

9   Gramsci, SPN 57.
10 Femia, Gramsci's Political Thought, 52.
11 Gramsci, SPN 235.
12 Femia writes that hegemony was 'the "normal" form of control in any post-feudal society, and, in particular [it was] the strength of bourgeois rule in advanced capitalist society, where material force is resorted to on a large scale only in periods of exceptional crisis.' (Femia, Gramsci's Political Thought, 31. See also Egan, Dialectic, 35–36.)
13 Gramsci, SPN 243.
14 Gramsci, SPN 239.
15 Karl Kautsky in Salvadori, Kautsky, 145.
16 Gramsci, SPN 206–7.
17 Gramsci, SPN 110 & 108.
18 Gramsci in Simon, Gramsci's Political Thought, 18.
19 Gramsci in Perry Anderson, 'The Antinomies of Antonio Gramsci,' *New Left Review* Number 100 November 1976-January 1977: 69. See also Gramsci, SPN, 238.

20 Karl Kautsky in Salvadori, Kautsky, 145.
21 Femia, Gramsci's Political Thought, 52.
22 Bhagwan Josh, *Struggle for Hegemony in India 1920–1947: The Colonial State, the Left and the National Movement. Volume II: 1934–41* (New Delhi: Sage Publications, 1992): 14, 18 & 48.
23 Josh, Struggle for Hegemony II, 48.
24 Gramsci, SPN 181–182. See also Simon, Gramsci's Political Thought, 42 & 61; Ali, Reading Gramsci, 243.
25 Gramsci, SPN 161.
26 Gramsci, SPN 243. In this context, he compares 'Gandhism' (which, with Tolstoyism, 'are naïve theorisations of the "passive revolution" with religious overtones') with the development of Christianity in the bosom of the Roman Empire. (SPN 107.)
27 Gramsci, SPN 229–230. Josh identifies Gramsci's three forms more specifically. Gandhi's strategy is a war of position; that of the Communist Party was a war of movement (an insurrectionary strategy); while India's revolutionary terrorists pursued underground warfare (Josh, Struggle for Hegemony II, 16).
28 Bipan Chandra, *The Writings of Bipan Chandra: The Making of Modern India from Marx to Gandhi* (Hyderabad: Orient Black Swan, 2012), 21.
29 Sujeta Mahajan, 'British Policy, Nationalist Strategy and Popular National Upsurge, 1945–46,' in *Myth and Reality: The Struggle for Freedom in India, 1945–47* ed. Amit Kumar Gupta (New Delhi: Manohar, 1987), 57–8.
30 Shashi Joshi, *Struggle for Hegemony in India 1920–1947: The Colonial State, the Left and the National Movement. Volume I: 1920–34* (New Delhi: Sage Publications, 1992), 14; Josh, Struggle for Hegemony II, 14; Mahajan, British Policy, 58.
31 Chandra, Writings, 22–23.
32 Josh, Struggle for Hegemony II, 51; Chandra, Writings, 43–44; Mahajan, British Policy, 58.
33 Chandra, Writings, 21.
34 Josh, Struggle for Hegemony II, 14–15.
35 Joshi, Struggle for Hegemony I, 16.
36 Bhagwan Josh II 14. See also 43–44; Shashi Joshi I 14.
37 Josh, Struggle for Hegemony II, 17.
38 Copland notes that 'many Gramsci-influenced scholars of South Asia… conclude that since the Raj was a stable and long-lived regime, its rule must have been, to some extent at least, hegemonic… Ranajit Guha being a notable exception.' (Ian Copland, 'The Limits of Hegemony:

Elite Responses to Nineteenth-Century Imperial and Missionary Acculturation Strategies in India,' *Comparative Studies in Society and History* 2007 49 (3): 639)

39 Ranajit Guha, *Dominance without Hegemony: History and Power in Colonial India*, Cambridge (Mass.): Harvard University Press, 1997, xii.

40 Ranajit Guha, 'Gramsci in India,' *Journal of Modern Italian Studies* 16 (2) 2011: 291 & 293. This echoes the position of the Communist Party of India in 1934: 'In India...there is no development of [a] parliamentary democratic form of government... The imperialist state in India bears the character of an absolute state...' (CC/CPI Draft Political Thesis 1934 cited in Josh, Struggle for Hegemony II, 49).

41 Guha, Dominance, 65.

42 Copland again: 'Ranajit Guha insists that the Raj was maintained solely by force... But the weight of scholarly opinion (and in my view the balance of the evidence too) is against him... British rule in India clearly aspired to be hegemonic.' (Copland, Limits, 661)

43 Guha, Dominance, 86.

44 Guha, Dominance, 66.

45 Guha, Dominance, 5.

46 Guha, Gramsci, 291.

47 Guha, Dominance, xiii.

48 As for the bourgeoisie, why they should have been expected to 'speak for the nation' through an armed revolution aimed presumably at socialism is mystifying to me. For an argument as to why and how the Indian bourgeoisie supported (but did not lead) the bourgeois revolution in India see David Lockwood, *The Indian Bourgeoisie: A Political History of the Indian Capitalist Class in the Early Twentieth Century* (London: IB Tauris, 2012).

49 Chandra, Writings, 97. See also Josh, Struggle for Hegemony II, 309.

50 Josh, Struggle for Hegemony II, 43. See also Mohandas Gandhi, 'Discussion with Philipose' (15 March 1939), *Collected Works of Mahatma Gandhi* (Electronic Book) Volume 75 (New Delhi: Publication Division, Government of India, 1999), 186–7.

51 Joshi, Struggle for Hegemony I, 15–24.

52 Chandra, Writings, 43 & 46.

53 'J.C.K.' 'Purposeful Politics', *Harijan* IX (19) 24 May 1942.

54 Joshi, Struggle for Hegemony I, 15–24.

55 See for example: Peter Brock, *The Mahatma and Modern India: Essays on Gandhi's Non-Violence and Nationalism* (Ahmedabad: Navajivan Publishing House, 1983); Mohandas Gandhi, *The Moral and Political*

Writings of Mahatma Gandhi (3 volumes), ed. Raghavan N. Iyer (Oxford: Oxford University Press, 1986–7).

56 Cited in Francis G. Hutchins, *Spontaneous Revolution: The Quit India Movement* (Delhi: Manohar Book Service, 1971), 247–8.
57 B. Pattabhi Sitaramayya, *History of the Indian National Congress 1935–47* (1969) cited in Josh, Struggle for Hegemony II, 50. Commenting on the struggle against Britain and its ruler in the princely state of Rajkot, Gandhi wrote that if the people maintained their non-violent stand, 'They will prove that they are the real rulers of Rajkot under the paramountcy of the Congress.' (Mohandas Gandhi, 'Rajkot' (4 February 1939), Gandhi, Collected Works Volume 75, 2.)
58 Gandhi cited in Joshi, Struggle for Hegemony I, 78; Joshi, Struggle for Hegemony I, 19.
59 Chandra, Writings, 8 & 41.
60 'Constructive Work—its value' (1 April 1940) in Gandhi, Collected Works Volume 78, 105; Gandhi in 1930 cited in Joshi, Struggle for Hegemony I, 213.
61 Gandhi writing in *Young India* (19 February 1930) cited in Josh, Struggle for Hegemony II, 78.
62 Mohandas Gandhi, 'Question Box,' *Harijan* IX (20) 31 May 1942.
63 Mohandas Gandhi, 'Talk with workers of the Rajkot Praja Parishad' (12 March 1939), Gandhi, Collected Works Volume 75, 175.
64 The British were reluctant to suppress these declarations lest they provoked the Congress. But some action had to be taken. The compromise: allow the processions, but arrest the speakers afterwards. (Joshi, Struggle for Hegemony I, 214–215.)
65 Joshi, Struggle for Hegemony I, 217–218.
66 Hitesranjan Sanyal, 'The Quit India Movement in Medinipur District,' in *The Indian Nation in 1942*, ed. Gyanendra Pandey (Calcutta: K.P. Bagchi & Company, 1988), 31.
67 'Mr Churchill on India,' *The Times*, 24 February 1931.
68 Cited in Josh, Struggle for Hegemony II, 70.
69 Home Department file 3/16/34 in Josh, Struggle for Hegemony II, 76.
70 See House of Commons, *Proposals for Indian Constitutional Reform* (London: HMSO, 1933).
71 Bipan Chandra et al, *India's Struggle for Independence, 1857–1947* (New Delhi, Penguin, 1989), 321 & 335.
72 Jawaharlal Nehru, *The Discovery of India* (London: Meridian Books Limited, 1947), 310 & 312.
73 See Chandra, Writings, 43.

74 Nehru, Discovery, 313.
75 Nehru in Chandra, India's Struggle, 334.
76 Speech reported in *Amrita Bazar Patrika*, 16 April 1939, 11.
77 Mohandas Gandhi, 'Interview with Gobind Bihari Lal (16 March 1939), Gandhi, Collected Works Volume 75, 189.
78 Morarji Desai, *The Story of My Life* (Volume 1) (Macmillan India 1974), 157. Hubert Evans described the Congress at this time as 'India's governing class on probation' (Hubert Evans, *Looking Back on India* (London: Frank Cass, 1988), 191).
79 N.S. Venguswamy, *Congress in Office* (Bombay: Bharat Publishing Co., 1940), 145. See also Nehru on the psychological effect and the 'sense of immense relief' that came with the Congress ministries (Discovery, 313–314).
80 Nehru, Discovery, 321.
81 Chandra, India's Struggle, 325.
82 Vengaswamy, Congress In Office, 86–144; on the communal problem, see Vengaswamy, chapter 8.
83 Vengaswamy, Congress In Office, 79–83. 'Their salaries were small, and we had the curious spectacle of a minister's secretary or some other subordinate belonging to the Indian Civil Service drawing a salary and allowances which were four or five times the minister's salary.' (Nehru, Discovery, 317.)
84 Nehru, Discovery, 312.
85 Chandra, India's Struggle, 329 & 331–2.
86 Simon Epstein, 'District Officers in Decline: The Erosion of British Authority in the Bombay Countryside, 1919 to 1947,' *Modern Asian Studies* XVI (3) 1982: 507.
87 Mahajan, 'British Policy', 60. See also Krishan on the establishment of 'an equality of legitimacy for the Congress organization.' (Shri Krishan, 'Crowd Vigour and Social Identity: The Quit India Movement in western India,' *Indian Economic and Social History Review* 33 (4) 1996: 464.)
88 B.R. Tomlinson, *The Indian National Congress and the Raj, 1929–1942: The Penultimate Phase* (London: Macmillan Press, 1976), 137.
89 Max Harcourt, 'Kisan populism and revolution in rural India: the 1942 disturbances in Bihar and east United Provinces,' in *Congress and the Raj: Facets of the Indian Struggle 1917–47*, ed. D.A. Low (London: Heinemann, 1977), 333.
90 K.M. Munshi, cited in Epstein, District Officers in Decline, 516,
91 Mohandas Gandhi, 'Jaipur Civil Disobedience,' *Harijan*, 1 April 1939 in Gandhi, Collected Works Volume 75, 213. See also Chandra, India's

Struggle, 338.
92 Gandhi, 'Jaipur Civil Disobedience'. See also Chandra, India's Struggle, 338.
93 Nehru, Discovery, 312.
94 Cited in Chandra, India's Struggle, 339.
95 Vengaswamy, Congress In Office, 84.
96 Mohandas Gandhi, 'Interview with *The Statesman*' (27 April 1939), Gandhi, Collected Works Volume 75, 304.
97 Mohandas Gandhi, 'Letter to Sampurnanand' (after 2 February 1942), Gandhi, Collected Works Volume 75, 21.
98 The Intelligence Bureau said that this resulted from the 1939 card renewal (aimed at corruption); defection of leftists (especially supporters of M.N. Roy); defection of supporters of the Muslim League and the Hindu Mahasabha; arrests; lack of patronage after resignation of provincial ministries; and the split in the Bengal Congress (Bhupen Qanungo, 'Preparations for Civil Disobedience, January-September 1940,' in *A Centenary History of the Indian National Congress. Volume Three: 1935–1947* ed. M.N. Das (New Delhi: All-India Congress Committee (I), 1985), 337).
99 Mohandas Gandhi, 'Answers to Questions at Gandhi Seva Sangh meeting' (5 May 1939), Gandhi, Collected Works Volume 75, 336; 'Speech at Subjects Committee', (Ramgarh 18 March 1940), Gandhi, Collected Works Volume 78, 7. See also Congress Encyclopaedia XII 334.
100 Mohandas Gandhi, 'Popular Violence in Ramdurg,' *Harijan*, 29 April 1939.
101 Gandhi, Answers to Questions at Gandhi Seva Sangh meeting (5 May 1939), Gandhi, Collected Works Volume 75, 336.
102 Mohandas Gandhi, 'A Discussion' (31 March 1939), Gandhi, Collected Works Volume 75, 220.
103 Mohandas Gandhi, 'Letter to Subhas Chandra Bose' (2 April 1939), Gandhi, Collected Works Volume 75, 224–5.
104 See for example the remarks of the Governor of Bombay, Sir Roger Lumley, in David Hardiman, 'The Quit India Movement in Gujarat,' in *The Indian Nation in 1942*, ed. Gyanendra Pandey (Calcutta: K.P. Bagchi & Company, 1988), 80.

3
1942

> *The golden opportunity for the people of India to win their independence has now come to the surface. The British-India negotiations led by Cripps did not bear fruit. The fact that it ended in utter failure makes us believe that India has given signs to depart from British rule and attain its independence spiritually. The spiritual foundation of Britain in India today has become extinct. The first historic step of India's independence has truly started.*
>
> –General Hideki Tojo, Prime Minister of Japan (May 1942).[1]

By the time General Tojo gave this speech in the Japanese Diet, Japan had taken Hong Kong, the Philippines, the Dutch East Indies, Malaya, Singapore and Burma. Tojo and other Japanese leaders spoke frequently at this time about India. In April Tojo declared 'It has been decided to strike a decisive blow against British power and [its] military establishment in India.'[2] A few days later he told Indians 'you should break off your ties with Britain and march forward for the realisation of your long-cherished goal of establishing a free India.'[3] Given that one of the premises of this book is that in 1942 there was a widespread belief that the Japanese were going to invade India, it seems reasonable at this point to examine whether this was the case. The victorious Japanese surge into South East Asia and Japan's proclamations about a future 'Co-Prosperity Sphere' gave rise to questions as to where the Japanese advance might stop. From the Indian point of view, the novelist and nationalist Mulk Raj Anand spoke for many when he wrote in 1942, 'while the whole of India will never be conquered by the Japanese, the situation for certain areas and the strategic points on the coast of India has passed the zero hour.'[4] Outside India, the view was the same. A Chinese Nationalist General, Wang Pun Shen, told Wilfred Burchett, 'Japan expects India to fall like a ripe apple when the tree is shaken. With radio broadcasts, and the "Indian Independence Army"...Japan is getting ready to shake the tree.'[5]

Japan, not unnaturally, was in confident mood. Flushed with victories, the regime decided to hold a general election in April 1942 (postponed from the previous year). Tojo stated, 'The reason for holding the general election while the War of Great East Asia is being fought is that it presents a good opportunity for consolidating our national strength.'[6] At first, however, the level of public interest was disappointingly low—perhaps because all the candidates uniformly praised the military and called for victory. But the first US air raid on Japan's home islands (the 'Doolittle Raid') on April 18, which killed fifty people in Tokyo, managed to unearth some patriotic fervour.[7] Tojo was able to claim in May that through the election 'the burning enthusiasm of the people was revealed in the form of surging waves of sincerity aimed at the prosecution of the Great East Asia war.'[8] Over 80 per cent of voters turned out (the highest number since 1930) and the Army's list of approved candidates received 66.3 per cent of the vote, delivering them 81.8 per cent of the seats in the Diet. This was not a surprising result, given the state's intimidation and suppression of rival candidates.[9] In the aftermath, the military regime formed up its legislators into the Imperial Rule Assistance

Political Association and proceeded to turn Japan into a one-party state.

Given political consolidation at home and continuing military success abroad, would Japan take the opportunity to push on beyond Burma?

Japan's stated aim was the formation of a Greater East Asia Co-Prosperity Sphere around it in order to challenge western imperialism in Asia. Such a scheme had been part of Japan's imperial vision for some years, but was given official voice by Prime Minister Konoe Fumimaro in 1938. It was reiterated by Foreign Minister Matsuoka Yosake in August 1940. Originally, the Sphere was based on Japan, Manchukuo and China, but Matsuoka expanded it to include the Dutch East Indies, French Indo-China, Hong Kong, Singapore, Thailand, British Malaya and Borneo, the Philippines and New Guinea.[10] The importance of the concept in Japanese policy can be gauged from the fact that at the Imperial Conference (a crisis meeting of the government with the Emperor) in July 1941, at which Japan committed itself to war with the western powers, 'choices were justified or rejected on the grounds they would promote, or impede, the establishment of the Great East Asia Co-Prosperity Sphere.'[11] The borders of the Sphere, Lebra suggests, were 'nebulous and elastic.' They stretched in proportion to Japan's military success. She continues:

> For some, by early 1941, the Greater Sphere, or sphere of influence, would sweep across Asia to embrace India, Australia and New Zealand within its compass. The concept of the Sphere grew as more of South East Asia fell under Japanese military occupation.[12]

A Ministry for Greater East Asia was established in November 1942 to cover 'all the countries and regions in the Greater East Asia Co-Prosperity Sphere under the influence of the Imperial Army and Navy.'[13] How the Sphere was going to be constituted, ruled or expanded was unclear. But its creation meant the destruction of western imperialism in the region and its replacement with some kind of Japanese alternative.[14] Once the war in Asia began, according to Hauner, the regime believed that 'after safeguarding their economic self-sufficiency by the conquest of the Co-Prosperity Sphere, they could stabilise their position within the defensive perimeter and await the peace proposals of the Western Powers.'[15]

The Assembly of the Greater East Asiatic Nations was convened in the Diet building in Tokyo in November 1943. In attendance were the representatives of Japan, China (the Nanjing regime), Burma, Thailand, Manchukuo and the Philippines. They were joined by the exiled Indian nationalist leader Subhas Chandra Bose, as an observer, representing the 'Provisional Government of Free India'.[16] The purpose of the conference was to underline the notion that Japan was fighting for a new order in Asia, untainted by colonial rule and racial discrimination.[17]

The status of the separate national units within the Sphere and their relationship to Japan soon became clear. They were to be under Japanese tutelage. This was increasingly the case as the war continued and Japan's need for their natural resources intensified. According to the Ministry of Foreign Affairs, their 'independence' would exist only 'within the New Order of East Asia and this conception differs from independence based on the idea of liberalism and national self-determination.'[18] Tojo declared that, initially at least, the Sphere would be under Japanese military administration—and, in any case, 'the areas essential for the defense of East Asia shall be controlled and dealt with by Japan herself.'[19] At the Greater East Asia Conference there were no representatives of Malaya, the Dutch East Indies or French Indo-China—areas vital to the Japanese war effort and therefore not to be risked in 'independence' experiments. Nor were there representatives of Japan's own colonies, Taiwan and Korea.[20] Even when Japan did start granting a kind of independence to some of the occupied countries (to Burma in August 1943, for example) it was a form of strategic opportunism, designed to bolster Japan's faltering war effort.[21]

Whether or not the Japanese considered that the Sphere would include India is a matter of some debate and is rather dependent on when the question is asked and by whom within the regime it is answered. Joyce Lebra is firm in her opinion that the Sphere was not intended to expand beyond Burma—and its purpose there was primarily to disrupt lines of communication between the Allies and China. Japan, however, did envisage India coming within her *political* sphere of influence.[22] Debchaudhury, on the other hand, argues that India was included for both strategic and economic reasons. There were those within the Japanese leadership, he says, who saw the Sphere as being based on Japan, China and India. By July 1940 'it was generally agreed in Japanese plans' that India would be a part of the Sphere—'but initially it was undecided when and how this was to be brought about.'[23] Others expand it even further. Mimura states 'in addition to the core region of Japan, Manchukuo, and China, the sphere would include Southeast Asia, Eastern Siberia, and possibly the outer regions of Australia, India, and the Pacific Islands.'[24] According to Richard Storry, the Research Section of the Ministry of War presented a 'Land Disposal Plan' for the Sphere in December 1941 in which India was carved up into regions: Ceylon and the south, Burma/Assam/Bengal in the north.[25] Hauner, more modestly, concedes that since India was important to the Japanese economy, it would be included in a post-war Japanese sphere of influence—but not as an integral part of the Sphere under Japan's tutelage.[26]

I would argue that it was not Japan's intention to include India in the original plans for the Sphere—though some within the regime, encouraged by Japan's military triumph, may have had ambitions in that direction for the future. As success lessened, and the demands of the Japanese war economy on the nations of the Sphere increased, notions of its expansion beyond Burma faded. According to Meo, Japanese military commanders on the ground felt that by November 1943, 'Greater East Asia was lost to Japan and [the countries within it] could be made to conform only by military pressure.'[27]

This brings us back to the question: did Japan intend to invade India, in part or in whole, in 1942? On the basis of their studies, both Lebra and Hauner say no.[28] But the good citizens of Calcutta and Bengal—and of India as a whole—were not privy to the inner secrets of the Japanese leadership. If they listened to the speeches of General Tojo and to other Japanese propaganda—and there is evidence that many of them did—they may have had every reason to be worried.[29] The Japanese stressed that, given the existence of British military installations in north-east India, the defence of their new empire necessitated an attack on them. Tojo told the Diet in May 1942:

> ...in India there still remains the skeleton structure of British domination...military facilities are still rooted and the country itself is still subjected to oppression. As long as there remain British and American military facilities in India, Japan is strongly determined to completely destroy them.[30]

The *Illustrated Record of the Greater East Asia War* declared in this regard:

> ...confronted with an absolutely intolerable situation in which our enemies are about to launch their highly-vaunted counter-attack against us with India as their base, the course which the Imperial forces should pursue is plain and self-evident.[31]

Tojo predicted great suffering for Indians if such an offensive were to take place. He apologised for this in advance: 'To our regret it is, indeed, unavoidable that in the progress of such [a] campaign some misfortune may befall innocent Indians.'[32] Such suffering could be avoided if Indians used a Japanese attack as 'a golden opportunity for India...to rid herself of the ruthless despotism of Britain.' If that came to pass, Japan 'will not stint herself in extending assistance to the patriotic efforts of the Indians.'[33] Tojo told the Greater East Asia Conference 'the Empire of Japan means to give India every possible aid so that she may free herself from the American and British yoke and attain her long-cherished ambitions.'[34] India will rise 'with an intrepid spirit, expel the Anglo-American forces as well as their influence completely from India and thereby realise the independence of their Fatherland.'[35]

It will be clear that, despite their threat to attack British and US military installations in northern India, the Japanese did not promise a full-scale invasion. Rather, the Japanese encouraged Indians to liberate themselves—and warned them of the consequences if they did not.[36] There had been Japanese support for Indian nationalism for some time. They encouraged the Indian Independence League (IIL) in its mission to unite the Indian diasporas in the struggle against the British. The Japanese were also instrumental in the formation of the first Indian National Army (INA) primarily from the Indian prisoners of war captured during the conquest of Malaya and Singapore. We shall learn more of the IIL and the first INA in Chapter Nine. Meanwhile, a series of conferences of Indian nationalists was held in 1942: in Singapore (early March); Tokyo (late March) and Bangkok (June).[37] Each of these, while acknowledging the military successes of Japan and the help that it would bring to the nationalist cause, avoided tying the Indian struggle to a Japanese invasion. The Tokyo conference resolved that 'military action against the British in India will be taken only by the INA under Indian military command' and that 'the forming of the future constitution of India will be left entirely to the representatives of the people of India.'[38]

Japan's most well-known collaborator was the radical Bengali Congress leader, Subhas Chandra Bose. A militant opponent of the British, Bose had diverged from the mainstream Congress leadership over (amongst other issues) the conduct of the struggle since the start of the European war. In May 1939, he grouped his followers within Congress into a new organization, the Forward Bloc. The Chief Secretary of Bengal reported in April 1940:

> His speeches are becoming more and more objectionable; his present line is to declare that Britain cannot win the war and that he for one will be glad if she loses.[39]

He was subsequently arrested during a demonstration calling for the removal of the monument to the victims of the 'Black Hole' of Calcutta and kept in gaol 'as a security prisoner pending his prosecution for a number of seditious speeches.'[40] But Bose took ill and was released into house arrest in December. The British were of the opinion that he was engaged in 'intrigue with Japan' but had little evidence to prove it.[41] On 17 January 1941, Bose made his famous escape from his Calcutta residence, turning up in Germany in April.[42]

Bose would spend all of 1942 in Germany. From May that year, he made a series of requests to the German authorities to be sent to Japan—from which he sensed a greater willingness (and greater resources) to join with the Indian cause.[43] For our purposes, Bose's political importance in 1942 came mainly from his broadcasts on the *Azad Hind* radio station, established in Berlin and beamed (quite successfully apparently) into India (see Chapter Eight). From these broadcasts and from various speeches, it is clear that Bose's collaboration during 1942 with Germany and then Japan did not hinge on an invasion of India by the Axis powers. In his message to the Bangkok conference in June he declared:

> ...the emancipation of India must be the work of Indians themselves...it is the Indian people who must determine the future destiny of the country and of the Free State.[44]

He said 'if we get [freedom] as a gift we shall not be able to retain it.' He specifically rejected being handed freedom by the Axis powers: 'we should not ask for any assistance as long as we can do without it.'[45] The positions of Bose and other nationalists would change. But in 1942, Indian nationalists in favour of collaborating with Japan were not relying on a Japanese invasion.

Nevertheless, Japanese statements, combined with the air raids of 1942 and British propaganda, convinced many that an invasion was inevitable and the threat remained after 1942.[46] The Japanese Imperial General Headquarters in Tokyo and the Southern Army Headquarters in Singapore had suggested that Japanese forces should enter Assam. Local commanders considered the terrain too difficult and the idea was dropped. It was revived in January 1944 in the form of 'Operation 21'—'an operation for the defence of Burma, aimed at the British bases in the Imphal Plain in Manipur State.'[47] This was exactly what the Japanese had threatened two years earlier: a defensive move into part of India, rather than an attempted invasion.[48] An enquiry by the British Cabinet Office concluded in May 1948 'the Japanese High Command did not seriously contemplate an invasion of India by land in 1944.'[49] In a limited way, Operation 21 was put into effect, but it turned out to be a military disaster for the Japanese—'up to that date, the most disastrous defeat the Japanese Army had known in its entire history.'[50]

In the years before Japan's entry into the war and the events of 1942, for most Indians a Japanese invasion seemed too remote a possibility to disturb imperial life. Nehru explained to the All-India Congress Committee in February 1938:

> Japan is further away from India...than England is. The land route is entirely closed and impossible of passage even for aircraft. The sea route is very long and terribly dangerous and cannot be negotiated till British sea power and air power have ceased to exist in the East and probably America has been wholly disabled. Japan cannot think of coming to India till she has absorbed the whole of China, a task almost certainly beyond her competence and resources.[51]

Even when hostilities with Germany commenced, there was Indian apathy towards Britain's war and Britain's war effort which we have already noted. This was reflected in Bengal in a lack of significant contributions to the War Fund. Worse still, there were those who greeted British setbacks in the war with glee and looked forward to the demise of the Empire.[52] 'Exultation of the Indian nationalists over British defeats and reverses continued unabated during the first eleven months of 1941,' writes Chaudhuri.[53] In the villages of the Ghazipur district some were singing, 'With Holland gone, and Poland gone, it's now turn of England!'[54] There were also those who believed that the European war would bring economic good times to India, in contrast to the 1930s.[55]

Japan's naval build-up produced warning notes in the press. The *Statesman* declared 'there is big trouble coming'; *Advance* pointed to 'a danger to Australia as well as to India'; and *Lokamanya* stated 'it is not a remote thing for Japan to think of invading India.'[56] Yet as late as December 1941 the Intelligence Bureau reported Indian opinion that 'no one seems to think that war with Japan would in any circumstances be comparable with the war that is being waged with Germany and no danger to India is anticipated.'[57]

Japanese entry into the war in December 1941 brought with it not only the fear (resulting in flight) that we noted in Chapter One, but also both a widespread *expectation* that Japan would invade, combined with considerable speculation as to what the British would do when they did. The Chief Secretary of Madras reported that Japan's entry was 'a very considerable and unpleasant surprise to the great majority'—exacerbated by the loss of HMS *Prince of Wales* and HMS *Repulse*. He went on: 'There is no doubt that the menace to India of the Japanese attack on Malaya is being more and more understood by all sections of the community.'[58] The Governor of Bengal declared 'It is no use blinking the fact that these reverses have led to the belief that we are unable to hold the Japanese.'[59] Intelligence reported rumours that the Japanese would attack Chittagong, Calcutta and Madras: 'An imminent collapse of British power had been taken for granted. In Bengal even some people started learning Japanese.'[60]

On the left, an invasion was a foregone conclusion. The Communist Party of India wrote to its members:

> After the fall of Singapore, our country is in imminent danger of foreign invasion. After the battle of Burma is over...a full-scale invasion is almost certain.[61]

The socialist M.N. Roy wrote that India 'is threatened with an invasion by a Fascist power... In the near future, Bengal may be overrun by the Japanese invaders.'[62] Other political parties were making other arrangements. A British intelligence agent reported on a meeting of the Muslim League's Working Committee in August 1942: 'the main item discussed was the possibility of the collapse of the Central Government following a Japanese invasion.' Muhammad Ali Jinnah was reported as saying that this 'would be a signal for the fight with the Hindus rather than with the Japanese who would naturally place the stronger party in power.'[63]

The Indian press did nothing to calm speculation. *Amrita Bazar Patrika* drew on events in Australia for Indian consideration. The Japanese raids on Darwin, headlined the newspaper, were more than likely 'A Prelude to Landing': 'Official view is that the Japanese will attempt a full scale attack before long.'[64] In Bihar, the *Searchlight* said 'An invasion of India now appears to be a matter of time.' *The Indian Nation* warned: 'The possibility of enemy parachutists attempting a landing on the Indian coasts as a preliminary to invasion in force is a very live possibility which we in India cannot ignore.'[65] Chaudhuri wrote later:

> Almost everyone I talked to in Calcutta, including high Bengali officials, believed that by the end of February 1942 or at least by March, the whole of Bengal including Calcutta would be occupied by the Japanese.[66]

S.K. Halder reported to a conference of District Officers in Calcutta that in his division (Burdwan), 'the people felt that the invasion would take place about October or November, just after the monsoon, a view for which there was the authority of astrologers.'[67]

The British too expected the worst. In 1940 and 1941 the view of the Indian General Staff had been that unless Japan took Singapore and the Dutch East Indies 'a landing operation against Indian and Ceylon was improbable and that eventual attacks were unlikely to exceed the scale of minor sorties.'[68] Once they were taken—and Burma invaded—an attempted invasion seemed inevitable. Jane Grice, daughter of the Managing Director of ICC (India) believed that 'The Japanese, having taken Hong Kong, Malaya and Burma, were now ready to swoop down on Calcutta.'[69] The Indian civil servant Philip Mason wrote in April 1942:

> There was no reason we could see why the Japanese should not land troops in India—only the blind hope that they must be getting rather tired and might have bitten off all they could manage.[70]

At a more official level, the same month Linlithgow wrote to the Secretary of State, 'It will not surprise me at any moment to hear of a Japanese landing somewhere in South India.'[71] General Slim and his colleagues 'passed full days and some anxious nights when scares of invasion called us from our beds...at the time it loomed constantly over us.'[72] The Governor of Bengal reported in February 1942, 'As soon as Rangoon falls, Bengal is liable not only to air attack but to invasion... As the threat is imminent, action is required at once.'[73] The official British history of the war with Japan compares India's situation after the fall of Rangoon with that of Britain after the retreat from Dunkirk.[74] The provincial government told the District Officers of Bengal at the end of March: 'in view of the present situation in Bengal heavy raids and perhaps invasion are definite possibilities.'[75] According to Prasad, 'the gravity of the situation...was fast deteriorating.'[76]

By now, the Joint Planning Staff (JPS) in India had no doubt that the Japanese could muster the resources for an invasion. The JPS considered Bengal, Assam, Orissa, Bihar, Madras and Ceylon under threat. Major-General Molesworth (Deputy Chief of the General Staff) predicted that the Japanese would attack India first through Burma and then through Ceylon.[77] A conference brought together in Calcutta by the Commander-in-Chief in March 1942 concluded:

> ...the Japanese would attempt a seaborne attack either in the Sundarbans area or directly on Calcutta or in its neighbourhood. A land attack on Assam coupled with infiltration up the east coast was also not improbable.[78]

Confidence in British ranks, both military and civilian, was not high. According to the Intelligence Bureau, after Singapore 'a large number of letters seen in censorship, mostly by British officers, are unrestrainedly critical and pessimistic.'[79] The gloom was exacerbated by the impression of unpreparedness for invasion and concern as to what would happen if one occurred. The Viceroy, speculating on the loss of Singapore, wrote to the Secretary of State:

> I am advised that India is at present wholly insufficiently protected against attack, and that direct attack on any considerable scale might produce an exceedingly difficult situation to hold in terms of security in this country.[80]

The Chief Secretary of Bengal commented in June 1942 that 'Nowhere...is there any considerable confidence felt or expressed in British strategy or in the quality of Imperial troops.'[81] Quite the contrary, according to a Women's Army Corps (India) officer: 'If the Japanese had known one division landed in the south of India would have been unstoppable.'[82] The Fortnightly Report from Bihar in February noted 'the feeling that India, if attacked, will be found as unprepared as the rest of the Far East.'[83]

Before the outbreak of war with Japan, the feeling in British defence circles was that eastern India was relatively secure. Invasion by land, sea or air was believed impossible without the enemy having bases in Burma, Indo-China and Thailand, and having taken Singapore. Thus by 1939, 'no schemes for the defence of the eastern frontier were prepared.'[84] As the European war situation worsened, some concern was expressed about India's vulnerability. The Chief Secretary of Bengal made the point in May 1940 'that the British Government alone is responsible for the comparatively defenceless position in which India finds itself today.'[85] Reassurance came from the military. The Commander-in-Chief (Far East) told the War Office in October 1941 that 'Japan is now concentrating her forces against Russia...the last thing Japan wants at this juncture is a campaign in [the] south.'[86] Some action was attempted before Japan entered the war. Eastern Command (India) wanted to improve the defences of the Bengal and Orissa coastlines.

> The Eastern Command...formulated an appreciation and a plan for defence, demolitions and inundations. Their appreciation was based on the vulnerability of India and the delay which might be involved in installing defences.

But Eastern Command's efforts were rejected by the General Staff. They felt that the only danger from Japan was of minor air raids: 'therefore no measures which would in any manner affect the primary task of sending reinforcements to the Middle East should be entertained.' On the eve of the Pearl Harbour attack, Eastern Command prepared another plan, 'based on giving minimum protection to the provinces of Assam, Bengal and Orissa'—but this too was rejected by the General Staff.[87] Prasad concludes:

> It is clear from the action taken up to the end of 1941 that the General Staff in India were suffering from a peculiar complacency, which prevented them from adopting effective measures to counteract any possible Japanese threat against Eastern India or her coastline.[88]

Thus it was that the Indian Chiefs of Staff reported to the Commander-in-Chief in March 1942 that naval defences would not be at sufficient strength to resist the Japanese for some months. 'We are in consequence greatly concerned regarding the possibility of an air or seaborne attack upon Calcutta,' they said.[89] At the same time a meeting at the Admiralty on the defence of eastern India concluded:

> For at least two months to come no determined attempt by the Japanese to send sea-borne forces e.g. to Ceylon, Madras, Vizagapatam, or to Calcutta could be successfully resisted.[90]

General Wavell described 'the forces available for defence' of India and Ceylon as 'dangerously weak'. He went on: 'our Eastern Fleet was powerless to protect Ceylon or Eastern India; our air strength was negligible'—and he warned 'I cannot, repeat not, be held against likely scale and method of Japanese attack.'[91] General Slim was most concerned about invasion by sea: 'we had no naval forces of any size nearer than East Africa. The airforce was insufficiently prepared to face the Japanese and there were not enough troops to hold the Sundarbans should invasion come that way.'[92] The situation led India Command to the conclusion in March 1942 that in the event of an invasion, it would have to choose between either dispersing its forces to protect ports, airfields and military bases, or withdrawing its forces 'from certain areas before they were inextricably committed, in order to hold one or more strategic positions strongly.' Those 'strategic positions' might not include Bengal. The paper continued: 'However desirable it might be to hold areas such as Bengal the fact that this might be impossible must be recognised.'[93] We shall examine this in more detail in the next chapter.

The inevitability of invasion was matched, for the British, by the expected breakdown of society in its aftermath. They believed that a pro-Japanese network was being put together across Bengal (and beyond) under the auspices of Bose's Forward Bloc.

Bose's brother (and long-time political collaborator) Sarat, it was reported, 'throughout the summer of 1941 was endeavouring to form a combination of secret terrorist groups under the banner of the Forward Bloc to give assistance to the Japanese invader.'[94] The Viceroy wrote to Amery at the beginning of 1942 that military authorities reported 'a large and dangerous potential 5th column in Bengal, Assam, Bihar, and Orissa, and that indeed [the] potential of pro-enemy sympathy and activity in eastern India is enormous.'[95] The Director of Intelligence at India Command telegrammed the War Office to report that 'In Bengal left wing speakers have professed readiness support Japanese invaders and danger active Fifth Column undoubtedly exists.'[96] Gandhi agreed. 'I have no proof,' he said, 'but I have an idea that the Forward Bloc has a tremendous organization in India.'[97]

In the paper referred to above, the JPS listed the following consequences of invasion:

a. a big refugee problem
b. a serious internal security problem
c. the problem of fifth column activities in Bengal
d. large scale desertion of labour from the threatened areas paralysing all industrial and transport activities
e. breakdown in civil administration
f. large-scale looting
g. general loss of morale throughout the population of India which could not escape having an effect on the Indian forces.[98]

Little wonder then that the Government of India felt the need to make some overtures to the Indian population in an attempt to engage them in the war effort.[99] But as we shall see, the moves that were made were rather too little and too late. 'British political policy failed to marshal Indian patriotism for the security of the country,' says Prasad.[100]

In this chapter, I have set out why the prospect of a Japanese invasion seemed very real to both Indians and Europeans, especially in the vulnerable coastal areas, despite Japan's initial reluctance and subsequent inability to invade. In the next chapter, I will delve more deeply into what the British intended to do to preserve the hegemony of the colonial state if and when invasion occurred.

Notes

1. Hideki Tojo, *Address by Hideki Tojo, Premier of Japan, at the Opening of the Imperial Diet* (27 May 1942), www.ibiblio.org/pha/policy/1942/1942-05-27a.html.
2. Joyce C. Lebra, *Jungle Alliance: Japan and the Indian National Army* (Singapore: Asia Pacific Press Pte Ltd, 1971), 64.
3. Milan Hauner, *India in Axis Strategy: Germany, Japan and Indian Nationalists in the Second World War* (Stuttgart: Klett-Cotta, 1981), 439.
4. Mulk Raj Anand, *Letters On India* (London: George Routledge & Sons, 1942), 14.
5. Wilfred G. Burchett, *Bombs over Burma* (Melbourne: F.W. Cheshire Pty Ltd, 1944), 187–8.
6. Sekijiro Takagaki, *The Japan Year Book 1942–43* (Tokyo: Japan Times Press, n.d. [1943]), 179–180; Ben-Ami Shillony, *Politics and Culture in Wartime Japan* (Oxford: Clarendon Press, 1981), 21.
7. Shillony, Wartime Japan, 26.
8. Hideki Tojo, *Address by Hideki Tojo, Premier of Japan, at the Opening of the Imperial Diet* (27 May 1942), www.ibiblio.org/pha/policy/1942/1942-05-27a.html.
9. Shillony, Wartime Japan, 23–6; Gerhard L. Weinberg, *Visions of Victory: The Hopes of Eight World War II Leaders* (Cambridge: Cambridge University Press, 2005), 70.
10. Sudata Debchaudhury, *Japanese Imperialism and the Indian Nationalist Movement: A Study of the Political and Psychological Impact of Possible Invasion and Actual Occupation, 1939–1945* (Ph.D. Dissertation, University of Illinois-Urbana, 1992), 101; Peter Duus, 'Imperialism without Colonies: The Vision of a Greater East Asia Co-Prosperity Sphere,' *Journal of Diplomacy and Statecraft* VII (1) 1996: 58–9; Hauner, India in Axis Strategy, 100–101.
11. Duus, Without Colonies, 62.
12. Lebra, Jungle Alliance, xi-xii.

13 Japan Year Book 1942–3, 140. The Ministry incorporated the former Ministry of Colonies, the Asian Affairs Bureau of the Foreign Ministry, the Bureau of Manchurian Affairs and the Asian Development Board (Shillony, Wartime Japan, 34).
14 Dechaudhury, Japanese Imperialism, 102; Duus, Without Colonies, 66.
15 Hauner, India in Axis Strategy, 300. By that time Japan believed that Britain would have been defeated, the Soviet Union neutralised by German attack and the US isolated (302).
16 Lebra argues that this indicates that India was not considered a part of the Sphere (Lebra, Jungle Alliance, 131).
17 Duus, Without Colonies, 69. Shillony points out that Tojo was under some political pressure at this time and used the conference to 'bolster his position and silence the critics.' (Shillony, Wartime Japan, 53.) The Japanese newspaper reporter Masuo Kato reveals that it was not an unqualified success in that regard. 'The affair soon bogged down in red tape, lack of co-ordination between the government departments sponsoring it, and the insistence of the army that it be permitted to make all the decisions without considering the advice of skilled civilian diplomats.' (Cited in Meo, Japan's Radio War.)
18 Debchaudhury, Japanese Imperialism, 103. Japan's Axis allies had already agreed to 'recognise and respect the leadership of Japan in the establishment of a new order in Greater East Asia.' (Richard Storry, *The Double Patriots: A Study of Japanese Nationalism* (Westport: Greenwood Press, 1976), 275.)
19 Tojo to the Diet in June 1942 cited in Meo, Japan's Radio War, 183. See also Japan Year Book 1942–3, 173.
20 Jeff Kingston, 'Pan Asian Dreams: The Greater East Asia Conference,' *The Japan Times* (9 November 2013): www.japantimes.co.jp; Duus, Without Colonies, 70.
21 Weinberg notes that moves by well-meaning Japanese officers towards real independence were 'quickly halted by Tokyo military authorities, who looked down on the peoples of the conquered lands not only on military but also on essentially racist grounds.' (Gerhard L. Weinberg, *Visions of Victory: The Hopes of Eight World War II Leaders* (Cambridge: Cambridge University Press, 2005), 73.
22 Lebra, Jungle Alliance, xii & 60. See also Mihir Bose, *The Lost Hero: A Biography of Subhas Bose* (London: Quartet Books, 1982), 191–192.
23 Debchaudhury, Japanese Imperialism, 103–111; for his critique of Lebra see 107–8.
24 Janis Mimura, *Planning for Empire: Reform Bureaucrats and the Japanese*

Wartime State (Ithaca: Cornell University Press, 2011), 171.
25 Storry, Double Patriots, 276 & 318–319.
26 Japan was the major importer of Indian textiles after the First World War; it was the biggest importer of raw cotton; from 1900 to 1939 Japan was India's most important trade partner in South East Asia (Hauner, India in Axis Strategy, 104–105 and 425).
27 Meo, Japan's Radio War, 186.
28 Lebra, Jungle Alliance, 64–5; Hauner, India in Axis Strategy, 601 & 607–8. Prasad maintains 'Whether [the invasion of Burma] was intended to be a ... jumping ground for the invasion of India ... it is difficult to say categorically' (Bisheshwar Prasad, *Official History of the Indian Armed Forces in the Second World War, 1939–45: Volume Two, The Retreat from Burma, 1941–42* (Calcutta: Orient Longmans, 1959), 61).
29 'It is reported that an increasing number of people now rely on broadcasts from Tokyo for news rather than on the All-India Radio.' (Fortnightly Report, Bengal 2nd half May 1942 in Bipan Chandra and Salil Misra (eds.), *Towards Freedom: Documents on the Movement for Independence in India, 1942* (New Delhi: Oxford University Press, 2016), 777.
30 Address by Hideki Tojo, May 1942.
31 'Blow Dealt [to] British Forces in India', *Illustrated Record of the Greater East Asia War* in Ian Nish, *The Japanese in War and Peace, 1942–48: Selected Documents from a Translator's In-tray* (Folkestone: Global Oriental, 2010), 154.
32 Tojo to the Diet, 27 May 1942 in Japan Year Book 1942–3, 184.
33 Tojo to the Diet, 16 February 1942 in Japan Year Book 1942–3, 178.
34 Moti Ram (ed.), *Two Historic Trials in Red Fort. An Authentic Account of the Trial by a General Court Martial of Captain Shah Nawaz Khan, Captain P.K. Sahgal and Lt. G.S. Dhillon and the Trial by A European Military Commission of Emperor Bahadur Shah* (New Delhi: Moti Ram, 1946), 370.
35 Tojo to the Diet, 27 May 1942 in Japan Year Book 1942–3, 184.
36 It is also argued that any invasion plans that did exist were shelved due to the strain on Japanese resources (see Debchaudhury, Japanese Imperialism, 108; Hauner, India in Axis Strategy, 102 & 104) and doubts about Indian stability in its wake (see Bisheshwar Prasad, *Official History of the Indian Armed Forces in the Second World War, 1939–45: Volume Twelve, Defence of India—Policy and Plans* (Kanpur: Combined Inter-Services Historical Section (India and Pakistan), 1963), 197; Hauner, India in Axis Strategy, 433; Debchaudhury, Japanese imperialism, 109.
37 Hauner, India in Axis Strategy, 433; Report on Indian Independence

Conference, Tokyo 28–30 March 1942 in Chandra and Misra, Towards Freedom, 565–7; Lebra, Alliance, 51.
38   Lebra, Alliance, 51; Report on Indian Independence Conference Tokyo 28–30 March 1942 in Chandra and Misra, Towards Freedom, 567–8.
39   Chief Secretary Report, 1st half April 1940. British Library, India Office Records (henceforward: IOR). Fortnightly Reports of Governors, Chief Commissioners and Chief Secretaries (1937–1948) L/PJ/5/146.
40   Police Department, Bengal. Report on the police administration in the Bengal Presidency 1940, 35. IOR
41   India Office memorandum, 22 October 1940. IOR: L/PLJ/12/217; Deputy Commissioner of Police (Bengal) to Assistant Director, Intelligence Bureau, 29 January 1941. West Bengal State Archive (henceforward: WBSA) 66/41 Bose activities.
42   The Governor of Bengal suggested that 'his disappearance is likely to detract further from his reputation in political circles' (Governor Report, 2nd half January 1941. IOR: Fortnightly Reports of Governors, Chief Commissioners and Chief Secretaries (1937–1948) L/PJ/5/148.).
43   Sisir K. Bose and Sugata Bose (eds.), *Azad Hind: Writings and Speeches, 1941–1943 by Subhas Chandra Bose* (Calcutta: Netaji Research Bureau, 2007), 100–101 & 107; Mihir Bose, *The Lost Hero: A Biography of Subhas Bose* (London: Quartet Books, 1982), 189.
44   S.C. Bose in Bose and Bose, Azad Hind, 115.
45   S.C. Bose, Azad Hind radio broadcast in George Orwell, *The War Commentaries* ed. W.J. West, (Harmondsworth: Penguin, 1987), 227; S.C. Bose, Azad Hind radio broadcast 17 June 1942 in Bose and Bose, Azad Hind, 119; SC Bose, Azad Hind radio broadcast 31 August 1942 in Bose and Bose, Azad Hind, 141. While in Germany, Bose outlined his plans for the future which are worth noting here as another contender for hegemony in India. The direction of his thought, perhaps influenced by his surroundings, seems clear. The future India would have to have a 'strong Central Government', backed up by 'a well-organized, disciplined all-India party, which will be the chief instrument for maintaining national unity.' Furthermore, 'All anti-national and disruptive elements will have to be firmly suppressed ... the law will have to be amended, so that offences against national unity may be punished heavily.' He endorsed Nazi policies on labour relations, extolling the virtues of various Nazi schemes for militarising the work force. He looked for economic, military and scientific aid from the Axis powers ('Free India and Her Problems August 1942 in Bose and Bose, Azad Hind 150–156).
46   Peter Stanley's comment on Darwin at about the same time is entirely

applicable to the situation in Bengal:

'Why was Darwin bombed? Simply because it was the main Allied base in northern Australia, and with the Japanese invasion of Timor about to begin, it made sense for the Japanese to try to damage as much as they could ... [But] the survivors of the raids assumed that they preceded a Japanese landing.' (Peter Stanley, *Invading Australia: Japan and the Battle for Australia, 1942* (Camberwell: Viking, 2008), 108.)

47 Louis Allen, 'Mutaguchi and the Invasion of India (Imphal, 1944)' in *War, Conflict and Security in Japan and Asia-Pacific, 1941–52: The Writings of Louis Allen*, ed. Ian Nish & Mark Allen (Folkestone: Global Oriental, 2011), 243, 246 & 249.

48 This was despite the individual ambitions of those like Lt-Gen. Mataguchi Renya, Maj-Gen. Sakura Tokutaro and Lt-Gen. Kawabe Masakuzu, who each harboured visions of a major thrust into, and occupation of, India. (Allen, Mitaguchi, 244–252; Louis Allen, *Burma: The Longest War 1941–45* (London: Guild Publishing, 1984), 154.)

49 Enquiry by Historical Section of the Cabinet Office, HMG: whether Japan seriously contemplated invasion of India (25 May 1948) in the Private Papers of Lt-Colonel G.D. Anderson. British Library: India Office Records, Mss Eur Photo Eur 397. General Slim disagreed. He maintained the Japanese believed that 'India, ripe as they thought for revolt against the British, would fall, a glittering prize, into their hands.' (William Slim, *Defeat into Victory* (London: Cassell and Company Ltd., 1956), 285.)

50 Allen, Mitaguchi, 244.

51 Nehru at the Haripura AICC meeting (10 February 1938) cited in Nicholas Owen, 'The Cripps Mission of 1942: A Reinterpretation,' *Journal of Imperial and Comonwealth History* 30 (1): 91. See also Nicholas Owen, 'The Cripps Mission of 1942: A Reinterpretation,' *Journal of Imperial and Commonwealth History* 30 (1): 69. Nehru wrote to Rajendra Prasad in May 1940, 'I do not think there is the slightest chance of a German or Japanese invasion of India.' (cited in Yasmin Khan, *India at War: The Subcontinent and the Second World War* (Oxford: Oxford University Press, 2015), 10.

52 Janam Mukherjee, *Hungry Bengal: War, Famine, Riots and the End of Empire* (Noida (India): Harper Collins, 2015), 37–8.

53 Nirad C. Chaudhuri, *Thy Hand, Great Anarch! India: 1921–1952* (London: The Hogarth Press, 1990), 582.

54 Gyanendra Pandey, 'The Revolt of August 1942 in Eastern UP and Bihar' in *The Indian Nation in 1942*, ed. Gyanendra Pandey (Calcutta: K.P. Bagchi & Company, 1988), 155.

55 Yasmin Khan, *India at War: The Subcontinent and the Second World War* (Oxford: Oxford University Press, 2015), 86.
56 Chief Secretary, Bengal Report 2nd half April 1940. Fortnightly Reports of Governors, Chief Commissioners and Chief Secretaries (1937–1948). IOR: L/PJ/5/146.
57 Intelligence Summary 14 December 1941. IOR: L/WS/1/317.
58 Chief Secretary, Madras Report 23 December 1941. IOR: Fortnightly Reports, Madras. L/PJ/205 1942.
59 Governor, Bengal Report 1st half February 1942. Fortnightly Reports of Governors, Chief Commissioners and Chief Secretaries (1937–1948). IOR: L/PJ/5/149.
60 Intelligence Report, February 1942 cited in Arun Chandra Bhuyan, *The Quit India Movement: The Second World War and Indian Nationalism* (New Delhi: Manas Publications, 1975), 22.
61 'To All Party Members,' CPI Party Letter IIA (7 March 1942) in Bipan Chandra and Salil Misra (eds.), *Towards Freedom: Documents on the Movement for Independence in India, 1942* (New Delhi: Oxford University Press, 2016), 475.
62 M.N. Roy, *War and Revolution: International Civil War* (Madras: Radical Democratic Party, 1942), 59–60. Roy advocated resistance to the Japanese organized by 'People's Councils'—which, after victory, would go on to organize the constitution of a free India (Debchaudhury, Japanese Imperialism, 130).
63 Statement by 'agent C.B. 29' (24 August 1942) E24/Cong/42-VIII in P.N. Chopra, *Quit India Movement: British Secret Report* (Faridabad: Thomson Press (India), 1976), 96.
64 The headlines in the same edition added: 'Plan of Assault on Australia; Possibility of Two-pronged Invasion of Port Moresby'; and, for good measure, 'Attack on Siberia seems imminent.' (*Amrita Bazar Patrika* 18 March 1942, 5.)
65 Fortnightly Press Report, Bihar 1st fortnight April 1942 in Chandra and Misra, Towards Freedom 1942, 745.)
66 Chaudhuri, Anarch, 592.
67 WBSA 362–42 (22) Proceedings. In December 1942, General Wavell made it known that he felt a Japanese invasion was then less likely. The Government of India at the same time issued a Press Note warning that 'it is possible that attempts will be made by the enemy to introduce enemy agents into India'. The *Amrita Bazar Patrika* countered: 'The object of introducing enemy agents can only be to facilitate invasion.' (20 December 1942, 2.)

68 Indian General Staff letter (13 February 1941) cited in Hauner, India in Axis Strategy, 440.
69 Quoted in Laurence Fleming (compiler), *Last Children of the Raj: British Childhoods in India 1939–1950* (London: Radcliffe, 2004), 144.
70 Philip Mason, *A Shaft of Sunlight: Memories of a Varied Life* (London: Andre Deutsch, 1978), 166.
71 John Barnes and David Nicholson (eds.), *The Empire at Bay: The Leo Amery Diaries 1929–1945* (London: Hutchinson, 1988), 727.
72 Slim, Defeat, 131. Writing on the Australian case (and arguing against the prospect of a Japanese invasion), Stanley says:
'In 1942 it was entirely understandable that an uninformed public would suppose that the Japanese, having conquered South-East Asia so swiftly, would keep going. Indeed the government (which for months knew no better) fostered this belief. Not to have faced the real threat would have been irresponsible. In early 1942 it was reasonable to believe that invasion was imminent.' (Invading Australia, 15.)
73 Governor's Report, Bengal 1st half February 1942. Fortnightly Reports of Governors, Chief Commissioners and Chief Secretaries (1937–1948). IOR: L/PJ/5/149.
74 S. Woodburn Kirby et al. *The War against Japan, Volume II: India's Most Dangerous Hour* (London, HMSO 1958), 106.
75 WBSA 177/42 Administration of Province 31 March 1942.
76 Prasad, Defence of India, 159.
77 Prasad, Defence of India, 151–2 & 161.
78 Cited in Prasad, Defence of India, 154; see also Khan, India at War, 94.
79 Intelligence summary 4 April 1942. IOR: L/WS/1/317.
80 Viceroy to Amery 21 January 1942 in Nicholas Mansergh (ed.), *The Transfer of Power 1942–7. Volume 1: The Cripps Mission, January-April 1942* (London: Her Majesty's Stationery Office, 1970), 46.
81 Chief Secretary's Report, Bengal. 2nd half June 1942. Fortnightly Reports of Governors, Chief Commissioners and Chief Secretaries (1937–1948). IOR: L/PJ/5/149.
82 Quoted in Christopher Bayly & Tim Harper, *Forgotten Armies: Britain's Asian Empire and the War with Japan* (London: Penguin, 2005), 191.
83 Fortnightly Report, Bihar 2nd half February 1942 in Chandra and Misra, Towards Freedom 1942, 713. A fortnight or so later, the Report said that 'The withdrawal from Rangoon is reported still further to have shaken confidence in British ability to withstand an invasion of India.' (Fortnightly Report, Bihar 1st half March 1942 in Chandra and Misra, Towards Freedom 1942, 723.)

84 Prasad, Defence of India, 136–7; see also S. Woodburn Kirby et al, *The War against Japan, Volume II: India's Most Dangerous Hour* (London, HMSO 1958), 49.
85 Chief Secretary Report, 1st half May 1940. IOR: Fortnightly Reports of Governors, Chief Commissioners and Chief Secretaries (1937–1948) L/PJ/5/146.
86 Telegram from Commander in Chief (Far East) to War Office 1 October 1941. IOR: Combined Actions against Japan L/WS/1/68.
87 Prasad, Defence of India, 145–7.
88 Prasad, Defence of India, 148.
89 Naval Appreciation from Chiefs of Staff to Commander in Chief (India) 18 March 1942. IOR: Scorched Earth. War Staff Series Files: File WS 17926. L/WS/1/124.
90 Meeting at Admiralty on defence of Eastern India (not dated: probably March 1942). IOR Scorched Earth. War Staff Series Files: File WS 17926. L/WS/1/124.
91 Prasad, Defence of India, 193; Hauner, India in Axis Strategy, 499. Bhattacharya refers to Wavell's 'cataclysmic reports' about the rapid erosion of British power' (Sanjoy Bhattacharya, 'An Official Policy that went awry: The WW II propaganda campaign against the Indian National Congress,' *International Institute of Asian Studies Newsletter* 13 Summer 1997: www.iias.nl).
92 Slim, Defeat, 128–9. On the disposition of India forces around the world see Kirby et al, War against Japan II, 47–8.
93 Joint Planning Staff Paper, 14 March 1942 in Prasad, Defence of India, 156.
94 SCB Conspiracy. India Office report (not dated). IOR: L/PJ/12/218.
95 Viceroy to Amery 21 January 1942 in Nicholas Mansergh (ed.), *The Transfer of Power 1942–7. Volume 2: 'Quit India', 30 April–21 September 1942*(London: Her Majesty's Stationery Office, 1971), 48.
96 Lt-Colonel Cawthorn to Major Mackenzie 15 February 1942 in Mansergh, Transfer of Poser I, 176.
97 Interview with Bombay suburban and Gujarat Congress members, 15 May 1942. Gandhi, Collected Works Volume 82, 284. Gandhi asked that the contents of this interview be kept secret.
98 Joint Planning Staff Paper, 14 March 1942 in Prasad, Defence of India, 153. The Joint Planning Staff repeated these forecasts in April and May 1942 (165 & 167).
99 See Khan, India at War, 93; Hauner, India in Axis Strategy, 121 & 463.
100 Prasad, Defence of India, 17.

4

THE BRITISH

> [T]he crisis of the ruling class's hegemony, which occurs either because the ruling class has failed in some major political undertaking for which it has requested, or forcibly extracted, the consent of the broad masses (war, for example), or because huge masses (especially of peasants and petit-bourgeois intellectuals) have passed suddenly from a state of political passivity to a certain activity and put forward demands which taken together...add up to a revolution...this is precisely the crisis of hegemony, or general crisis of the State.
>
> —Antonio Gramsci, *Selections from the Prison Notebooks*.[1]

An important feature of British hegemony in colonial India was its ability to hold India together as a single, geographical unit. The British Government and the Government of India did this by enacting and enforcing national laws, by making concessions interspersed with bouts of repression—and, probably most importantly, by demonstrating their ability to defend India from its enemies. These hegemonic cornerstones were threatened by the prospect of a Japanese invasion.

The surest way to defend British hegemony was to successfully defend India against the Japanese. The necessity for this clearly informed a lot of British decision making. But the record for the British, thus far, had not been an auspicious one. The retreat through Malaya, the fall of Singapore and the flight from Burma inspired no confidence in the ability of the British and British-controlled armed forces to stop the Japanese. From the Indian point of view, reassuring defence would have been forward defence—that is, pushing the Japanese back from India's borders. The prospects of that looked exceedingly dim in 1942.

The British would have been in a far stronger defensive position if they had been able to raise the Indian nation in its own defence. Given a non-consensual war, continuing political crisis and their refusal to give any guarantees to the national movement in the event of victory, it is not surprising that this was beyond the capacity of the colonial authorities. Much of the force that could fight the Japanese (beyond conventional armed forces) was, from the British point of view, at best apathetic and at worst anti-British and pro-Japanese. To fight the Japanese, the British needed Indian support. But they were not prepared to make the necessary concessions to win it.

The alternative was flight. This would deal a mighty blow to British hegemony since it would obliterate the cornerstones referred to above in the areas abandoned. However, withdrawal from areas that could not be held or were militarily unimportant might strategically have been the best option—provided that it could be done in an organized and equal manner. Some remnants of hegemonic respectability might have been saved. Once again, the examples of Malaya, Singapore and Burma did not indicate that such a thing could be done. Withdrawal necessitated hard decisions: what would be abandoned and what defended? Who would be left behind? How much infrastructure would have to be destroyed? The very act of planning withdrawal led to a further loss of faith in the colonial state's ability to defend its people.

The fact was that both these strategies, if carried out seriously, contained within them the potential to undermine British hegemony. Defence demanded concessions to the national movement which the British would not consider during the war crisis. Withdrawal necessitated an authoritarian regime which, despite some vigorous attempts, the British were not able to impose. We will examine the options in more detail.

FIGHT

Let us return for a moment to the Calcutta Racecourse. In August 1942, the Royal Calcutta Turf Club approached the military authorities as to whether the usual cold weather race meetings could be held later that year. The Bengal Home Department was also consulted. From there, P.D. Martyn, the Deputy Secretary, objected strenuously to any such scheme. He pointed out that an air attack could probably not be prevented and, if one occurred, the racing crowds would not be able to take shelter in time. But the main thrust of his objection was the impression that 'racing as usual' would create. It would imply, Martyn argued, that preparations for a race meeting were more important than pressing military matters. The government would appear to be at great pains to ensure that the well-heeled racing fraternity was not inconvenienced by the war. To allow the cold weather racing, said Martyn, would be 'proclaiming from the housetops that everything is normal and at the same time expect[ing] the general public to believe that [the government is] seriously concerned with maintaining the war spirit and war effort.' Martyn's views were echoed by his department. Despite this, the Club took their case to the Viceroy himself, with the result that the racing went ahead—even though it was agreed that the Government of Bengal could provide no special protection in the event of an air raid.[2] A tiny incident perhaps, but one that well illustrated the British dilemma. Creating an image of carrying on regardless was meant to exude a confidence in victory that would help create the necessary fighting spirit in Europeans and Indians alike. But what was that fighting spirit for? In the case of the Royal Calcutta Turf Club, it seemed to be deeply imbued with the preservation of the traditions, privileges and superiorities that lay at the heart of the Empire.

If there was to be a fight, how would it be organized? We have noted some early preparations in the previous chapter. Indian defence plans were reviewed at a Commander-in-Chief's conference on March 17, 1942. There was general agreement that Calcutta had to be held, mainly because 'the chief war industries area in eastern Bengal must not be given up.'[3] The Governor of Bengal noted that in his discussion with the Commander-in-Chief:

> It was agreed that Calcutta should be completely defended with all resources available and that consequently there should be no question of evacuation of plant or personnel beyond a request that "ineffectives" who desire to leave should do so.[4]

Back at the conference, it emerged that 'There was, however, difference in regard to the local defence of Calcutta.' While Eastern Command felt that the loss of the city would be 'a serious disaster', the General Staff were more concerned with defending industrial areas rather than the metropolis itself.[5] The question clearly remained unresolved because a month later Governor Herbert wrote to the Viceroy (and through him to the Secretary of State and the Prime Minister):

> The abandonment of the Calcutta area would not only deprive India of more than half her war production but would be such a severe blow to prestige that any belief in our ability to resist the enemy would disappear. The loss of Calcutta would prove tantamount to the loss of India.

He added that it would be 'a fatal and irretrievable mistake to undertake the defence of Calcutta and then fail.' The Viceroy commented to Amery, 'Herbert has been a great nuisance about this.'[6] Either way, the defence that was being discussed was the defence primarily of urban centres and military bases. Hutchins remarks, 'The retreating army would confine itself to the defence of certain strategic enclaves, leaving villagers to their fate with a hearty slap on the back and a promise to return.'[7]

Successful resistance required a galvanised—or at least non-hostile—Indian population. Amery's view in May 1940 was an optimistic one:

> My whole conception is that of India humming from end to end with activity in munitions and supply production and at the same time with the bustle of men training for active service of one sort or another, the first operation largely paying for the cost of the second.[8]

This failed to materialise. Later, it was felt that the imminence of invasion might have a positive effect. It was reported from Orissa in March 1942: 'there are indications that the anxiety concerning India's Eastern border is resulting in greater willingness on the part of the general public to co-operate in Government's efforts to defend themselves and the country.'[9] Vigorous propaganda for the Allied cause was undertaken. A Government of India publication for the guidance of its officers, *The Fifth Column as a Weapon in War*, advised, 'Counter defeatism by emphasising the success of our arms, the rottenness of Axis propaganda and an unfailing belief in ultimate Victory.'[10] But, as has been noted, the task of rousing Indians to defend the status quo was, in the end, an impossible one. Unless the war effort was for a 'people's war'—for Indian war aims under Indian leadership—the prospects of proper defence were dim.[11] Sir Frederick Puckle (head of the Central Board of Information) saw danger in a real mobilisation:

> Even were it possible...to awaken the masses of the people to the seriousness of the war, it is open to question whether it would be wise. Once the masses begin to stir, anything may happen.[12]

Hauner concludes:

> A direct appeal to the Indian population to defend the country against the Japanese invaders...was never seriously considered by the authorities. A "People's War" was clearly an anathema in India as far as the British military were concerned.[13]

Stafford Cripps understood this. He stressed to Churchill in April 1942 'the importance from a Defence point of view of getting the Indian leaders into the job of controlling, encouraging and leading the Indian people. This cannot be done under existing circumstances by any Britisher.'[14] But only Britishers were on offer. Given the lack of Indian engagement, blame was laid on Indians not understanding the war effort. Commissioner Larkin (Dacca division), commenting on the denial policy (see below) at a Bengal Commissioners' Conference, said

> If there were a general understanding that present sacrifices were for the ultimate good of the sufferers and there were a real desire to co-operate in an all-out War effort, there would be little trouble. Unfortunately, this is not the case...'[15]

Alternatively, they were accused of being indifferent to the powers that ruled them. Sir Henry Twynam wrote to the Viceroy:

> There is no hope of arousing a national spirit in India such as exists in China: it simply is not there. The mass of the people regard government as belonging by right to any power which is strong enough to maintain itself and...the vast majority would acquiesce in Japanese rule without hesitation...[16]

In political terms, it was not lack of understanding or indifference that prevented Indian enthusiasm. It was a refusal to identify the defence of India with the defence of the Empire. The Communist Party expressed it in this way:

> India's war effort, to be effective, must be a free and voluntary effort of its entire people and this means the existence of democratic rights and civil liberties. India's effort, to be worthy of the Indian nation, must be directed and planned by a National Government and not by the present foreign Government.[17]

The British, of course, could not give up on the project. Sporadic attempts were made to engage the people in defence, but these were often half-hearted or fell afoul of one section or another of the British administration. In March 1942, the Chittagong Commissioner suggested 'watcher patrols' along the Chittagong and Noakhali coasts, 'to report the approach of enemy troops or boats suspected to contain enemy troops.'[18] The Chief Secretary of the Province had championed such a scheme since 1940.[19] It had the enthusiastic support of the Governor. The military authorities, however, were not keen on involving Indian civilians, prompting the Governor to declare 'if the military are likely to delay this organization, it would be best to proceed on our own at once.'[20] Without the backing of the military, the scheme languished. Elsewhere, the possibility of training guerrilla forces to fight the invader was raised. In Darjeeling, senior police officials and the District Commissioner discussed this in July 1942. W.J. Buchanan, a local military officer, reported that such a guerrilla force could be used 'for the defence of the District should Bengal be overrun and for guerrilla warfare should infiltration or invasion of the District by the enemy be successful.' The officials were optimistic that 'the normal population is capable of being trained to a high degree of efficiency [for the] type of work required.' More than a month later an Indian Civil Service official noted that nothing had been done and wrote that 'it should surely be possible to do something about it, but is this really a civil job?' The officer recognised that it was necessary for the Government to make a political decision and for the military to put it into operation. The scheme (and the file) lapsed in September 1942.[21]

In the absence of Indian engagement, British attempts to take serious steps to fight the war tended to make the situation worse. In March (on the eve of the Cripps Mission), the Viceroy announced the formation of a 'National War Front' in an attempt to unite Indians against the Japanese. He emphatically explained this to the Governor of the United Provinces (who was urging the arrest of Nehru instead):

> If we can show that we *have* got another answer besides putting people in jail, that we are *not* incompetent, and that we *can* lead and help people in the present emergency, we shall have done more to discredit Nehru than any number of prosecutions.[22]

The formation of the National War Front is described by Joselyn A. Zivin, in her study of British propaganda in India, as an attempt to 're-hegemonise' India and 'to manufacture a nation at war.'[23] It seems to have elicited little enthusiasm. Linlithgow was decidedly pessimistic about its prospects when he wrote to Amery only a few weeks later:

> I confess that I am not even now confident that it will have any very considerable success in the country, but at least it can do no harm and it may well serve to rally and hearten the many people of goodwill.[24]

But by April he was still having to urge Provincial Governors 'to infuse real life into it.' And he was forced to admit that leaders had not been appointed in most provinces 'because persons sympathetic towards the objects of the Front were reluctant to come forward.'[25] The Chief Secretary of Bengal emphasised the need for vigorous propaganda against the enemy 'bringing home to the people that the actual occupation of Bengal's soil by the Japanese...would ensure upon their getting a foothold in Bengal.'[26] British propaganda emphasised the ill-treatment of Indians under Japanese rule as well as the economic hardship that they encountered.[27] Indians may have been more concerned about their own situation under the British. National War Front speakers in Bengal were heckled in December on questions of economic hardship.[28] Undoubtedly accurate reports of Japanese brutality were undermined by the British portrayal of the Burma debacle as a 'brilliant delaying manoeuvre which had allowed the Allied forces to regroup in India.'[29]

At the same time, the British were attempting to tighten up their political control. This was not new. The Governments of India and Bengal kept a constantly watchful eye on those they regarded as subversive elements. War gave this an added importance. Zivin comments: 'it was at the moments of the gravest effects of war in India that the imperial fist in the liberal glove of British rule was most exposed.'[30] At the beginning of the war, a Bengal Police Administration Report had pointed out:

> In brief, during 1939 all the subversive forces have strengthened and reorganized their parties and have been preparing for the furtherance of their ideal, viz., an armed mass revolution to overthrow the British connection in India.[31]

The report of the following year detailed unrest and resistance to police authority in rural areas. 'It was found necessary,' the report continued, 'to extern a number of active communists from the industrial areas in order to frustrate their attempts to cause serious labour unrest.' Twenty-one were arrested under the Defence of India Rules. At the same time, terrorist organizations (specifically the Bengal Volunteers Group and the Anushilan Samiti) 'appeared to be growing so rapidly that the

Government felt itself compelled to disorganize them.' Twenty-five Bengal Volunteers and ninety-two Anushilan Samiti members were arrested under the Defence of India Rules and made security prisoners.[32] Under those rules, repression was unleashed against those conducting anti-war propaganda, spreading alarmist rumours and 'staging objectionable dramas.'[33] Even after the Indian communists had decided to support the war effort, state vigilance could not be relaxed. At a conference of Bengal Commissioners in 1942, the Burdwan commissioner, Mr Halder, 'observed that these people [communists and anti-fascists] wanted to keep Japan out of India but at the same time wanted ultimately to bring about a mass revolution.'[34] The Secretary of State mused that it might be best 'to go back more to the spirit of the Mutiny days and revive British Rule in its most direct and, if necessary, ruthless form.'[35] The National War Front itself, as well as projecting the positive side of the war effort, was also designed to combat subversion. Linlithgow described this aspect of its operations as a 'process of infiltration by which ultimately there will be members of the movement in every village, hunting out, reporting and contradicting rumours and loose talk and helping in every way possible to stiffen morale.'[36] His vision may have brought forth results from less hostile ground. As it was, when the National War Front's seeds were sown on ground that was, to say the least, stony, they withered and died.

Other aspects of fighting seriously elicited some hilarity, but, more generally, annoyance on the part of Indians. In December 1942, the illegal All-India Congress Committee News Bulletin reported that the Government had ordered ten thousand 'Dummy Aeroplanes' made of wood, 'to be distributed over Indian aerodromes to deceive the people that they have plenty of planes.'[37] When Japanese bombing raids started, it was soon evident that there was a serious shortage of air raid shelters. British forces soon set about providing a modern shelter with all sorts of facilities for the Viceroy (under Viceroy's House) and a number of Anderson shelters for British administrators. Everyone else had to make do with slit trench shelters which provided minimal protection.[38]

More seriously, many Indians were faced with the hardships that real warfare produced—the intrusion of the military into their lives being one. In Medinipur (Bengal):

> A number of villagers were evacuated for building army camps, aerodromes and other military establishments. But in many places, the angry reaction of the people led to open clashes with the military.[39]

At the Commissioners' conference:

> Mr Townsend [Presidency district] remarked that there was a certain amount of anti-British feeling in the 24-Parganas [district] owing to various reasons, viz. stationing of troops, passing of orders to withdraw from cultivable lands, digging of trenches in private lands, etc.[40]

In other words, the very act of preparing to fight produced hostility and fear from Indians. The Chief Secretary of Bihar reported in April that because they believed that the Government intended to commandeer the wheat crop, farmers in the northern districts 'are reported to have harvested the crop before it was time to do so.'[41] The Governor of Bengal wrote to P.D. Martyn that 'Congress propaganda' had convinced people that they would be prevented from entering the 'denial area' (see below). He concluded 'there is a likelihood that they will riot or otherwise indirectly assist the [Quit India] movement. There is of course the further danger that the crop will not be got in.'[42] Khan comments:

> To many in Bengal it appeared that war was bringing devastation with or without a new foreign occupier and that the incursion of an occupying force could not be more destructive than the defensive actions already being taken.[43]

Indeed, according to Biswamoy Pati, 'every major step taken by the colonial administration seemed to strengthen the feeling of an "impending doom".[44]

Simultaneously, there was a feeling that not *enough* was being done and that British efforts lacked seriousness and efficiency. The Chief Secretary of Bengal was of the opinion that 'the thinking public is sceptical of the chance of an effective resistance by the armed forces.'[45] Nehru wrote later:

> There was no sense of hurry and speed, of tension and getting things done. The system they represented had been built up for another age and with other objectives. Whether it was their army or their civil services, the objective in view was the occupation of India and of suppression of any attempts of the Indian people to free themselves.[46]

Indian misgivings led in turn to British distrust. 'Defeatism' was a constant preoccupation for the authorities. It was, they felt, encouraged 'by enemy broadcasts and objectionable speeches.'[47] *The Punjab* reported 'the stories of evacuees and refugees from the Far East and of soldiers on leave, alarmist letters from Bengal and Calcutta, the defeatist tone of the Hindu vernacular press, and enemy broadcasts, which are now widely listened to and discussed, have combined to create an atmosphere of insecurity and defeatism.'[48] Governor Herbert detected 'a strong inclination to hedge on Japanese victory', reflected in the desire of War Front donors to remain anonymous. He also feared 'the danger of communal strife, and even of uprisings.'[49] The Viceroy detected more sinister stirrings:

> I suspect that the moment they think that we may lose the war or take a bad knock, their leaders would be much more concerned to make terms with the victor at our expense than to fight for the ideals to which so much lip-service is given...[50]

It was but a short step to suspecting the entire Indian population—and not a few Europeans as well—of real or potential disloyalty.

In the Government of India's 1942 pamphlet, *The Fifth Column as a Weapon in War*, sure enough, all were suspect. Citing the experience of Fifth Column activities in Malaya, Singapore and Burma, the pamphlet warned:

> The real danger of the Fifth Column comes from within. The British subject, the allied subject, the local resident, the members of the household in which one lives...it is these persons amongst whom the most dangerous agents of the Fifth Column are to be found.[51]

A dire warning was issued against 'subversive organizations':

> The enemy has no need to organize this type of internal disruption nor to spend money in keeping the unrest alive: it is itself a complete Fifth Column playing, even though subconsciously, a role most advantageous to the enemy.[52]

In terms of fighting then, the British found themselves in something of a dilemma. They were unable to make this a 'people's war' without engaging Indians in their *own* defence rather than that of the existing structures of the Empire. To do so would have seriously undermined the hegemony of the colonial state. In the absence of Indian engagement, the attempts at serious defence preparation provoked the distrust and the hostility of the Indian population.

FLIGHT

The other option for the British, in the event of invasion, was withdrawal—preferably an organized and calmly-executed withdrawal rather than a panic-stricken rout. Unfortunately, as we have noted, experience in Malaya, Singapore and Burma had not been positive in this regard. We will focus particularly on events in Burma since in that country (according to the 1931 census) there resided well over a million Indians, three-fifths of them having been born in India. The capital, Rangoon, was a majority-Indian city. The Indians were not well-loved by the Burmese, who tended to regard them as imperial imports.[53] In turn, Indians looked to the British authorities for their protection. When Japan invaded Burma in January 1942, replete with propaganda about 'Burma for the Burmese', Indians' faith in British protection was sorely tried; it wavered and finally broke.

After two heavy air raids on Rangoon in late December 1941, thousands of Indians left the city.

> The city was denuded of all servants, menials, subordinate employees and coolies. All essential services, air raid services, municipal services, transport services, Post and Telegraph clerks, the Ordnance and Military works, Telephone Exchange personnel and, above all, dock labour, left Rangoon. The dead were left unburied for three days, the railways ceased working in the dock and town areas, delivery of mails ceased, shops, markets and hotel were closed and food supplies broke down...the docks went completely out of action.[54]

The Government of Burma's Chief Press Adviser, judging that 'there is a perceptible lack of balance in the presentation of news', issued 'personal warnings' to newspaper editors, warning them against the use of 'scare headlines'.[55]

Much of the Indian exodus attempted to move off from Rangoon to Prome, across the Irrawaddy River. Some took the week-long sea journey to Calcutta (750 miles) or to Madras (1000 miles). But the Government was reluctant to let them go. As can be seen above, Rangoon depended on them for municipal services and dock labour.[56] The instruction was to stay. As for those who had already left, Government officers were despatched to stop them crossing the Irrawaddy and turn them back to Rangoon where they were promised accommodation in Government camps near the city and timely evacuation if it became necessary.[57] Many were persuaded to return and they were followed by those convinced more by the lack of further air raids than by British assurances. The Government tried to prevent them from leaving again by ordering that no adult Indians could travel as deck passengers on ships, thus making boat travel too expensive for ordinary Indians.[58] Despite this, there was a second mass exodus in mid-January 1942 'as a result of rumours, which proved to be false, that Rangoon was to be subjected to fifteen days' concentrated bombing.' By the end of that month, the population of Rangoon had been halved.[59]

The Japanese advance continued and there were further air raids on Rangoon. Any notions of a planned evacuation of the Indian population began to fall apart. The Government of Burma had been encouraged to prepare for this moment. Back in February 1941 a group of Indian politicians and others in Rangoon had set up a Committee for Evacuation and submitted a plan to the Government. But the Burmese authorities had rejected it on the grounds of expense.[60] Sensing what was going to happen, Robert Hutchings, the Government of India's representative in Burma, urged New Delhi to take over the evacuation since the Government of Burma was 'suffering from a degree of disintegration'. This was not done.[61]

Officially, the Government of Burma eventually planned the evacuation of the civilian population of Rangoon in three stages. The first stage was to commence with the transmission of 'Signal E'—which was done on February 20. The official war history tells us:

> From the time that Signal E was given law and order broke down in Rangoon. Nearly all the police had left. A wave of incendiarism swept the city and large areas were burnt out. Looting of shops and private houses took place on a large scale.[62]

After this there was no organized evacuation and 'the Indians had to join in the general stampede for safety.' By this stage, as far as the British were concerned, 'Military needs were paramount and the civilians must face the consequences.'[63] Before Rangoon fell on March 18, some 70,000 Indians had been evacuated by sea, while 4,801 had managed to get out by air with the British. The remaining Indians were left to their own devices and many, not willing to face either the Burmese or the Japanese, attempted to get out on foot.[64]

There was a general sense that the British had abandoned the Indians in Burma—and this seemed to reflect previous experience in Malaya and Singapore. George Seabridge, editor of *The Straits Times*, wrote a report for the British Government on the withdrawal in Malaya.

> From Penang, for example, every European, male and female, except about six men who refused to leave, fled. Government officers and men in essential services got out as quickly as possible. Much the same thing happened elsewhere and there were many bitterly sarcastic references among asiatics to subjects of the Protecting Power who were concerned only with protecting their own skins and leaving the 'Protected' to face whatever might befall.[65]

Some 400,000 Indians attempted to leave Burma by land, traversing an area six hundred by two hundred miles which had few real roads, the rest being covered by forest and the whole subject to heavy rains. As if the terrain were not enough, they were also afflicted by class and race discrimination. Those who had escaped by air had had to pay ₹280 to be flown out of Magwe and Shwebo in the north: 'in other words, only the professional and business classes got out.' The ban on Indians leaving Rangoon as deck passengers had a similar effect.[66]

In general there was a racial divide in the evacuation process. The British were seen to be getting their own out first with Indians coming a distant second, often abandoned altogether.[67] Rizvi describes the evacuation as 'a dismal picture of racial discrimination under stress,' while Khan says it 'became emblematic of a two-tier system based on racial privilege.'[68] It may be thought that the general misery of evacuation on foot would impose an austere equality of suffering. It was not so. Initially, the Monywa-Sitang-Tamu-Palel route into Manipur (India)—generally regarded as the easier one—was *reserved* for whites, Anglo-Burmans, Anglo-Indians and others with 'special recommendations'. The Kalewa-Tamu-Mintha-Hiroika route, which was longer and more difficult, was set aside for the Indians. This situation seems to have remained in force until Rangoon fell.[69] In an interview with two American journalists, Gandhi commented:

> Hundreds, if not thousands on their way from Burma perished without food and drink, and the wretched discrimination stared even these miserable people in the face. One route for the whites, another for the blacks. Provision of food and shelter for the whites, none for the blacks! And discrimination even on their arrival in India!'[70]

The lessons of Malaya and Burma were stark—to none more so than British officials in India. The Governor of Madras reported in January 1942, 'The fact that Europeans were evacuated from Penang whilst Indians were not, has done a great deal of harm... there is a pretty bitter feeling about it.'[71] Cripps wrote to Churchill in April:

> The anti-British feeling is running very strong and our prestige is lower than it has ever been owing to events in Burma and more particularly Singapore. The stories circulating on all sides as to Malaya and Singapore convey an impression of incompetence which is indeed alarming.[72]

Many of the Indians in Malaya and Burma were from Madras, Bihar and the eastern United Provinces. They took their accounts of British evacuation or flight home with them and, on the way, passed them into Assam and Bengal. The physical state of the refugees as well as the stories they told undermined the morale of the Indian soldiers at the border.[73] Amidst the details of deprivation, discrimination and incompetence, the refugees' conclusion was a simple one:

> For the refugees the outcome of the war was not in doubt, a Japanese victory was certain. They had witnessed the Allied defeat; they *knew* the empire was to end.[74]

If experience of withdrawal in Malaya and Burma was anything to go by, it was going to be difficult for the British authorities to persuade Indians that withdrawal from eastern Indian would be anything less than a terrifying and life-threatening event.

From the British point of view, if there was to be a withdrawal in the face of a Japanese invasion, then military logic dictated that useful infrastructure, equipment and supplies should not be left behind for the enemy to use. That which could not be taken should be destroyed, or at least made ready for destruction. Once again, Burma was an object lesson. There, Prasad points out, 'Since a wholesale denial scheme was not enforced, the supply problem of the Japanese…was made easy.'[75] Indians feared that the colonial government would implement a drastic 'scorched earth' policy of widespread confiscation and destruction (which, by all accounts, was in operation in the Soviet Union in the face of Nazi advances).[76]

Initially, the British Government clashed with the Government of India on this question. On or about January 30, 1942, the former requested from the latter a plan of denial to the enemy forces that was:

> Ruthless. It should aim at total destruction for indefinite period and should not be compromised by any desire to recover resources essentially intact when the enemy withdraws… Destruction is much better than concealment… experience shows that principal danger lies in leaving matters too late.[77]

However, the Government of India, in its defence plan, stated that:

> No attempt will be made to carry out a "scorched earth" policy as such...it must be remembered that we intend to reoccupy any area which is temporarily in enemy hands. Wholesale destruction is therefore not contemplated.[78]

The Government of India seems to have stuck to this position despite pressure from London. Nevertheless, its plan also stated that in the event of withdrawal, 'Calcutta port will be destroyed' and 'Chittagong port will be prepared for destruction'. Furthermore, 'A plan for collecting all river craft and, if necessary, sinking or destroying them will be prepared.'[79] Work on denial plans started for Assam, Bihar, Orissa and, especially, Bengal. The scheme concentrated on rice stocks and boats, rather than the potential destruction of the industrial plant. District Officers were instructed not to discuss the matter with the owners of industrial enterprises: 'The situation at the moment is such that any such discussion would be bound, however tactfully it was done, to lead to misapprehension and misconception and only lead to trouble.'[80] Instead, the scheme entailed 'the denial to the enemy of any form of transportation, and removing surplus stocks of paddy and rice from the threatened coastal districts.' A month later, the Governor of Bengal reported that both aspects of the policy had 'led to difficult problems in certain districts.'[81] District Officers were told on March 31:

> It is to be noted that there is no intention of adopting a scorched earth policy on the Russian model. The object of the denial policy is to remove what is surplus to local requirements and to deny the enemy material which would be of value to him in an attack on other parts of India. Officers must avoid all references to scorched earth policy.[82]

On April 7 the Government of Bengal issued a press note, reported in *Amrita Bazar Patrika*:

...it is not impossible that at some stage attempts may be made by the enemy to land on the coast of this province. Any such attempt would be met by formidable and ever-growing military strength, but it is naturally not impossible that temporary landings may be effected. As such it would be most unwise to ignore the lessons of Burma and fail to take such measures as experience has shown are necessary.

This would necessitate the removal of cars, bicycles and boats.[83] In its editorial in the same issue, the *Amrita Bazar Patrika* congratulated the Government for assuring the public that an invasion would be resisted. Clearly in the belief that doing something was better than doing nothing, and perhaps not realising the implications of the policy, the editorial approved the removal of motor boats, bicycles and country boats from threatened areas.[84]

The humble boats—both the motorised and (more commonly) the 'country' variety—were the Government's first targets.[85] The Government decided that 'all boats in coastal districts are to be removed 20 miles from the coast.' The Governor warned in his report, 'The task will not be easy, for in some areas in Eastern Bengal boats are essential for marketing purposes and their removal may involve considerable economic dislocation.' But this, after all, was war. The Governor concluded: 'Nevertheless the work will be done.'[86] On April 8, the order went out to remove all boats from extensive coastal areas—within nine hours. Samanta contends that in the Midnapur district villagers were given only three hours to remove boats to a distance of thirty to ninety miles from the coast. The impossibility of carrying out these instructions led to widespread attempts to bribe officials and, where this did not avail, to the destruction or sinking of the offending boats. Compensation was either inadequate or non-existent.[87] The economic dislocation foreseen by the Governor inevitably ensued.

> To deprive the estuarial and the coastal people of the canoe is to deprive them of their lifeline. It almost completely disrupted the normal life of the estuarial and coastal areas. Trade almost ceased and they soon ran short of supplies of the essential commodities.[88]

In addition to boats, most buses were removed from the threatened areas. The few that remained were allowed so little petrol that their operation soon halted. There then followed the compulsory registration and removal of bicycles.[89]

In line with the denial policy, the Government of Bengal proceeded to appropriate 'surplus' rice from the coastal and eastern areas of Bengal. It was estimated that 123,000 tons of rice was available.[90] Mukerjee points out:

> It is far from clear who made the crop estimates in these 'denial' areas...district-level officials gauged the area under cultivation as well as possible yields... [However] these administrative personnel had no expert knowledge of agriculture...'[91]

It is commonly argued that over-enthusiastic appropriation in the cause of denial was critical in the onset of the Bengal famine, which would hold the province in its devastating grip from 1943.[92]

These processes encouraged rumours of even more swingeing denial policies on the horizon—that the government was stockpiling sickles and scythes in order to destroy crops in the event of invasion, or that villages within three miles on either side of the Grand Trunk Road were to be compulsorily evacuated.[93] The reality, however, was bad enough. When plans were first laid for the denial policy, Gandhi appealed to the Government to abandon any idea of a scorched earth policy.[94] Some weeks later, a correspondent asked him:

> But what about the destruction that is going on of crops, wells, tanks, houses, boats, cycles etc., in the name of

preparation for war? The people are summarily driven out of their villages and houses in the cities.

Gandhi agreed and pointed to 'the crores [of rupees] already drained from the country for warding off a threatened danger.' Regarding dispossession of tenements he said, 'To the poor it is like taking away their bodies.' And further: 'To deprive the people of East Bengal of their boats is like cutting off a vital limb.' But he stopped short of advocating resistance to the authorities' depredations.[95] Resistance there was, however. Protests erupted against the removal of boats and the clearing of land for military purposes. Transportation of appropriated rice was subject to attack and looting. Such resistance was met by force.[96]

On the British side, there were those who considered the denial policy ineffective—and that if it was made effective it would be impossible to implement. The Commissioner for Comilla wrote to the Government in June:

> What is worrying me mainly is, not so much the details of the [denial] policy (though these are troublesome), as whether the policy is likely to achieve its object without a disastrous effect on the economic life of the country...the main point is that the denial policy, if it is to be effective, [has] got to be pushed beyond the point at which you can possibly expect local cooperation. It is vastly expensive and upsets civil morale. My own opinion is that it is not worthwhile even from the military point of view.[97]

In Indian political circles, the idea that Britain would abandon Bengal was running very strongly. A leading member of the Congress Working Committee (CWC), Abul Kalam Azad, wrote later:

> I came to know that Government had decided to abandon Calcutta [in the event of a Japanese invasion]. A secret circular had been issued to selected officers instructing

them about the stages at which they should leave Calcutta, Howrah and the 24 Parganas and the routes they should follow... The Government had also decided that in the case of a Japanese attack, something like the scorched earth policy must be followed... Plans for the destruction of the Iron and Steel Factory at Jamshedpur had somehow become known and there was great anxiety and unrest in the whole area.[98]

Nehru also felt that British withdrawal was likely. He wrote to Roosevelt's representative in India, Lampton Berry, on the likely effect:

> Even if the intention is to offer determined resistance at a later stage, the mere fact that Bengal has fallen will have far-reaching repercussions all over India. It is quite likely that in many rural areas, far away from troop concentrations, civil administration may gradually fade away.

'Such indications,' he said, 'do not encourage resistance.'[99]

If there was to be a withdrawal, who would withdraw and under what circumstances? The Governor demanded answers to these questions in early February 1942. Noting that 'Schemes for defence are still largely on paper', he asked for:

> ...definite instructions regarding the policy to be followed in the event of invasion...it is becoming a matter of urgency to let District officials know exactly what they are to do in an extreme emergency, particularly in the Chittagong and sea-based areas.[100]

District officials were requesting advice. In December 1941, the District Magistrate of Hooghly had asked the Chief Secretary, should he remove his records? Should he suspend normal work in the offices? Should he keep lorries and buses on standby in case of an emergency?[101] Others began to take action on their own account. The Fortress Commander at Chittagong had prepared a plan to evacuate the port within five hours, reported the Assistant Inspector General of Police to the Governor. This, it was thought, would be time enough for the RAF to destroy the aerodrome and more besides. 'No attempt will be made to hold Chittagong.' Five thousand six hundred personnel would be evacuated: 'This figure represents all military, police, Govt servants, railway personnel, B.O.C. and bank staff at [District] H.Qrs.' On receiving this news, an aide to the Governor noted that the Fortress Commander 'has apparently taken the bit between his teeth'. But he went on, 'the Fortress Commander's action is totally opposed to the Government of India's policy, particularly when the enemy are 200 miles away!'[102]

Meanwhile, still in the absence of a plan, military officers began to air opinions as to the best way forward. General Molesworth (Deputy Chief of the Indian General Staff) told the Rotary Club in Delhi in April 1942 that if the Japanese came, 'we shall hold vital places which it is necessary to hold in order to make India safe, but we cannot hold everyone.' There would be places 'where we are unable to put troops or air or naval forces... We cannot arm all.' The general went on to make the suggestion that 'The people can work in bands and give trouble and delay and destroy [the] invasion.'[103] Perhaps the general was suggesting a 'people's war'—but, as we have seen, that was a project that the British were incapable of initiating.

As far as one can tell, there was no generally accepted plan to abandon Bengal (or other parts of eastern India) if the Japanese made a move. But the disparate pieces that made up British policy clearly gave rise to that fear. The Commander-in-Chief, India, and the Governor of Bengal agreed in March that 'last minute evacuation [from Calcutta] would be confined to key personnel and key parts. It was understood that there could be no large-scale evacuation of women and children, at the last minute.'[104] The Government, therefore, told its officers in April:

Government would strongly advise all Government servants who can do so to send their families away <u>at once</u> to places outside the coastal belt...transport facilities might become difficult, if not non-existent in an emergency resulting from an attack.[105]

An evacuation plan was put in place for the European population of Vizagapatam.[106] The Indian Tea Association had its own plan regarding the eastern tea gardens in place by June, European families would be moved out westwards, 'quietly, unobtrusively and without fuss or demonstration'—otherwise, 'labour might be adversely affected.' No 'special steps' would be taken 'with regard to the evacuation of the families of the Indian clerical staffs or the garden labourers.'[107] Elsewhere, the lessons of Burma had had more effect. The District Magistrate of Chittagong was told, 'In preparing any evacuation scheme moreover Government cannot permit any racial discrimination to be made.'[108] Back in the tea gardens, the European supervisory staff were expected to remain at their posts 'until either this became untenable or they were ordered out by the military'—at which point they were to 'destroy all things of immediate use to the enemy.'[109]

In early 1942, the Government of India's Home Department considered whether district officials should stay or go if the Japanese arrived. Initially it was decided that they should follow the (official) policy that had been laid down in Burma: they were to stay at their posts, aid the local population and obey 'the reasonable orders of the enemy commanders' (this had hardly been followed to the letter in Burma, but that was set aside). There was clearly some idea that a form of the existing administration could be kept going under the Japanese and that, in any case, the enemy occupation would be temporary. In the Home Department's defence, it might be remembered that at this stage, Rangoon had not fallen and the reality of the Japanese occupation was not altogether clear. Nevertheless, the policy was greeted with a great deal of dismay. Protests were voiced by the Governors of Bengal, Madras and Orissa, who pointed out that Japanese behaviour thus far did not inspire confidence and that the Government of Burma itself had abandoned this policy.[110] The policy was slightly modified to the effect that officials, while staying at their posts, should try to avoid capture. 'It is the Government's intention that their officers should not fall into the hands of the enemy if this can be avoided,' declared the Government of Bengal on April 9. In the same memorandum, the Government felt it important to point out:

> It is to be clearly understood that any officer who fails to obey an order or who disappears during or after an air raid or through fear of invasion will automatically be regarded by Government as dismissed and will lose all claim to pension or provident fund.[111]

A defence conference at Government House in Calcutta on April 14 reiterated that while 'civil officers are not to retire at the first threat of danger', they were to remain only 'as long as is consistent with the avoidance of their capture by the enemy'.[112]

Such was the hostility (among the British) to the 'stay put (but avoid capture)' policy that the Government of India withdrew it later in the year. Officials were now instructed that they should remain only as long as there was a possibility of helping the local population.[113] Despite the warning that 'the withdrawal of officials should be neither hasty nor unregulated', the new policy was clearly a welcome green light for withdrawal at the first sign of Japanese approach. The Governor of Madras commented:

> I am very glad indeed that the decision about Civil Officers in the event of invasion has been reversed. The previous orders were very hard on them as it would be death or prison if they remained behind, and they would have been of no use to the local inhabitants.[114]

There remained the question of the non-European, lower-ranked officials. The Government's new policy added, 'Municipal and local officials should, however, be encouraged to remain behind.' This was rapidly modified by the Government of Bengal. P.D. Martyn (of the ICS) suggested to a Bengal Conference of Commissioners in June 1942:

> ...there should be no directions to subordinate officers or their staff to remain at their posts where superior officers are directed to withdraw... It has been suggested that it would be difficult to expect the civilian population to 'stay put' when every officer of the Provincial Government is arranging to depart, and that such a policy would have a bad effect on propaganda for the war effort and the National War Front.[115]

The conference decided that 'for non-gazetted and menial officers every opportunity should be given to them to remain unless they wished to withdraw.'[116]

On her mission for Gandhi to Orissa in May 1942 (see next chapter), Mirabehn (Madeleine Slade) reported back:

> I had an interview with two English officials of the then Advisory regime. Since we were in possession of the fact that the Government officials were to retire to the hills, forty or fifty miles inland, the moment that there was news of the Japanese coming and such files as they could not take in their motor-cars were to be burnt and all bridges were to be blown up, my object at the interview was to request them to retire in an orderly fashion, leaving the administrative machinery in our hands. I specially pleaded with them to hand us over the keys of the jails and also not to take away the doctors and medical supplies of the civil hospitals.[117]

CONCLUSION

As has hopefully been demonstrated in this chapter, the two apparent options for the colonial state on the eve of a Japanese invasion were both fraught with difficulty. A determined defence against the Japanese meant a defence of the status quo—from the British point of view, a war (which they appeared to be losing on all fronts) was not the time to restart the process of political reform. On the contrary, the defence of the Empire in India entailed a stiffening of its authoritarian sinews. A war which prolonged and intensified the oppression of Indians was not designed to engage their support. This option, therefore, could only be carried out in the face of Indian opposition. Their consent was an increasingly rare commodity. To fight, then, was necessarily to undermine the colonial state's hegemony.

Flight—or more politely, strategic withdrawal—was equally difficult. Malaya and Burma (and points in between) had demonstrated the kinds of chaotic depths that this could reach. British experience thus far did not inspire confidence. As we have seen, serious preparations in this regard were liable to produce panic and exodus. Even a properly organized withdrawal would necessarily have left many (mostly Indians) behind to face the Japanese on their own. M.N. Roy wrote in *War and Revolution* (1942), 'The Government of a country is supposed to be responsible for the defence of life and property.'[118] To sanction flight meant that the British were in peril of jettisoning this fundamental guarantee of the hegemonic state to its citizens.

It may be, however, that at this point some among the British rulers had another long-term objective in mind. While India had always been an important military base (or series of bases) and a rich source of recruits, it is widely recognised that India's strategic significance increased from the end of the First World War through to the end of the second one—outstripping imperial bonds and even commercial profit.[119] The Viceroy, Lord

Linlithgow, entertained few sentimental feelings about 'the Raj' and considered India in a purely instrumental way. He wrote to the Secretary of State in January 1942:

> ...India and Burma have no natural association with the Empire, from which they are alien by race, history and religion, and for which as such neither of them have any natural affection, and both are in the Empire because they are conquered countries which had been brought there by force, kept there by our controls, and which hitherto it has suited to remain under our protection.[120]

He stressed the strategic connection between Britain and India to the exclusion of almost everything else. Some months later he wrote to Churchill to assure him that, once the Quit India movement had been suppressed, 'We shall then be able to offer you India as a sound platform for future operations in any direction.'[121] The British government emphasised strategic priorities in the postwar world. 'The loss of India,' wrote Amery to Anthony Eden, 'will, of itself, disastrously weaken our whole position in the Middle East and in all the British countries round the Indian Ocean.'[122] Bevin raised the question of 'India's place in the scheme of defence of the British Commonwealth' at the War Cabinet in June 1943. These considerations were for military ties with India, not colonial ones.[123] Moore states:

> In one way or another not only the possibility but also the necessity of sustaining formal imperial control over India had receded.[124]

If formal control was no longer vital, military interests still demanded a settlement with Indians in which, while colonialism as such could disappear, strong defence arrangements would continue. In the meantime, the defence of all the coastline and territory of eastern India may have lessened in importance. If this was the direction of (some) British thinking, it may have been concluded that strategic defence—the defence of certain important military outposts—was all that was necessary. And for that, perhaps, an elaborate and complex system of hegemony was not required.

Antonio Gramsci notes two features of the crisis of hegemony: firstly, the failure by the ruling class to gain mass consent for a major political undertaking ('war, for example'); secondly, a shift amongst the people from political passivity to 'a certain activity'. The first of these features was complete in 1942. The second, we will examine in the next two chapters. The 'general crisis of the State' was sure to follow.

Notes

1 Antonio Gramsci, *Selections from the Prison Notebooks of Antonio Gramsci* ed. Quintin Hoare & Geoffrey Nowell Smith (New York: International Publishers, 1975), 210.
2 West Bengal State Archive (henceforward WBSA) Question whether Racing should be allowed in Calcutta during Present Emergency. W–709/42.
3 Bisheshwar Prasad, *Official History of the Indian Armed Forces in the Second World War, 1939-45: Volume Twelve, Defence of India—Policy and Plans* (Kanpur: Combined Inter-Services Historical Section (India and Pakistan), 1963), 162.
4 British Library, India Office Records (henceforward IOR). Governor of Bengal to Commander in Chief, March 1942. Defence of East Bengal R/3/2/27.
5 Prasad, Defence of India, 163.
6 Herbert to Viceroy, 12 April 1942. Nicholas Mansergh (ed.), *The Transfer of Power 1942-7. Volume 1: The Cripps Mission, January-April 1942* (London: Her Majesty's Stationery Office, 1970)—henceforward Transfer of Power I—763.
7 Francis G. Hutchins, *Spontaneous Revolution: The Quit India Movement* (Delhi: Manohar Book Service, 1971), 240.
8 Wm. Roger Louis, *In the Name of God, Go! Leo Amery and the British Empire in the Age of Churchill* (New York: W.W. Norton & Company, 1992), 129.

9   Fortnightly report, Orissa 2nd half March 1942 in Bipan Chandra and Salil Misra (eds.), *Towards Freedom: Documents on the Movement for Independence in India, 1942* (New Delhi: Oxford University Press, 2016), 727.
10 The writer goes on: 'watch the "local" situation from day to day ... This cannot be done from the bar stool, [nor] yet from a chair in the Institute or Club.' Government of India, *The Fifth Column as a Weapon in War* (New Delhi: Government of India Press, 1942), 27.
11 The Communist Party, which by now was generally supporting the war effort, called for 'the people's war' to be placed in the hands of the people (CPI Letter II (4), 7 March 1942 in Chandra and Misra, Towards Freedom, 1942, 476).
12 Frederick Puckle, 'A Review of War Publicity, December 1939 to February 1941,' in Joselyn A. Zivin, *The Projection of India: Imperial Propaganda, the British State and Nationalist India, 1930–47* (Department of History, Duke University: PhD Dissertation, 1994), 50.
13 Milan Hauner, *India in Axis Strategy: Germany, Japan and Indian Nationalists in the Second World War* (Stuttgart: Klett-Cotta, 1981), 440.
14 Cripps to Churchill, 1 April 1942 in Mansergh, Transfer of Power I, 601. Such advice fell on profoundly deaf ears, as we shall see in the collapse of the Cripps mission.
15 Conference of Commissioners of Divisions held in July 1942. Proceedings. WBSA 362 (22)/42.
16 Sir Henry Twynam (Governor, Central Provinces and Berar) to Viceroy, 24 March 1942. Mansergh, Transfer of Power I, 473.
17 *Forward to Freedom*, CPI pamphlet in Puran Chand Joshi, *People's 'Warrior': Words and Worlds of P.C. Joshi*, ed. Gargi Chakravartty (New Delhi: Tulika Books, 2014), 119.
18 Chittagong Commissioner, 25 March 1942. IOR: Defence of East Bengal R/3/2/27.
19 Chief Secretary's Report 1st half June 1940. IOR: Fortnightly Reports of Governors, Chief Commissioners and Chief Secretaries (1937–1948). L/PJ/5/146.
20 IOR: Defence of East Bengal R/3/2/27. General Slim was particularly derisive about the worth of such a scheme. He wrote later: 'There were no telephones in the area, and reports, hurriedly written in imperfect English, went by boat or runner to the nearest civil telegraph office. There, the local telegraph clerks transmitted them to Calcutta and they were eventually delivered to my office.' Getting to the telegraph office

was not the end of the watchers' travails. Slim continues: 'a sweating messenger arrived at the telegraph office with a report of alleged hostile shipping, only to be told that, as it was Sunday, and he had not the extra fee with him, the signal could not be sent.' (William Slim, *Defeat into Victory* (London: Cassell and Company Ltd., 1956), 129)

21 Constitution of battalions of irregulars and organization of observers in Darjeeling. WBSA W–733/42.
22 Viceroy to Sir M. Hallett, 24 February 1942 in Mansergh, Transfer of Power I, 237.
23 Joselyn A. Zivin, *The Projection of India: Imperial Propaganda, the British State and Nationalist India, 1930–47* (Department of History, Duke University: PhD Dissertation, 1994), 173.
24 Viceroy to Amery, 10 March 1942 in Mansergh, Transfer of Power I, 393.
25 Viceroy to Governors 17 April 1942 in Mansergh, Transfer of Power I, 794; Viceroy to Amery 26 April 1942 in Mansergh, Transfer of Power I, 857.
26 WBSA 362 (22)/42. Proceedings.
27 Sanjoy Bhattacharya, 'British Military Information Management Techniques and the South Asian Soldier: Eastern India during the Second World War,' *Modern Asian Studies* XXXIV (2) April 2000: 499.
28 Chief Secretary Report 1st half December 1942. IOR: Fortnightly Reports of Governors, Chief Commissioners and Chief Secretaries (1937–1948). L/PJ/5/149.
29 Batthacharya, British Military Information, 498.
30 Zivin, Projection, 172.
31 Report on Police Administration in Bengal, 1939, 30. IOR: Bengal, Police Department. Report on the Police Administration in the Presidency, 1936–1947. V/24/3207.
32 Report on Police Administration in Bengal, 1940, 35. IOR: Bengal, Police Department. Report on the Police Administration in the Presidency, 1936–1947. V/24/320.
33 Report on Police Administration in Bengal, 1940, 36–7. IOR: Bengal, Police Department. Report on the Police Administration in the Presidency, 1936–1947. V/24/3207.
34 WBSA 362 (22)/42. Proceedings.
35 Amery's Diary 17 February 1942 in Louis, Name of God, 150–151.
36 Linlithgow to Provincial Governors, 17 February 1942 in Mansergh, Transfer of Power I, 194.
37 Hutchins, Spontaneous Revolution, 236.

38 Yasmin Khan, *India at War: The Subcontinent and the Second World War* (Oxford: Oxford University Press, 2015), 110.
39 Hitesranjan Sanyal, 'The Quit India Movement in Medinipur District,' in *The Indian Nation in 1942*, ed. Gyanendra Pandey (Calcutta: K.P. Bagchi & Company, 1988), 29.
40 WBSA 362 (22)/42. Proceedings.
41 Hutchins, Spontaneous Revolution, 233.
42 Governor of Bengal to P.D. Martyn, 17 October 1942. WBSA Propaganda against Congress activities in the denial area. W–268/42 (XLVIII).
43 Khan, India at War, 97.
44 Biswamoy Pati, 'The Climax of Popular Protest: The Quit India Movement in Orissa,' *Indian Economic and Social History Review* 29 (1) 1992: 11.
45 Chief Secretary Report 2nd half February 1942. IOR: Fortnightly Reports of Governors, Chief Commissioners and Chief Secretaries (1937–1948). L/PJ/5/149. Commenting on Burma, Slim wrote '... when all is said, the real reason the Burman civilian, like his soldier brother, left his post was because he doubted that we, the [British] soldiers and airmen, could hold back the Japanese.' (Slim, Defeat, 35.)
46 Jawaharlal Nehru, *The Discovery of India* (London: Meridian Books Limited, 1947), 386.
47 Chief Secretary Report Bihar 1st half May 1942 in Hutchins, Spontaneous Revolution, 233.
48 Fortnightly Report Punjab 1st half February 1942 in Chandra and Misra, Towards Freedom 1942.
49 Herbert to Viceroy to Amery, 12 April 1942, Mansergh, Transfer of Power I, 763.
50 Viceroy to Amery, 21 January 1942 Mansergh, Transfer of Power I, 149.
51 Government of India, Fifth Column, 8.
52 Government of India, Fifth Column, 9. The C-in-C India reported to the War Office in early October (cabled by Amery to the Viceroy) that the thousands of Indian refugees coming in from Burma, 'Obviously include proportion fifth columnists ... Indications point to intensification Japanese efforts introduce subversive agents and spies.' (Amery to Viceroy, 13 October 1942, Mansergh, Transfer of Power III, 127).
53 See Louis Allen, *Burma: The Longest War 1941–45* (London: Guild Publishing, 1984), 80; Hugh Tinker, 'A Forgotten Long March: The Indian Exodus from Burma, 1942,' *Journal of Southeast Asian Studies* VI (1) March 1975: 2; Indivar Kamtekar, 'The Shiver of 1942,' *Studies in History* XVIII (1) 2002: 83.

54 Bisheshwar Prasad, *Official History of the Indian Armed Forces in the Second World War, 1939–45: Volume Two, The Retreat from Burma, 1941–42* (Calcutta: Orient Longmans, 1959), 74. See also S. Woodburn Kirby et al. *The War against Japan, Volume II: India's Most Dangerous Hour* (London, HMSO 1958), 93.
55 Chief Secretary Report, Report 2nd half December 1941. IOR: Fortnightly Reports of Governors, Chief Commissioners and Chief Secretaries (1937–1948). L/PJ/5/148.
56 'The Government of Burma ... were reluctant either to let them go or to admit that they were essential to the economy of the country— which would have spoiled the arguments they had been using for some years.' (Philip Woodruff [Philip Mason], *The Men Who Ruled India. Volume II: The Guardians* (London: Jonathan Cape, 1965), 315.)
57 Tinker, Long March 4–5; Allen, Longest War, 81.
58 Tinker, Long March 5.
59 War against Japan II 93.
60 Tinker, Long March 4.
61 Tinker, Long March 5–7. Hutchings was able to persuade the Government of India to send ships to pick up evacuees.
62 Woodburn Kirby, War against Japan II 93–4.
63 Tinker, Long March 5 & 8.
64 Tinker, Long March 2. Prasad says that in the evacuation of one southern Burmese town, 'Another thing to be regretted was that the jailers and the Public Works Department staff who were Indians and who should have been evacuated were left behind.' (Prasad, Retreat from Burma, 91.)
65 George Seabridge, Notes by Mr Seabridge; Editor of the *Straits Times*. 11 February 1942. National Archives (UK): WO 106/2609B C 704351. Understandably, these people were seriously disoriented. Seabridge goes on to report that when they reached Singapore: 'Civil servants who had evacuated from the Malay states sought to set up temporary departments for no other apparent reason than the preservation of their jobs ... Even the Federated Malay States Income Tax Department set itself up in Singapore after the last Federated State had fallen into Japanese hands.'
66 Allen, Longest War, 81–84.
67 See Nehru, Discovery, 389; Sanyal, Medinapur, 28; Khan, India at War, 119.
68 Gowher Rizvi, 'The Congress Revolt of 1942: A Historical Revision,' *Indo-British Review* XI (1) December 1984: 34; Khan, India at War, 119.
69 Bhupen Qanungo, 'The Quit India Movement, 1942,' in *A Centenary History of the Indian National Congress. Volume Three: 1935–1947* ed.

    M.N. Das (New Delhi: All-India Congress Committee (I), 1985), 476.
70 M.K. Gandhi, 'An Important Interview', *Harijan* IX 22 14 June 1942.
71 Governor Report, Madras 4 January 1942. IOR: Fortnightly Reports, Madras. L/PJ/205.
72 Cripps to Churchill, 1 April 1942 in Mansergh, Transfer of Power I, 601.
73 Sanyal, Medinapur, 29; David Arnold, 'Quit India in Madras', in *The Indian Nation in 1942*, ed. Gyanendra Pandey (Calcutta: K.P. Bagchi & Company, 1988), 208; Kaushik Roy, 'Military Loyalty in the Colonial Context: A Case Study of the Indian Army during World War II', *Journal of Military History* 73, April 2009: 513.
74 Kamtekar, Shiver, 84.
75 Prasad, Retreat from Burma, 392.
76 Indian merchants and businessmen were particularly alarmed at the prospects of scorched earth policies (see David Lockwood, *The Indian Bourgeoisie: A Political History of the Indian Capitalist Class in the Early Twentieth Century* (London: IB Tauris, 2012), 155–156; David Hardiman, 'The Quit India Movement in Gujarat', in *The Indian Nation in 1942*, ed. Gyanendra Pandey (Calcutta: K.P. Bagchi & Company, 1988), 81. It may be noted that several Allied countries prepared scorched earth plans for possible invasion. This included Australia (see Sue Rosen (ed.), *Scorched Earth* (Sydney: Allen & Unwin, 2017); Stanley, Invading Australia, 123–4).
77 Secretary of State to Government of India Defence Department 30 January 1942. IOR: War Staff 'WS' Series files: Scorched Earth L/WS/1/1942.
78 IOR: Scorched Earth file. Plan for Defence of North East India (para 13: Demolition Policy). WS 17926 L/WS/1/1942. Confirming this, Prasad adds that scorched earth 'would have spread panic and disaffection or resulted in large-scale evacuation of the bulk of the population.' (Retreat from Burma, 393.
79 IOR Scorched Earth file. WS 17926 L/WS/1/1942.
80 Government of Bengal memorandum to District Officers (not dated). WBSA W–268/42.
81 Governor Bengal Report 2nd half March 1942; Governor Bengal Report 1st half April 1942. IOR: Fortnightly Reports of Governors, Chief Commissioners and Chief Secretaries (1937–1948). L/PJ/5/149.
82 Administration of the Province in the event of hostile action in India. WBSA 177/42.

83 Government of Bengal press note reported in *Amrita Bazar Patrika* (henceforward ABP), 7 April 1942, 5.
84 'A Timely Warning,' ABP 7 April 1942, 4.
85 'Country boats' were simple wooden vessels providing cheap transport and haulage along Bengal's inland waterways.
86 Governor Report 2nd half March 1942. IOR: Fortnightly Reports of Governors, Chief Commissioners and Chief Secretaries (1937–1948). L/PJ/5/149.
87 Satish Chandra Samanta, Syamadas Bhattacharyya, Ananga Mohan Das & Prahlad Kumar Pramanik, *August Revolution and Two Years' National Government in Midnapore* (Calcutta: Orient Book Company, 1946), 7; Sanyal, Medinapur, 39–40. See also Khan, India at War, 95–6.
88 Sanyal, Medinapur, 29.
89 Sanyal, Medinapur, 39; Samanta, August Revolution, 6 & 8; Governor Report 2nd half February 1942. IOR: Fortnightly Reports of Governors, Chief Commissioners and Chief Secretaries (1937–1948). L/PJ/5/149.
90 Mukherjee, Hungry Bengal, 59.
91 Madhusree Mukerjee, 'Bengal Famine of 1943: An Appraisal of the Famine Inquiry Commission,' *Economic and Political Weekly* XLIX (11) 15 March 2014: 73.
92 See for example, Janam Mukherjee, *Hungry Bengal: War, Famine, Riots and the End of Empire* (Noida (India): Harper Collins, 2015). The British were at great pains to deny that their actions contributed in any way to the horrifying events that followed. The Famine Commission, set up in 1944, was aimed 'not towards explaining the famine, but towards observing the role played by His Majesty's government in precipitating and aggravating the famine.' (Mukerjee, Bengal Famine of 1943, 72.) In private however, the Secretary of State believed that the famine had been caused by the over-exploitation of Indian resources for the British war effort. (Mukerjee, Bengal Famine of 1943, 71.)
93 Biswamoy Pati, Climax, 12.
94 M.K. Gandhi, 'Scorched Earth,' *Harijan* 22 March 1942, Collected Works 82, 121–2.
95 M.K. Gandhi, 'To every Briton,' (11 May 1942) Collected Works 82, 272.
96 See Chandra and Misra, Towards Freedom 1942, 750–753; Mukherjee, Hungry Bengal, 61–2.
97 Letter from Comilla Commissioner to Blair, 14 June 1942. Commissioners Conference Proceedings. WBSA 362 (22)/42.
98 Maulana Abul Kalam Azad, *India Wins Freedom: An Autobiographical Narrative* (Bombay: Orient Longmans, 1959), 72.

99   Nehru to Lampton Berry, 23 June 1942 in Jawaharlal Nehru, *A Bunch of Old Letters* (London: Asia Publishing House, 1960), 492 and Jawaharlal Nehru, *Nehru: The First Sixty Years, Volume Two* ed. Dorothy Norman (London: The Bodley Head, 1965), 106.
100 Governor Report 1st half February 1942. IOR: Fortnightly Reports of Governors, Chief Commissioners and Chief Secretaries (1937–1948). L/PJ/5/149.
101 Instructions in view of the Public Declaration of a State of Emergency in the province of Bengal. WBSA W–4/42. He was told: wait for Revenue Department instructions; only if necessary; transport could be requisitioned when the time came.
102 Defence of Bengal R/3/2/27.
103 The speech was extensively quoted by by Mahadev Desai in *Harijan* 'How to be Worthy of Our Heritage', Harijan IX 13.
104 IOR: Defence of East Bengal R/3/2/27.
105 Government of Bengal Home Department memorandum 9 April 1942 IOR: Defence of East Bengal R/3/2/27.
106 Roland Hunt and John Harrison, *The District Officer in India, 1930–1947* (London: Scholar Press, 1982), 215.
107 Indian Tea Association Calcutta, 'Emergency Measures in the Tea Districts', 6 June 1942. IOR: MSS EUR F 174/382.
108 Memorandum to District Magistrate, Chittagong (not dated). WBSA: Administration of the province in the event of hostile action in India. 177/42.
109 Indian Tea Association Calcutta, 'Emergency Measures in the Tea Districts', 6 June 1942. IOR MSS EUR F 174/382.
110 Home Department War Histories. IOR: Mss Eur F161/151/9: 1940s, 33.
111 Memorandum to all District Magistrates 9 April 1942. WBSA: Administration of Province 177/42.
112 Note on a Conference held at Government House 14 April 1942. IOR: Defence of East Bengal R/3/2/27. Officials in Chittagong were instructed that 'the administration should continue to function as long as is consistent with the avoidance of Government officials falling into the hands of the enemy.' (Governor's Report 1st half April 1942. IOR: Fortnightly Reports of Governors, Chief Commissioners and Chief Secretaries (1937–1948). L/PJ/5/149).
113 Home Department War Histories. IOR: Mss Eur F161/151/9: 1940s, 34.
114 Madras Governor Report 3 of 1942. IOR: Fortnightly Reports, Madras L/PJ/205.
115 'Maintenance of civil administration', Commissioners' Conference.

WBSA 362 (22)/42.

116 The Inspector General of Police (Gordon) told the conference that he approved of 'constables taking off their uniforms and merging with the general population'—though 'The possibility of such constables being exposed to the enemy by the general inhabitants' was pointed out. (Proceedings of Commissioners' Conference. WBSA: 362 (22)/42.)

117 Mirabehn's note, 31 May 1942 in Mohandas K. Gandhi, *The Collected Works of Mahatma Gandhi: Volume 82* (Chief Editor: Shri R.P. Dhasmana. Delhi: Publications Division, Ministry of Information and Broadcasting, 1958–1994), 352.

118 M.N. Roy, *War and Revolution: International Civil War* (Madras: Radical Democratic Party, 1942), 78.

119 See for example, Johannes H. Voigt, 'Co-operation or Confrontation? War and Congress Politics 1939–42.' in *Congress and the Raj: Facets of the Indian Struggle 1917–47*, ed. D.A. Low (London: Heinemann, 1977): 349–350. Robin Moore points to the decline of the commercial aspects of the Indian Empire in Robin J. Moore, *Escape from Empire: The Attlee Government and the Indian Problem* (Oxford: Clarendon Press, 1983), 24–27.

120 Viceroy to Amery 21 January 1942. Mansergh, Transfer of Power I, 49.

121 Viceroy to Churchill 19 August 1942. Mansergh, Transfer of Power II, 755.

122 Amery to Eden 9 May 1943 in Moore, Escape, 19.

123 Moore, Escape, 19.

124 Moore, Escape, 28.

5

CONGRESS AND THE WAR

> *I do not know what I shall ask you to do... I have impenetrable darkness before me regarding the future course of action. I have no mysteries. I do not know how I shall lead, what action I shall put before you. I hope that any action we may take will be worthy of the Congress traditions and of the occasion.*
>
> —Mohandas K. Gandhi, Speech to the All-India Congress Committee, Bombay, September 15, 1940.[1]

We left the Congress in a somewhat dispirited state following the overreach of the Provincial Ministerial experience. To recover, it would have to grope its way back to a counter-hegemonic strategy. This was made all the more difficult by the outbreak of the Second World War. This chapter will cover the reconstruction of Congress' counter-hegemonic strategy, which will emerge as the Quit India movement. The next chapter will examine how that strategy was put into operation.

The Congress Working Committee, meeting on October 23, 1939, instructed all the Provincial Congress ministers to resign.[2] This was, to be sure, in protest against British Government actions, but it was also a matter of great relief to the central

Congress leadership. Given the problems that had arisen around the Congress ministries (see Chapter Three), their destruction was, at least in part, a blessed release. Gandhi was reported as saying that the resignations were 'to cover the fact that we were crumbling to pieces.'[3] Nehru had wanted to get out of provincial government for six months before the decision was made, so dismayed was he at the effect that office was having on the Congress. 'It was believed,' writes Pandey, 'that the measure would strengthen the organization and establish the control of the High Command over the provincial congresses.'[4] Some on the Congress Left, believing that the best remedy for post-ministerial doldrums was immediate mass action, urged the rapid commencement of civil disobedience against British rule and the British war. Gandhi, however, feared that the Congress was in no shape to launch such a campaign at this time.[5] The Congress session in Ramgarh in March 1940 reiterated this position. Although declaring that the resignation of the ministers 'must naturally be followed by civil disobedience, to which the Congress will unhesitatingly resort', this would only be done 'as soon as the Congress organization is considered fit enough for the purpose, or in case circumstances so shape themselves as to precipitate a crisis.' The session endorsed Gandhi's undertaking that he would only lead civil disobedience 'when he is satisfied that they are strictly obeying discipline and are carrying out the Constructive Programme.'[6]

Once hostilities commenced on September 3, 1939, the Congress approach to the war became an ongoing problem which revealed distinct differences within the Congress leadership. Gandhi condemned warfare as a whole and could therefore be expected to shun the British war effort. This was, however, confusingly combined with sentimental support for Britain. For most of the other Congress leaders, the nature of the war—if it could be agreed on—would determine Congress' immediate strategy towards Britain, the Government of India and their war effort. At one level, the war was clearly an inter-imperialist conflict revolving around, in the first instance, which of the imperialist powers (or groups of powers) would dominate Europe—and, in the second instance, which would dominate Asia. Congress hostility towards this sort of conflict was longstanding. The Madras session in 1927, surveying the rising international tension, declared that India had no quarrel with other countries and that, if Britain tried to involve India in a war, it was the duty of the Indian people to resist. This was reiterated at subsequent sessions, from Calcutta (1928) to Lucknow (1936). With the emergence of fascism, Nazism and militarism, the Congress condemned the regimes in Italy, Germany and Japan but equated them with the older imperialist powers, including Britain.[7] Conflicts between these powers were of an inter-imperialist nature and therefore to be opposed outright.

At another level, however, the war was being fought against Nazism, fascism and militarism, forces that threatened the democracies and—perhaps more importantly—the prospects of democracy, especially in the colonial world, for many years to come. Congress took a firm stand against fascism and in support of Chinese resistance to the Japanese occupation.[8] Nehru was the most forthright Congress exponent of this analysis of the war. He had been closely associated with the antifascist Left in Britain, a prominent supporter of the Spanish Republic and a constant ally of the Chinese in their struggle against Japan. From 1938 to 1939 he visited Spain, Britain and China which undoubtedly strengthened his anti-fascist/nazi/militarist views. Meanwhile, on the left of the Congress, Subhas Chandra Bose saw the war primarily as an opportunity to push forward the freedom struggle at full speed, and was not much interested in the differences between the two sides.

Congress therefore spoke with a number of voices as far as the nature of the war was concerned. Nevertheless, just before it began, in May 1939, the All-India Congress Committee reaffirmed its opposition to any Indian involvement and to any use of Indian resources in a war that had not the consent of the Indian people.

To this end, in the second week of August, the Congress Working Committee advised its provincial ministers not to co-operate with the war effort and to prepare their letters of resignation.[9]

Distinct streams of thought on the war remained within the Congress leadership even after Japan had joined the fray. Bhattacharya lists three: those of Gandhi, of Nehru and Azad and of Rajagopalachari.[10]

Gandhi's position until the end of 1941 was still essentially a pacifist one. He rejected the war on grounds of non-violence—not, like the other Congress leaders, on the grounds that it was an imperialist war into which India had been forced.[11] Abul Kalam Azad was reported explaining to the All-India Congress Committee at Wardha in January 1942:

> Gandhiji was opposed to participation in the war on the pure ground of non-violence whereas they (Azad and Nehru) were opposed to it on political grounds. Gandhiji had declared that he would not have the independence of India if secured at the cost of non-violence and on the condition that the country should participate in war... He (Azad) was prepared to accept the independence of the country at any time it was available; whether in times of peace or under the shadow of war.[12]

Gandhi felt able to extend a 'moral sympathy' for Britain's plight in the European war and 'benevolent neutrality' towards the war effort.[13] At the same time (and increasingly), he felt able to express support for other Congress leaders in their efforts to fit war strategy into the struggle for freedom. Nehru and Azad wanted an immediate declaration of independence in return for India's support for the war. This was not a strategy of non-violence. Nehru had begun to make the effective defence of India conditional on this demand. He told a public meeting in Delhi in February 1942:

> ...if administration of the country is entrusted to us today it is questionable whether we can prepare ourselves in several weeks or months to defend our country with arms. But we will not surrender to anybody and we will not refuse responsibility for defending the country merely because it is entrusted to us at a dangerous time.[14]

Rajagopalachari, the Congress leader from Madras, worked on the same theme, stressing the inability of the British to resist the Japanese. The Chief Secretary of Madras, reporting on a speech by Rajagopalachari on Independence Day in 1942, said, 'His main argument for the demand of independence was that Britain was no longer in a position to defend this country.'[15] Rajagopalachari's solution was radically different from Nehru's. He urged Congress to join the Government's war effort to defend India and to make concessions to the concept of 'Pakistan' to preserve national unity.[16]

Amidst these positions, a kind of consensus around the 'Nehruvian centre' emerged. While declaring support for the struggle against fascist/nazi/militarist imperialism and for the victory of the democracies (and the Soviet Union), that support did not stretch to encompass the forces of the British Empire. The struggle against imperialism remained and would impede India's participation in the war until she was made free. Only then could Congress support the war. The question remained as to whether Indian freedom had to be immediate, delayed (until the end of the war) or conditional (on an Allied victory).

In the meantime, what was the Congress leaders' advice on how Indians should react to the worsening situation and the imminence of invasion? Gandhi told the press in December 1941 that 'Those who do not wish to run any risk would do well quietly to leave their cities.' He added: 'I would not like it said of us as a nation that we run about like mad men on the approach of the slightest danger.'[17] The Congress Working Committee told

Congress members in January that they 'must remain at their posts and continue their service of the people.'[18] Gandhi again advised emigration for city dwellers to the villages the following month.[19] Nehru and Rajagopalachari were advising people not to leave. They were of the view that 'It was the duty of Indian leaders to see that India, if it could not be saved from invasion, was at least free from the horrors of panic and fear.'[20] Resistance was also envisaged. Unpublished instructions of the Congress Working Committee at the end of December 1941 had set out that, in the event of invasion, 'Congressmen can on no account submit to [invasion] or co-operate with it even if the consequences of such non-cooperation be death.'[21]

From the outbreak of the European war until early 1942 there took place a tactical joust between the British and the Congress, designed, on the part of the British, to bring about Indian participation in the war effort and, on the part of Congress, to bring about Indian freedom and *therefore* (as they saw it) victory over enemy forces. The Congress Working Committee met at Wardha just after hostilities commenced. The meeting reaffirmed that questions of war and peace had to be decided by the Indian people. Congress would resist Indian resources being used for imperialist ends. The Committee demanded clarification of Britain's position. If the war was being fought for the *status quo ante* (imperialism and colonies) they would have nothing to do with it. But if Britain was fighting for democracy—and that would have to include self-determination for India—then Indian co-operation was possible. The Committee, therefore, awaited a declaration of British war aims.[22]

The British were not inclined to set out their war aims in the manner requested. Nevertheless, the Congress Working Committee edged a little closer towards co-operation in July 1940. It declared that if the British acknowledged the independence of India for a future date (preferably just after the successful conclusion of the war), Congress would participate fully in organizing national defence. Despite some resistance to this at the All-India Congress Committee later that month in Poona, the Working Committee's recommendation was accepted, ninety-five votes to forty-seven. Gandhi was, predictably, unhappy at the direction of Congress policy.[23]

Rather than a clarification of war aims, the British response was the 'August Offer' of 1940, which proposed an expansion of the Viceroy's Executive Council, the establishment of a National Defence Council and, after the war, a body to devise a new constitution for India as a Dominion.[24] Congress rejected this as grossly inadequate. It entirely missed the point of Congress representations as to who would make decisions for India in wartime.

Since the idea of British concessions for Congress support in the war had now been swept aside, the division between Gandhi and the other Congress leaders lessened. British intransigence had moved them back towards each other. But not entirely. In late December 1941, the Congress Working Committee met at Bardoli to consider the situation now that Japan had entered the war. Despite British rejection, the Committee reiterated its willingness to aid national defence if independence was granted. For this reason, Gandhi once again backed away from the leadership, stating that even if independence were granted he would not give up non-violence to defend India.[25] However, while the British refused any concession, the differences between Gandhi and the Committee were minimal. He urged the All-India Congress Committee to adopt the Working Committee's resolution because 'The resolution throws on the Government the entire burden of wooing the Congress by meeting its legitimate demands and securing its participation in the war effort. That nothing much is to be expected from the Government is probably too true.'[26]

What then was the Congress actually going to do? When the provincial ministries resigned, there had been a general expectation among Congress members that they would move back towards mass action. But, in the aftermath of the ministerial experience and in the midst of the war-charged atmosphere, Gandhi did not believe that the moment was right. He told the Congress session in March 1940 that neither the conditions nor the Congress membership were ready for mass struggle.[27]

> I feel you are not prepared...you do not understand what this preparation means. Your General finds that you are not ready, that you are not real soldiers and that if we proceed on the lines suggested by you, we are bound to fail.[28]

Later he said that civil disobedience 'should wait till the heat of the battle in the Allied countries subsides and the future is clearer than it is. We do not seek our independence out of Britain's ruin.'[29] Gandhi's concern over the preparedness of the Congress for civil disobedience was linked to his expectation of the level of repression such a movement was to expect from the colonial authorities. Speaking at Sevagram in October 1941 he warned:

> If I launch a mass movement, people may perhaps jump into it. What will the British do in that case? They will enact another Jallianwala Bagh. I am not afraid of it but I do not want to give them an opportunity to do so.[30]

He was to hold this view until about April 1942. In the meantime, he encouraged Congress members to work diligently at implementing the constructive programme.

Pressure for some kind of action was mounting, however, from both British intransigence and his fellow Congress leaders. Nehru was worried that inaction was breeding 'an atmosphere of approaching compromise' which arose 'from the excessive desire to avoid conflict at all costs, and to get back the shreds of power we had previously.' Some in the Congress were looking forward to a re-run of the ministerial experience:

The effort of several months to keep undesirable elements out of the Congress has partly failed because of this sudden change in the Indian atmosphere which led them to believe that the compromise was imminent.[31]

In April 1940, the Congress Working Committee voted in favour (8:4) of a civil disobedience campaign—but 'the General' would not mobilise his troops.[32] Britain's August Offer, however, convinced Gandhi that something had to be done. The Congress President, Abul Kalam Azad, advised 'Now that Britain has rejected all the offers made by the Congress we have only one thing left to do and that is to non-co-operate in every way with the war effort.'[33] Gandhi was still very wary of a mass campaign. Instead, he authorized a campaign of individual *satyagraha* in protest against the British wartime clampdown on free speech and civil liberties. Hand-picked individuals would make speeches against the war and court arrest.[34] There would be a gradual expansion of the campaign from the select few to the Congress rank and file from its launch in October 1940 into 1941. By mid–1941, over 25,000 had been convicted for individual civil disobedience.[35]

For the British though, this was an irritant rather than a serious threat. Due to leftist influence in Bengal, it was particularly unpopular in that province. The Inspector-General of the Bengal Police, A.D. Gordon, reported that 'It started in Bengal on the 30th November but aroused no enthusiasm and by the end of the year only 21 persons had offered *satyagraha*.'[36] In December the Chief Secretary noted 'The *satyagraha* movement arouses decreasing interest throughout the Province.'[37] Commenting in late 1941, Gordon concluded 'By the middle of the year the movement in Bengal was dead.'[38] The campaign was called off by the Congress Working Committee in December 1941.

Two events seem to have brought Gandhi's mind into clearer focus on what the Congress should do next. They were the retreat from Burma and the Cripps Mission. The first convinced him that the British were incapable of defending India against the Japanese and that, in the event of retreat, it would be Indians who would suffer most. The second convinced him that the British were steadfast in their determination not to change their methods of rule in order to defend India—and in their likely defeat they were willing to take India down with them.

The All-India Congress Committee pointed in January 1942 to instances of discrimination in the evacuation of Burma.[39] The Bengal Congress Committee reported on discrimination suffered by Indian evacuees—being excluded from 'reserved' railway carriages, for example.[40] Within a few months reports of ill-treatment and discrimination during the evacuation were rife—spread by the refugees themselves, by the soldiers that passed by them and by the citizens of the Indian cities that received them. At the end of April 1942, the All-India Congress Committee fired off a salvo of bitter criticism at British behaviour.

> As war approaches India, the lessons of Rangoon and Lower Burma are full of meaning for this country, for the same type of official wields authority here...inefficient and irresponsible officials, who have, in addition, no contacts with the people of the country... It is the misfortune of India, at this crisis in her history, not only to have a foreign government, but a government which is incompetent and incapable of organizing her defence properly or of providing for the safety and essential needs of her people.

The resolution went on:

> Such arrangements for evacuation as were made were meant principally for the European population and at every step racial discrimination was in evidence. Because of this and also because of the utter incompetence, callousness and selfishness of those in authority, vast number of Indians in Malaya and Burma have not only lost all they possessed but

have also undergone unimaginable suffering, many dying on the way from lack of the necessaries of life, from disease, or from attacks from anti-social elements.[41]

Publication of this resolution was suppressed by the Government of India.[42]

In March 1942, the British Government despatched Sir Stafford Cripps to India at the head of a mission, the ostensible purpose of which was to effect a political settlement. The Cripps Mission proposed a weak central government for India—made weaker by giving provinces the opportunity to opt out of Indian political structures. The Mission was clearly a response to British defeats in Southeast Asia and an attempt to resolve things politically in India in order to get on with the war.[43] Stafford Cripps himself could see the importance of engaging Congress leaders in the war effort. Prasad notes that most of the British War Cabinet, including Churchill and Amery, 'did not attach any importance to this.'[44] Gandhi commented:

> Sir Stafford is a very good man, but he has entered bad machinery—British Imperialism. He hopes to improve that machinery, but in the end it will be the machinery that will get the better of him.[45]

Talks with Congress broke down over a number of issues, including the British refusal to countenance a cabinet-style Executive Council and their open-ended approach to a future Pakistan. Khan suggests that Congress was also 'unwilling to be jointly responsible for the economic and social fiasco unfolding in India.'[46] By April, Congress had decided to reject the Cripps Mission proposals.[47]

The most important issue on which the talks foundered was the control of India's defence. The issue was whether the Defence portfolio in the Viceroy's 'cabinet' could be given to an Indian—most likely, a member of the Congress. Harold Laski, an adviser to the British Labour Party, declared:

> It is...clear that any endeavour to withdraw Defence from Indian control will bring the whole policy [the Cripps proposals] under suspicion, and that it constitutes the ultimate proof that these proposals are *bona fide*.[48]

If political concessions were made and independence promised, Congress was willing to arouse the people to defend a potentially new India. But this could only be done, in the words of Mulk Raj Anand, 'by an Indian Defence Minister whose sympathy with the aspirations of the people would muster the necessary response from the masses.'[49] The members of the British War Cabinet tried to brush this aside as a deliberate distraction from 'the essential features' of the Cripps proposals. The War Cabinet added 'There could, of course, be no question of our accepting a nominee of Congress to some office connected with the defence responsibilities of the Government of India.'[50] Nehru wrote later that the Indians were told they could not command the Indian army because it was, in fact, a section of the *British* armed forces. So jealous was the British state of its monopoly of armed forces, says Nehru, 'It was further doubtful if we would be allowed to raise any separate forces like militias or home guards.'[51] Louis Fischer remarks that during the Cripps negotiations, 'the efforts of Azad, Nehru and Rajagopalachari were directed to expanding the responsibility and activity of Indians in the war effort; the British, on the other hand, sought to limit them. It was on this point that the talks broke down.'[52] The furthest the British would go in this regard was to split Defence between a British Commander-in-Chief (who would also become the War Minister) and an Indian Defence Minister. The former would command the armed forces and control the conduct of the war; the latter could occupy himself with public relations, canteens, stationery, forms and other ephemera.[53] Rejecting the Cripps proposals, the Congress Working Committee resolved on April 11, 1942:

> To take away Defence from the sphere of responsibility at this stage is to reduce that responsibility to a farce and nullity, and to make it perfectly clear that India is not going to be free in any way and her Government is not going to function as a free and independent Government during the pendency of the war... What is most wanted is the enthusiastic response of the people, which cannot be evoked without the fullest trust in them and the devolution of responsibility on them in the matter of Defence.[54]

The impossibility of a political solution based on the Cripps proposals, the behaviour of the British during the evacuation of Burma and the miserable prospects of a successful defence of India that these events portended forced the focus of Indian politics back to the question of Indian independence. Starting from there, Gandhi evolved a new strategy which would not only reunite him with the rest of the Congress leadership but also provide the basis for a new mass mobilisation.

Since the resignation of the Provincial Ministries in 1939, the Congress leadership had been strategically floundering—reacting spasmodically to war events and British actions. The concept of counter-hegemony had faded. Congress policy had been a series of negatives: against the ministries, against the war, against Cripps. Down this path lay either a tightened-up British Raj or a Japanese occupation of unknown (but well signposted) brutality. Gandhi was convinced that Congress could do better than this and, although for a time obscure, his new strategy was a return to counter-hegemonic basics. It was for the Congress—not the British or the Japanese—to put forward a vision of India's future and to start, as best it could, putting that vision into practice. Gandhi arrived at this view probably in late April 1942, though he failed to have it entirely adopted by the Congress Working Committee at that time.

Gandhi's new starting point was that India's problems in 1942 did not originate from the war, from the Japanese, from Indian apathy, from defence unpreparedness, from corruption in the Congress or from the communal question. To be sure, these were real problems. But their root cause was the presence of the British. Congress had offered the British its help but had been rejected. 'The Congress,' he wrote, 'with all the will in the world to defeat Nazism, cannot thrust its help on Great Britain which evidently does not want it or about which it is at least indifferent.'[55] That being the case, the continued British presence in India was of no use to Indians—in fact, it was a danger to them.

> I feel convinced that the British presence is the incentive for the Japanese attack. If the British wisely decided to withdraw and leave India to manage her own affairs in the best way she could, Japan would be bound to reconsider her plans.[56]

If Japan did not, 'free India will be better able to cope with the invasion. Unadulterated non-co-operation will then have full sway.'[57] Continued British rule pushed India into a passive role in the war and it was this that made Indians apathetic towards the struggle and even favourable towards the Japanese. There is a distinct change in Gandhi's tone here.

> India is not playing any effective part in the War. Some of us feel ashamed that it is so and, what is more, we feel that if we were free from the foreign yoke, we should play a worthy, nay, a decisive part in the World War which is yet to reach its climax. We know that if India does not become free *now*, the hidden discontent will burst forth into a welcome to the Japanese, should they affect a landing.[58]

Gandhi warned 'The Japanese may free India from the British yoke, but only to put on their own instead... I have no enmity against the Japanese, but I cannot contemplate with equanimity their designs upon India.'[59]

The continued presence of the British Empire in India would subject parts of the country to scorched earth, turn other parts into battlefields and then leave them to the mercies of the Japanese.[60] Much of this had been said before. Gandhi's point was that something could be done about it—and that it was the responsibility and within the power of the Congress to do it. He told the Rashtriya Yuvak Sangh in June:

> ...my attitude has undergone a change. I feel that if I continue to wait I might have to wait until doomsday... We have to take the risk of violence to shake off the greater calamity of slavery.[61]

The tension between those from Hindu and Muslim backgrounds in India had long been laid at the door of the British by the nationalists. It was nevertheless regarded as an issue to be resolved before (or in the process of) liberation. Gandhi himself said in April 1942 that 'Attainment of Independence is an impossibility till we have solved the communal tangle.'[62] His new strategy was based on the belief that, while the British remained, unity between the communities was impossible.

> I have been asking myself why every whole-hearted attempt made...to reach unity has failed and failed so completely...the third power [the British], even without deliberately wishing it, will not allow real unity to take place.[63]

Unity was impossible 'until British power is wholly withdrawn from India' because until that time 'all parties will be looking to the foreign power.'[64] Indians, he argued, could only take ownership and responsibility for the problem when they were free to do so.

Gandhi did not want to stand by and watch the British at war, nor to have Indians suffer as a result of British war preparations, nor to conduct further fruitless negotiations. He wanted the Congress to attack the root cause of India's problems, which was, he believed, the British presence—and, having persuaded the British to leave, to set about Indian solutions to Indian problems. He told the *News Chronicle* in May:

> It has cost me much to come to the conclusion that the British should withdraw from India, and it is costing me still more to work out that conclusion... They and we are both in the midst of fire. If they go, there is a likelihood of both of us being safe... Under my proposal, they have to leave India in God's hands, but in modern parlance to anarchy.[65]

He believed that there was a chance, if the British left, that the Japanese would leave India alone.[66] On various occasions he repeated the term 'anarchy' in the wake of British withdrawal in order to emphasise his view that it was not for the British to determine what would happen in India afterwards.[67]

Gandhi also felt that withdrawal would be a positive move for Britain. Britain's 'real safety' lay 'in orderly and timely British withdrawal'. Britain could then concentrate on the war in the west 'and leave the East to adjust her own position'.[68] He appealed 'To Every Briton' in May 1942 'to support me in my appeal to the British at this very hour to retire from every Asiatic and African possession and at least from India.'[69]

Everything in Gandhi's new strategy depended on freedom—the withdrawal of the British. As the illegal Congress Radio put it during the Quit India campaign, 'the Congress demand is for freedom to defend India and to defend the freedom of India.' If defence were left to the British (and the Americans) and somehow they succeeded, 'they will claim to rule us afterwards.'[70] The strategy sought to avoid invasion but also to provide the basis for resistance to it. Freedom would lead to a change in the Indian attitude: 'Independence sheds all fear—fear of the Japanese, of anarchy, and of the wrath of the British lion,' wrote Gandhi in May.[71] Mahadev Desai wrote in *Harijan*:

> But defeat—irretrievable defeat—stares us in the face, if we choose the wrong weapons. It is the spirit that we have to weigh against the planes... All that is needed is the spirit, the will to resist, the will to shake off our lethargy, cowardice,

inertia—the will not "to live routine lives".[72]

As has been noted, Gandhi felt that if the British left, the Japanese might leave India alone. 'I am confident,' he wrote to Nehru in April, 'that after this Government goes, we shall be able to deal adequately with the Japanese.'[73] But he did not rule out an invasion: 'it is equally likely that they will want to invade India in order to use her ports for strategic purposes. Then, I would advise the people to...offer stubborn non-violent non-co-operation.'[74] Part of the strategy was to inspire that non-co-operation. Gandhi called for non-violent resistance to the Japanese which encompassed a refusal to obey orders, to accept bribes or favours, or to surrender land to the Japanese. Some thousands might be killed—but the Japanese would have to give up.[75] The invaders 'will find that they have to hold more than they can in their iron hoop. They will find it much more difficult than Britain has. Their very rigidity will strangle them.'[76]

Nehru, among others, found this aspect of Gandhi's strategy particularly hard to accept—and it must be admitted that some of his statements on it were pretty hair-raising. He told foreign journalists in April, 'you can see that the Japanese cannot have India without mowing down 350 million people...If Japan will kill every man and woman, we will be the better for it.'[77] Nehru favoured armed resistance and guerrilla warfare against the Japanese. Gandhi expressed sorrow at Nehru's advocacy of guerrilla warfare. 'But I have no doubt that it will be a nine days' wonder. It will take no effect. It is foreign to the Indian soil... Guerrilla warfare can take us nowhere. If it is practised on any large scale, it must lead to disastrous consequences.'[78] The difference between them in this regard was never really resolved.

In considering Gandhi's non-violent approach, it is perhaps worth noting that, up to this point, the most powerful armies that imperialism could put in the field had not been able to stop the Japanese by traditional military methods, despite the enormous loss of life on both sides that had occurred. An alternative method of resistance may not have seemed altogether implausible. Even Nehru would observe, sometime later:

> Many people criticized with considerable sarcasm what seemed to them the absurd notion of resisting an invading army with these methods of non-violent non-co-operation. Yet far from being absurd, it was the only method, and a very brave method, left to the people.[79]

Gandhi put forward the same remedies—British withdrawal and non-violence—for the communal problem. After the British left he expected that 'all the parties will fight one another like dogs, or will, when real responsibility faces them, come to a reasonable agreement. I shall expect non-violence to arise out of that chaos.'[80] At that point, it would be an Indian problem, to be solved by Indians without the intervention of 'the third party'. When Rajagopalachari was calling for concessions to 'Pakistan', Gandhi told him:

> But all this can only happen when the British Power is entirely withdrawn and the Japanese menace has abated. Till then there is neither Pakistan nor Hindustan or any other 'stan'. It is today Englishstan and may be tomorrow Japanistan if we do not take care.[81]

Gandhi now had to convince the rest of the Congress leadership to drop the consensus that had arisen that India's main problem was the war and return them to the position that the problem was the British.[82] This was not an easy task. Nehru was apparently 'flabbergasted' at Gandhi's new position and he was not alone.[83] According to Arnold, the period leading up to the new movement was 'revealing of the tensions, conflicts and contradictions in the national movement and the Congress party. It was an important internal crisis—of identity, method and purpose.'[84]

Gandhi's opening salvo came at the Allahabad meeting of the Congress Working Committee in late April, called to consider the situation after the fall of Burma and the failure of the Cripps Mission. Gandhi did not attend, for either diplomatic or health reasons. He sent, instead, Mirabehn with a draft motion for the Committee, which was further worked on by his supporter, Rajendra Prasad. Mirabehn presented the points in Gandhi's draft:

- That the British Government should 'clear out'
- India has become a war zone because of British imperialism
- No foreign assistance was needed for the freedom of India
- India had no quarrel with any country
- In the event of a Japanese invasion, it would be met with non-violent resistance
- The form of non-co-operation was laid down
- Foreign soldiers are a menace to Indian freedom[85]

Gandhi's motion declared that Britain and India had different interests in Indian defence: 'There is an eternal conflict between Indian and British interests. It follows that their notions of defence would also differ.' India had no quarrel with Japan; therefore 'If India were freed her first step would probably be to negotiate with Japan.' But if Japan were to attack India, 'the Committee would expect all those who look to the Congress for guidance to offer complete non-violent non-cooperation to the Japanese forces and not to render any assistance to them.' The motion stated: 'The All-India Congress Committee [to which the Working Committee resolution would be recommended] is therefore of [the] opinion that the British should withdraw from India.'[86] Gopal comments: 'This draft clearly moved away from the whole trend of Congress policy, since the beginning of the war.'[87]

Much too far away, it seemed, for Nehru and his supporters (notably Azad and Rajagopalachari), who found 'the whole attitude of defeatism and sympathy with Japan which underlay this resolution' unacceptable.[88] Nehru told the Committee:

> Japan is an imperialist country. Conquest of India is in their plan. If Bapu's [Gandhi's] approach is accepted we become

passive partners of the Axis powers...the whole thought and background of the draft is one of favouring Japan.

Rajagopalachari said that if it were accepted, 'The entire policy of the Congress will be reinterpreted and the new interpretation will go against us. Japan will say "excellent".[89] Nehru put forward an alternative draft which, while very similar in many respects, removed the idea of negotiations with Japan and placed greater emphasis on anti-fascist, anti-Japanese resistance. It seemed that he wanted to offer, once again, support for the Allied cause in return for concessions. Vallabhbhai Patel, standing with Gandhi, took Nehru to task on this point:

> The draft [Gandhi's draft] says to the British: "you have proved your utter incompetence. You cannot defend India. We cannot defend it either because you won't let us... But if you withdraw there is a chance for us"... It is time the door is finally closed after the repeated insults heaped upon us. I agree with the draft before us. If there is any pro-fascist hint in the draft let it be removed.[90]

Rajendra Prasad agreed, pointing out, 'We cannot produce the proper atmosphere unless we adopt Bapu's draft. The Government has closed the door on armed resistance. We have only unarmed resistance to offer.'[91]

The Committee voted 11:6 on the morning of May 1 in favour of Gandhi's draft, as it had been revised by Rajendra Prasad. That afternoon, however, the Congress President (Azad) reopened the question, pleading with Gandhi's supporters to accept Nehru's draft and thus make the decision unanimous. This they agreed to do.[92] Regardless of the exact wording of these resolutions, the question, whether Congress would take up Gandhi's new position clearly remained unresolved after the Allahabad meeting. Gandhi went to work to persuade his fellow Congress leaders and the Congress rank and file of its correctness.

His task was made somewhat easier by increasing pressure

from the British after the failure of the Cripps Mission. This culminated in a police raid on the Congress offices in Allahabad resulting in the capture of the April Congress Working Committee minutes and draft resolutions. Much was made of Gandhi's draft, with its suggestion of negotiations with the Japanese after British withdrawal. British propaganda now branded the Congress as, at best, appeasers, and at worst, traitors.[93] These moves hardened the attitude of the Congress leadership towards the British and increased support for Gandhi's position.

Gandhi's most important task was to convince Nehru. Undoubtedly, Nehru shared Gandhi's fear that continued inaction would lead to passivity and eventual collaboration with the invader—especially from those currently collaborating with the British: 'They had perfected the art of collaboration and would find no difficulty holding on to that basis even though the superstructure had changed.'[94] Nehru later described the emergence of Gandhi's new position: '...Gandhiji wrote a number of articles which suddenly gave a new direction to people's thoughts, or as often happens, gave shape to their vague ideas.' India had to be free and only a free India could meet aggression and invasion. Nehru points out that this was not a new demand, 'but there was a new urgency and passion in his speech and writing. And there was the hint of action.'[95] The real difference in Gandhi's position (though Nehru does not say this) was its emphasis that freedom (British withdrawal) had to be achieved *before* India could be aroused for defence. Nehru goes on:

> Some of us were disturbed and upset by this new development, for action was futile unless it was effective action, and any such effective action must necessarily come in the way of the war effort at a time when India herself stood in peril of invasion... These were obvious difficulties and we discussed them at length with Gandhiji without converting each other.[96]

'I argued with him for days together,' Gandhi reported, 'He fought against my position with a passion which I have no words to describe.'[97] Gandhi had already conceded that 'negotiations with Japan' should be removed from the Congress Working Committee position. He stiffened his position against the Japanese in China and in India. In July he declared in an open letter 'To Every Japanese', 'we will not fail in resisting you with all the might that our country can muster.'[98] He also agreed that if the British withdrew some part of their military forces might remain. He wrote to Chiang Kai-shek in June:

> To make it perfectly clear that we want to prevent in every way Japanese aggression, I would personally agree that the Allied powers might, under treaty with us, keep their armed forces in India and use the country as a base for operations against the threatened Japanese attack.[99]

These shifts all brought the position of Nehru and the other Congress leaders (with the exception of Rajagopalachari) closer to that of Gandhi. But Nehru argues that it was a change in the attitude of the people that really brought them around.

> While we were doubting and debating, the mood of the country changed, and from a sullen passivity it rose to a pitch of excitement and expectation. Events were not waiting for a Congress decision or resolution: they had been pushed forward by Gandhi's utterances, and now they were moving onwards with their own momentum.[100]

By June Nehru appears to have been convinced. Gopal says 'Jawaharlal was reluctantly dragged to the conclusion that the ending of British rule was the primary issue.' Pandey states that 'In June, he [Nehru] began to realise that there was probably no alternative to Gandhi's plan of action.'[101] A month later, Nehru wrote to Sampurnanand (a nationalist leader):

> I have been worried and disturbed beyond measure. Yet gradually I have come to this conclusion that there is no other way out. I am convinced that passivity is fatal now...somehow in my bones I feel some terrible shake-up is necessary for our country. Otherwise we shall get more and more entangled in communal and other problems, people will get thoroughly disillusioned and will merely drift to disaster.[102]

Abul Kalam Azad was also not immediately convinced of Gandhi's position. In June 1942, Gandhi had told him that, if the British withdrew, Japan would have no reason to invade. Azad wrote:

> I could not accept his reading and in spite of long discussions we could not reach agreement. I found Sardar Patel held the same view... We therefore parted on a note of difference.[103]

Azad was afraid of 'any word or action which could offer encouragement to the Japanese.' He advocated a 'wait and see' approach and was therefore hesitant to adopt Gandhi's position. He continued to oppose a mass campaign at the July Congress Working Committee meeting (where Gandhi's position was finally accepted), arguing that the British would immediately arrest the Congress leadership and the movement would then degenerate into violence or passivity.[104] In his memoirs, Azad reprints the Working Committee's July resolution but does not indicate whether he supported it. He acknowledges however that the Congress resolution 'created an electric atmosphere in the country...at last Congress was launching a mass movement to make the British quit India.' Azad supported the Quit India resolutions at the Congress Working Committee and All-India Congress Committee meetings in August.

Having grasped Gandhi's position, Nehru became one of its strongest proponents. He wrote to Lampton Berry in June that having independence and a National Government would 'make all the difference in the world.' It would enable Indians to resist as the

Chinese were resisting: 'A spirit of passive resignation gives place to active opposition and resistance.'[105] 'This movement,' he told an interviewer in late July, 'is born of an utter lack of confidence in the British ability to defend India.'[106] At a meeting in Delhi, he declared:

> We want to create a spirit in India which will make people fight for every inch of ground and not be dismayed by a single military defeat... We want to check the dangerous turn which the anti-British feeling in India is taking. In the opinion of Gandhiji the only method to do it is to create a spirit of non-submission against foreign domination of Britain or Japan.[107]

How was this spirit to be created? How would the movement work? It appears that Gandhi had given little consideration to these questions up to the passing of the Quit India resolution in August.[108] At a press conference in June he was asked:

> Now about your plan; you are reported to have plans for launching some big offensive?'

He replied:

> There are certainly many plans floating in my brain. But just now I merely allow them to float in my brain... I may have to do something. That something may be very big, if the Congress is with me and the people are with me.[109]

Azad writes that at the Congress Working Committee meeting, 'When I pressed him to tell us what exactly would be the programme for resistance, he had no clear idea.' Gandhi only said in this movement people should resist arrest and submit only to physical force.[110] Nehru concurs, writing later that 'Gandhiji...said nothing at all about the nature of this action.' He only mentioned 'some kind of non-co-operation and a one-day protest *hartal* or cessation of all work in the country.'[111] Up until the All-India

Congress Committee meeting (from roughly May through to August), Gandhi's main preoccupation was to construct his own position—that the main problem was British colonialism, the main solution was the reassertion of India as a nation and that all else followed from that—and to convince as many of the Congress leaders as he could of its correctness. The tactical decisions came afterwards. And as Azad suggests, Gandhi may have believed that the British would take no precipitate action once the movement was declared; 'He would therefore have time to work out details of the movement and develop its tempo according to his plans.'[112] In fact, the nature of the movement (if not its finer details) had been laid down in the decades of counter-hegemonic Congress practice. We will examine this in more detail in the next chapter.

The Congress Working Committee met from July 6 to 14 at Wardha. The Gandhi position was put and endorsed to go forward to the All-India Congress Committee in Bombay on August 7. The Working Committee noted 'a rapid and widespread increase of ill will against the British and a growing satisfaction at the success of Japanese arms.' The Congress wanted to call a halt to this, to avoid a repeat of Malaya and Burma, to build up resistance to foreign aggression—but this could only be done if India were free.[113] Gandhi 'expressed the fear that if something of the kind was not done, the very existence of the Congress would be in danger owing to inactivity.'[114] He told foreign correspondents that the movement was aimed at averting the 'catastrophe' of large numbers of Indians siding with the Japanese.

> We are determined so far as it is humanly possible to secure our independence, so that no Indian worth the name would then think of going over to the Japanese.[115]

An important part of the Working Committee's July proceedings was the position it took against the Indian and Bengal Governments' programmes of 'denial'. Gandhi had already expressed bitter opposition to the measures that were being taken.[116] The

Committee demanded fair and immediate compensation for property and goods requisitioned—in its absence, resistance was advocated. It also declared that 'all restrictions on organization for self-protection should be disregarded.'[117] Here we can see the beginnings of the Quit India movement, at the heart of which would be the question: who is to rule? The Committee's resolution against 'denial' and its sanctioning of resistance to it was a direct challenge to colonial hegemony and the start of an avalanche of such challenges. The British were immediately aware of the nature and the implications of the resolution. Amery telegrammed the Viceroy, describing the resolution as orders issued by 'a parallel authority acting in defiance of established Government in respect of measures necessary for the prosecution of the war. Such action here would, of course, involve not only internment but prosecution and drastic punishment.' Which is exactly what Amery recommended.[118] The War Cabinet noted:

> The Congress Working Committee, claiming the position of an authority parallel to that of the Government, deliberately instructed people to resist the Government's actions in regard to measures such as the removal of boats or vehicles. This was an intolerable challenge...'

It promised the Viceroy full support for repressive measures.[119]

The Congress Working Committee approved the Quit India resolution and forwarded it to the All-India Congress Committee for consideration at its meeting on August 7. The *Amrita Bazar Patrika* reported on the meeting:

> Tickets for admission of visitors to the pandal, ranging in price from Rs.10/- to Rs.500/- [had] been sold out two days before the session, and hundreds of eager man and women who were unable to obtain admission stood outside listening to the loudspeakers installed in the pandal.[120]

Opening the session, Azad devoted his entire speech to the

Congress and the War ♦ 143

proposition that *if* India is to be defended and *if* India is to make a contribution to the war, then India must be free—because Indians must feel they are defending their country.[121] A majority of the All-India Committee's 250 members passed the resolution and set Gandhi's new exercise in counter-hegemonic struggle in motion. Gandhi issued the mantra: Do or Die.[122]

Notes

1. Mohandas K. Gandhi, 'Speech to the All-India Congress Committee', 15 September 1940 in *The Collected Works of Mahatma Gandhi* (Chief Editor: Shri R.P. Dhasmana. Delhi: Publications Division, Ministry of Information and Broadcasting, 1958–1994 (henceforward MK Gandhi, Collected Works), Volume 79, 219 & 226.
2. B.N. Pandey, *Nehru* (London: Macmillan London Limited, 1976), 210; Arun Chandra Bhuyan, *The Quit India Movement: The Second World War and Indian Nationalism* (New Delhi: Manas Publications, 1975), 6.
3. Nehru's notes on Gandhi's talk (18 June 1940) in Nicholas Owen, 'The Cripps Mission of 1942: A Reinterpretation', *Journal of Imperial and Commonwealth History* 30 (1): 210.
4. Pandey, Nehru, 210.
5. Sudata Debchaudhury, *Japanese Imperialism and the Indian Nationalist Movement: A Study of the Political and Psychological Impact of Possible Invasion and Actual Occupation, 1939–1945* (Ph.D. Dissertation, University of Illinois-Urbana, 1992), 171.
6. Resolution of 53rd (Ramgarh) Session in A.M. and S.G. Zaidi (eds.), *The Encyclopaedia of the Indian National Congress. Volume Twelve: A Fight to the Finish* (New Delhi: S. Chand & Company, 1981), 368.
7. Bhuyan, Quit India Movement, 1–3.
8. Congress funded the dispatch of an ambulance unit to aid the Chinese Communist Party's 8th Route Army (Milan Hauner, *India in Axis Strategy: Germany, Japan and Indian Nationalists in the Second World War* (Stuttgart: Klett-Cotta, 1981), 104).
9. Bhuyan, Quit India, 3.
10. General Editor's Preface in Bipan Chandra and Salil Misra (eds.), *Towards Freedom: Documents on the Movement for Independence in India, 1942* (New Delhi: Oxford University Press, 2016)—henceforward Chandra and Misra, Towards Freedom 1942—xix. Debchaudhury adds a fourth, that of

'Bose and the pro-Japan group' which, since it was soon to be outside the Congress leadership, we will not consider here (Debchaudhury, Japanese Imperialism, 178).

11. See Gandhi's 'Letter to Abul Kalam Azad' and 'Statement to the Press' (both 30 December 1941) in MK Gandhi, Collected Works, Volume 81, 398 & 400.
12. Speech of Azad, AICC Wardha, 15–16 January 1942 in Chandra and Misra, Towards Freedom 1942, 17.
13. Bhuyan, Quit India, 4; Debchaudhury, Japanese Imperialism, 169–170, 196.
14. Summary of a speech by Nehru, 11 February 1942 in Viceroy to Amery, 12 February 1942 in Nicholas Mansergh (ed.), *The Transfer of Power 1942–7. Volume 1: The Cripps Mission, January-April 1942* (London: Her Majesty's Stationery Office, 1970) (henceforward Transfer of Power I), 155–6.
15. Madras Chief Secretary Report 2nd half June 1942. See also Madras Governor Report, 2 of 1942, 22 March 1942. British Library: India Office Records (henceforward IOR): Fortnightly Reports of Governors, Civil Commissioners and Chief Secretaries (1937–1948) L/PJ/205
16. Madras Congress Committee's resolutions for AICC (undated) Chandra and Misra, Towards Freedom 1942, 791.
17. Statement to the press, 19 December 1941. MK Gandhi, Collected Works, Volume 81, 385.
18. CWC Instructions in *Harijan*, 25 January 1942 in MK Gandhi, Collected Works, Volume 81, 511.
19. 'Plea for Calmness', *Harijan*, 22 February 1942.
20. Congress Annual Report 1940–1946 in Zaidi, Congress Encyclopaedia XII, 585.
21. CWC Instructions (drafted by Nehru), 30 December 1941 in Bhupen Qanungo, 'The Quit India Movement, 1942', in *A Centenary History of the Indian National Congress. Volume Three: 1935–1947* ed. M.N. Das (New Delhi: All-India Congress Committee (I), 1985), 479.
22. Bhuyan, Quit India, 4–5. The AICC, endorsing the Working Committee's resolution, wanted to give 'every opportunity for the war and peace aims of the British Government to be clarified with particular reference to India.' While this position was clearly not that of Gandhi, the Congress continued to declare its confidence in him as a strategic leader who would eventually lead them in civil disobedience (see report on the Ramgarh session of Congress, *Amrita Bazar Patrika* (henceforward ABP) 19 March 1940, 11).

23 Bhuyan, Quit India, 11.
24 See Linlithgow's speech of 8 August 1940 in Victor A.J.H. Linlithgow, *Speeches and Statements* (Delhi: Government of India (Bureau of Public Information), 1945), 250–2.
25 Gandhi's statement to Bardoli CWC and letter to Maulana Azad (both 30 December 1941) in Chandra and Misra, Towards Freedom, 7.
26 Gandhi's speech to the AICC 15 January 1942 in Chandra and Misra, Towards Freedom, 19.
27 Reports of the Ramgarh Congress session in ABP 19 March 1940, 9; 24 March 1940, 7.
28 Gandhi's speech at the 53rd Congress session, 19 March 1940 in Zaidi, Congress Encyclopaedia XII, 341–2.
29 *Harijan* 1 June 1940.
30 Speech at Sevagram 12 October 1941, MK Gandhi, Collected Works Volume 81, 190.
31 Letter to Gandhi, 4 February 1940 in Jawaharlal Nehru, *A Bunch of Old Letters* (London: Asia Publishing House, 1960), 427.
32 Discussion at CWC meeting, Wardha 15–19 April 1940 in MK Gandhi, Collected Works, Volume 78, 156.
33 Bhuyan, Quit India, 13.
34 For a description of the campaign, see Mridula Mukherjee, *Peasants in India's Non-Violent Revolution: Practice and Theory* (New Delhi: Sage Publications, 2004), 204. Nehru is said to have reacted angrily against it (Pandey, Nehru, 221)—nevertheless, he was the second person to take part in the campaign.
35 See Debchaudhury, Japanese Imperialism, 176–177; Bhuyan, Quit India, 17.
36 Report on Police Administration in Bengal 1940, 34. IOR: Bengal. Police Department: Report on the Police Administration in the Presidency, 1936–1947. V/24/3207.
37 Chief Secretary Report 2nd half December 1940. IOR: Fortnightly Reports of Governors, Chief Commissioners and Chief Secretaries (1937–1948). L/PJ/5/147.
38 Report Police Administrationin Bengal 1941, 29. IOR: Bengal. Police Department: Report on the Police Administration in the Presidency, 1936–1947. V/24/3207. In one of the few positive comments about the campaign, Khan maintains 'it did solidify and give form to a strong strand of anti-war feeling.' (Yasmin Khan, *India at War: The Subcontinent and the Second World War* (Oxford: Oxford University Press, 2015), 58).
39 AICC meeting Wardha 15–16 January 1942 in Zaidi, Congress

Encyclopaedia XII, 385.
40 Bengal Provincial Congress Committee Report in Chandra and Misra, Towards Freedom 1942, 720.
41 AICC Draft Resolution 29 April 1942 in Chandra and Misra, Towards Freedom 1942, 794–5.
42 Bhuyan, Quit India 23.
43 Partha Sarati Gupta, 'Imperial Strategy and the Transfer of Power, 1939–51', in *Myth and Reality: The Struggle for Freedom in India, 1945–47* ed. Amit Kumar Gupta (New Delhi: Manohar, 1987), 3; Khan, India at War, 132; Hauner, India in Axis Strategy, 451; Debchaudhury, Japanese imperialism, 178–9.
44 Prasad, Cripps Mission, 151.
45 Interview to Eve Curie, *Harijan* 19 April 1942, MK Gandhi, Collected Works, Volume 82, 156.
46 Khan, India at War, 134.
47 See report in ABP 8 April 1942, 5.
48 Owen, The Cripps Mission, 74.
49 Mulk Raj Anand, *Letters On India* (London: George Routledge & Sons, 1942), 11–12. See also Prasad, 'Cripps Mission', 143.
50 War Cabinet minutes 2 April 1942 TOP I 612.
51 Nehru, Discovery, 296.
52 Louis Fischer, *The Life of Mahatma Gandhi* (New York: Harper & Brothers Publishers, 1950), 359.
53 Anand, Letters, 12; Bhuyan, QI, 28.
54 CWC Resolution, 11 April 1942 in Transfer of Power I, 747–8.
55 'What if Germany wins?' *Harijan*, 15 February 1942 in MK Gandhi, Collected Works, Volume 82, 6.
56 'Are You Not Inviting the Japanese?' *Harijan*, 3 May 1942 in MK Gandhi, Collected Works, Volume 82, 236.
57 'One Thing Needful' *Harijan*, 10 May 1942 in MK Gandhi, Collected Works, Volume 82, 258.
58 'Plea for Reason' *Harijan*, 26 July 1942 in Chandra and Misra, Towards Freedom 1942, 909.
59 Question Box, *Harijan*, 26 April 1942 in MK Gandhi, Collected Works, Volume 82, 217–218.
60 See the perceptive comments of R. Tottenham, Additional Secretary to the Government of India in a letter to the Secretary of State, 19 February 1944 in P.N. Chopra, *Quit India Movement: British Secret Report* (Faridabad: Thomson Press (India), 1976), 5.
61 Gandhi's speech in *Sarvodaya*, June 1942 in MK Gandhi, Collected

Works, Volume 82, 339.
62 'That Ill-Fated Proposal' *Harijan*, 19 April 1942. A few days later he declared that 'national independence is an impossibility until Indians have solved the communal problem' ('Unity is Vital in India,' *Bombay Chronicle*, 25 April 1942), both in MK Gandhi, Collected Works, Volume 82, 190 & 194.
63 Notes, *Harijan*, 21 June 1942.
64 Interview to the Press, *Harijan*, 24 May 1942 in MK Gandhi, Collected Works, Volume 82, 286. Gandhi advised the Muslim League that 'it must first free the home before partitioning it.' (*Harijan*, IX (21) 7 June 1942.)
65 Interview with *News Chronicle*, 14 May 1942, in MK Gandhi, Collected Works, Volume 82, 279.
66 'Foreign Soldiers in India,' *Harijan*, 26 April 1942 in MK Gandhi, Collected Works, Volume 82, 216.
67 See *Harijan*, IX (19) 24 May 1942; (22) 14 June 1942.
68 'Foreign Soldiers in India,' *Harijan*, 26 April 1942 in MK Gandhi, Collected Works, Volume 82, 216.
69 'To Every Briton' *Harijan*, 17 May 1942 in MK Gandhi, Collected Works, Vollume 82, 271.
70 Congress Radio Part IV, Gandhimedia.org. 'Indian Underground Radio', Parts 1–4. http://www.gandhimedia.org/cgi-bin/gm/gm.cgi?action=view&link=Audio/Radio_Programs/English&image=AURPEN0010.mp3&img=&tt=mp3.
71 'Question Box: The Difference' *Harijan*, 24 May 1942 in MK Gandhi, Collected Works, Volume 82, 296.
72 Mahadev Desai, 'How to be Worthy of Our Heritage,' *Harijan* IX (13) 12 April 1942.
73 Letter from Gandhi 24 April 1942 in Nehru, Letters, 484.
74 *News Chronicle* interview in *Harijan*, 24 May 1942 in MK Gandhi, Collected Works, Volume 82, 280.
75 For Gandhi's advice on non-violent resistance, see 'Non-Violent Resistance,' *Harijan*, 12 April 1942 in MK Gandhi, Collected Works, Volume 82, 167–9; 'With Foreign Correspondents,' *Harijan* IX (14) 19 April 1942.
76 'Foreign Soldiers in India,' *Harijan*, 26 April 1942 in MK Gandhi, Collected Works, Volume 82, 216.
77 'With Foreign Correspondents,' *Harijan* IX (14) 19 April 1942.
78 'Question Box,' *Harijan*, 26 April 1942 in MK Gandhi, Collected Works, Volume 82, 218–219.

79 Jawaharlal Nehru, *The Discovery of India* (London: Meridian Books Limited, 1947), 400.
80 'An Important Interview,' *Harijan* IX (22) 14 June 1942.
81 'For Rajaji,' *Harijan*, 31 May 1942 in MK Gandhi, Collected Works, Volume 82, 320. Clearly, Gandhi was guilty of underestimating the deep roots that communalism had struck even by 1942. He asserted at this time, 'Communalism is an urban product fated to flourish only on urban soil. In rural areas the people are too poor and too interdependent to find time for communal quarrels.' ('Vacation Work,' *Harijan* IX (12) 5 April 1942.)
82 The British interpreted this, Muni suggests, as an attempt by Gandhi to regain control over the Congress leadership in the wake of the Cripps Mission and the failure of individual *satyagraha* (S.D. Muni, 'The Quit India Movement,' *International Studies* XVI (1) January-March 1977: 159).
83 Bhuyan, Quit India, 40–41.
84 David Arnold, 'Quit India in Madras' in *The Indian Nation in 1942*, ed. Gyanendra Pandey (Calcutta: K.P. Bagchi & Company, 1988), 207.
85 This account comes from an enclosure in Sir Maurice Hallett's (Governor, United Provinces) letter to the Viceroy on 31 May 1942 which he says 'appears to be a record of the discussion in the Congress Working Committee on the "war resolution".' (Enclosure to Number 13, Nicholas Mansergh (ed.), *The Transfer of Power 1942–7. Volume 2: 'Quit India', 30 April–21 September 1942* (London: Her Majesty's Stationery Office, 1971 (henceforward Transfer of Power II)), 157.)
86 MK Gandhi's draft motion for the CWC (before 24 April) in Chandra and Misra, Towards Freedom 1942, 788.
87 Sarvepalli Gopal, *Jawaharlal Nehru: A Biography. Volume One: 1889–1947* (Cambridge (Mass.): Harvard University Press, 1976), 289.
88 Gopal, Nehru, 289.
89 Enclosure to Number 13, Transfer of Power II 158–9 & 161.
90 Enclosure to Number 13, Transfer of Power II 160.
91 Enclosure to Number 13, Transfer of Power II 160.
92 Enclosure to Number 13, Transfer of Power II 164.
93 Sanjoy Bhattacharya, 'An Official Policy that went awry: The WW II propaganda campaign against the Indian National Congress,' *International Institute of Asian Studies Newsletter* 13 Summer 1997: www.iias.nl.
94 Nehru, Discovery, 403–4.
95 Nehru, Discovery, 405–6.

96 Nehru, Discovery, 406.
97 Louis Fischer, Mahatma Gandhi, 377.
98 'To Every Japanese' *Harijan*, 26 July 1942 in MK Gandhi, Collected Works, Volume 83, 116.
99 'Letter to Chiang Kai-shek,' 14 June 1942 in MK Gandhi, Collected Works, Volume 83, 27.
100 Nehru, Discovery, 408.
101 Gopal, Nehru, 292; Pandey, Nehru, 231.
102 Nehru to Sampurnanand, 28 July 1942 in Pandey, Nehru, 232.
103 Maulana Abul Kalam Azad, *India Wins Freedom: An Autobiographical Narrative* (Bombay: Orient Longmans, 1959), 73.
104 For this, Gandhi asked for his resignation as Congress president—a request he then withdrew (Azad, Freedom, 74–7).
105 Nehru to Lampton Berry 23 June 1942 in Nehru, Letters, 493.
106 Miss A. Moore, notes on interview with Nehru, 28 July 1942 in Chopra, British Secret Report, 309.
107 Nehru speech in Delhi 18 July 1942 in Chandra and Misra, Towards Freedom 1942, 894–896.
108 As Gopal puts it, '... Gandhi, as usual, had no clear idea as to the way in which Britain could be induced to quit India.' Gopal, Nehru, 292.
109 Press Interview, *Harijan* IX (21) 7 June 1942.
110 Azad, Freedom, 74.
111 Nehru, Discovery, 409.
112 Azad, Freedom, 74.
113 CWC Final Quit India resolution, 14 July 1942 in Chandra and Misra, Towards Freedom 1942, 880–881.
114 CWC Wardha proceedings 6–14 July 1942 in Chandra and Misra, Towards Freedom 1942, 867.
115 Gandhi to foreign correspondents 15 July 1942 in Chandra and Misra, Towards Freedom 1942, 885.
116 See 'Scorched Earth,' *Harijan*, 22 March 1942; 'To Every Briton,' 11 & 17 May 1942 in MK Gandhi, Collected Works, Volume 82, 272; 'Implications of Withdrawal,' *Harijan*, 24 May 1942.
117 CWC proceedings 6–14 July 1942 in Zaidi, Congress Encyclopaedia XII, 467–9; CWC resolution, 10 July 1942 in Transfer of Power II, 362–4.
118 He suggested 'immediate arrest pending prosecution' of 'Gandhi and Working Committee' (Amery to Viceroy, 13 July 1942 in Transfer of Power II, 374–5. See also John Barnes and David Nicholson (eds.), *The Empire at Bay: The Leo Amery Diaries 1929–1945* (London: Hutchinson, 1988), entry for 13 July 1942, 819.

119 War Cabinet minutes, 13 July 1942 in Transfer of Power II, 377–8. Mukherjee suggests that 'the proposed resistance to "denial" was central to the brutality with which the "Quit India" movement would be dealt.' (Janam Mukherjee, *Hungry Bengal: War, Famine, Riots and the End of Empire* (Noida (India): Harper Collins, 2015), 70.
120 ABP 8 August 1942, 5.
121 ABP 8 August 1942, 6.
122 AICC Bombay proceedings 7–8 August 1942 in Zaidi, Congress Encyclopaedia XII, 390–395.

6

THE FOUNDATIONS OF QUIT INDIA

> *When the people failed to obtain desired reforms from the communal authorities, they seceded, with the support of prominent individuals from the commune, and after forming an independent assembly they began to create their own magistracies similar to the general systems of the commune... The people, then, came to dominate the commune, overwhelming the previous ruling class ...*
>
> —Antonio Gramsci, writing on 13th century Italy in 1930.[1]

The commencement of the Quit India campaign is often portrayed as a leap into the dark by Congress—the launching of a movement with no plan and no structure, made more confusing by the arrest of the Congress leadership the day after the Bombay All-India Congress Committee meeting. In fact, the *nature* of the movement—its general outline and its objects—were known and understood, for they had been laid down by the practice of Congress counter-hegemony over the previous two decades. It will be remembered that this did not consist primarily in confronting the enemy, but in moving into positions that the enemy had conceded or abandoned, pushing the enemy aside, replacing—and being seen to replace—the enemy as a source of authority. 'A non-violent revolution,' said Gandhi in the summer of 1942, 'is not a program of seizure of power. It is a program of transformation of relationships ending in a seizure of power.'[2] Structures were required to put this into effect: the constructive programme, volunteer organizations and self-help committees to fill the gaps that the British were leaving. As Bhagwan Joshi puts it, the aim was 'to build an alternative hegemony and its political organization in the form of a state within a state.'[3] All of this had begun to proliferate after the resignation of the Congress ministries and under the pressure of wartime conditions. Gandhi wrote at the beginning of 1942, 'If we wish to achieve Swaraj through truth and non-violence, gradual but steady building up from the bottom upwards by constructive effort is the only way.'[4] The building of these organizations was simultaneously a method of self-organization, a means of self-defence and a challenge to British authority. Nehru told a press conference after the breakdown of the Cripps negotiations:

> Only the State can defend the country. We cannot now raise an army; nevertheless, since this crisis came we have started an intensive programme of self-sufficiency and self-protection in rural and urban areas in respect of food and clothing if and when transportation fails. Naturally [the] units [that have been formed] could not resist an invading army, [but] they form the background of any resistance...the State or we might organize.[5]

One further point should be noted. The Congress leadership was seriously worried at this time that a combination of opposition to British rule, alienation from the war effort, the resignation of the Congress ministries and the collapse of the Cripps Mission were giving rise to demoralisation and apathy among the people—which could lead, not to resistance, but to a sullen acceptance of either British or Japanese rule.[6] The building up of alternative structures before the Quit India campaign was designed to combat demoralisation and apathy—and to promote a positive opposition to the British and the Japanese. As Chandra argues, 'it was necessary to draw them out of this demoralized state of mind and convince them of their own power.'[7]

The starting point for the Congress remained the constructive programme. Even before his new strategy became clear, Gandhi was convinced that this was where its basis lay. He told the press in January 1942, 'Strange as it may appear, I suggest that ceaseless occupation in [the] constructive programme is the best preparation to face danger.'[8] The Congress Working Committee declared two weeks later that 'The constructive programme...is of particular importance at this juncture. It [will] bring about unity and promote self-reliance and the co-operative spirit.'[9] The All-India Congress Committee echoed the call, urging all Congress members to take up anew the constructive programme.[10]

Work in the programme was seen as a preparatory step for the struggle to come. The Congress Independence Day pledge in 1940 had stated that 'non-violent action in general and preparation for non-violent direct action in particular require successful working of the constructive programme of Khadi, communal harmony and removal of untouchability.'[11] Moving the resolution at the Bardoli All-India Congress Committee in January 1942, Nehru emphasised 'There is plenty of work to do. The constructive programme will keep our hands full preparing the country to be self-sufficient.'[12] It would also help to rejuvenate the Congress and its members—all of whom, the Working Committee had demanded in June 1940, 'are expected to take a continuous and active part in Congress work.' The Congress 'should not be merely a roll of vast numbers of inactive members,' said the Committee.[13] The programme would turn the Congress outwards, towards 'the task of strengthening the organization and reviving and maintaining contacts with the people in the villages and towns.'[14]

The constructive programme was also the basis on which the

Congress could emerge as the mainstay of the people. For in the new strategy, Congress was moving on to become an economic organizer, a food provider and a means of defence. Gandhi wrote:

> The Congress will cease to be popular if it cannot deserve popularity in times of stress. If it cannot provide work for the workless and hungry, if it cannot protect the people from depredations or teach them how to face them, if it cannot help them in the face of danger, it will lose its prestige and popularity... Nobody thinks of mass revolt at the present moment. The best, quickest and most efficient way is to build up from the bottom... Every village has to become a self-sufficient republic.[15]

Shankar Rao Deo, a Congress leader, told Congress workers 'it is the Congress alone which can establish order in an emergency.'[16] Nehru advised various audiences that 'disorder and panic can only be avoided by the Congress' and that '*Shanti sena* [peace armies—volunteer organizations] should be organized in every village for the preservation of internal peace and order.'[17] Nehru was also confident that 'if the administration at any time breaks down, especially in the countryside, the people themselves will have the opportunity to take up the responsibility of running the government.'[18]

Congress was not just advocating that village life should be defended and preserved. Self-defence and self-sufficiency would be the vehicles of social change. Gandhi even saw a ray of hope in the exodus from the cities in this regard. He urged those leaving to take up the constructive programme in the villages. 'Thus they will identify themselves with the villagers and become a kind of co-operative society with an ordered programme of economic, social, hygienic and political reconstruction.' This 'must result in a silent re-organization of villages.'[19]

But the greatest change of all would be the replacement of British administration. If a sufficient network of Congress volunteer organizations were in place '[w]hen government ends,' said Nehru, 'You can even carry on the administration of *Swaraj* government through that organization.'[20] Similarly, Azad speculated to a public meeting of some 25,000 in Punjab that in the event of an invasion:

> If Congress could by that time set up a parallel administration it would be in a position to build up a new India in the same way as a new China was being born.[21]

Congress was now acting on the assumption that 'no reliance can be placed on Central or Provincial governments functioning in India to act effectively and intelligently in times of emergency.' The people had to organize themselves on the basis of self-sufficiency and self-protection.[22]

In preparation for the new policy, Gandhi sent agents into the provinces most likely to face invasion: Bengal, Orissa and Assam.[23] The most well-known of these was Mirabehn (Gandhi's staunch acolyte, Madeleine Slade), who visited Orissa. She reported back to Gandhi on the suffering and resentment created by boat confiscation, the emptying of canals and the compulsory clearing of land (including villages) for aerodromes.[24] In part, her mission (and that of the other Congress agents) was precisely what the British perceived it to be:

> Her general plan no doubt [said the Governor of Orissa] is to develop Congress propaganda on the lines that if trouble comes here, the Government will withdraw and desert the people; but even if the districts are overrun by invaders Congress will stay with the people and look after them.[25]

But an important element was missed here. The Congress agents were also charged with fighting against apathy and passive acceptance of an invasion, were it to come. Mirabehn reported extreme antipathy towards the British, particularly over racial discrimination during the evacuation of Malaya and Burma and the scorched earth policy. In these circumstances, she said, it was hard to argue for neutrality and even for non-co-operation with the Japanese.

> The strongest feeling is fear and distrust of the British, which is growing day by day on account of the treatment they are receiving. Anything that is not British is therefore something welcome.[26]

Gandhi, in reply, encouraged his representatives to emphasise that the Japanese too must be resisted, albeit non-violently.

> Remember that our attitude is that of complete non-co-operation with [the] Japanese army... One thing they [the people] should never do—to yield willing submission to the Japanese... Their attitude therefore must always be of resistance to the Japanese.[27]

VOLUNTEERS

Organizations of 'Congress Volunteers' had been established since the early 1920s to provide security and keep order at Congress functions—and later, especially in the villages, to organize self-defence. In 1921, Congress established a National Volunteer Corps.[28]

The constructive programme always contained the seeds of an alternative political power. The 1920–21 Non-Co-Operation Campaign in the Midnapur district, for example, emphasised the 'rural reconstruction activities of the Congress', which included 'a settlement of disputes through arbitration.' Chakrabarty maintains that 'what became a gigantic movement in 1942 was the result of sincere efforts of Congress volunteers since 1920.'[29]

From 1926 the *Amar Kutir* organization established a self-help co-operative community near Santiniketan in Bengal. According to the (still existent) group's museum, 'this organization involved itself in the task of nation-building through a nationalist-economic endeavour' and became closely linked with the freedom movement. It set up an 'ancillary unit' ostensibly to undertake social work. But 'behind the smoke-screen of social work' they campaigned against the British and established 'a secret camp where recruits were given martial training.' The object, according to the caption on a photograph of training in June 1940, was 'the formation of a *People's Army*.' During the Quit India campaign, the local anti-British actions were organized by the *Amar Kutir*.[30]

Less dramatically, but along the same lines, in the Tamluk sub-division (Bengal) in 1939, Congress workers organized khadi training, a camp for training women activists, nine schools for *harijans*, two adult night schools and a Hindi language school.[31]

Voluntary organizations of all kinds blossomed from the outbreak of the war. The Government of India banned military drill by such organizations in August 1940 and uniforms and training camps in August 1944.[32] In protest at the 1940 ban, Nehru toured the United Provinces in the uniform of the Congress Volunteers and urged local volunteer groups to continue their activities.[33] In preparation for the individual satyagraha campaign (October 1940-December 1941), volunteer organizations and training camps had been set up.[34] It seems that government bans on volunteer organizations were generally ineffective, not least because the Government itself started trying to set up similar organizations—Civic Guards, Home Guards and the ARP.[35]

Ignoring government bans, in January 1942 the Congress Working Committee sent out instructions that 'volunteers should be organized in both the urban and rural areas. Such organizations should be formed on the basis of strict non-violence.'[36] It was emphasised that the main purpose of these organizations was to preserve order in the event of Japanese invasion, British collapse, or both. Congress volunteers were urged 'to remain cool and collected and on no account to give way to nervousness or excitement'. In the emergencies to come, their role was to protect the people and prevent disorder.[37] The volunteers were no longer confined to Congress members. J.B. Kripalani, Congress General Secretary, said in an All-India Congress Committee circular:

> The volunteer organization that we contemplate for meeting the needs of the present situation is broad-based. Our previous volunteer organizations were subject to many rules and a fairly severe disciplinary code and were confined to congressmen. This time we have thrown open the doors of the organization to all our countrymen irrespective of political affiliation, the only condition being adherence to peaceful methods... The drive therefore to enlist members of all communities and all political parties for the volunteer organization should be further intensified.[38]

One of the first tasks that Bengali Congress volunteers turned their attention to (in the absence of official action) was aid to the refugees from Burma. The Bengal Congress Committee started making arrangements for the reception and relief of evacuees coming into the province. Meanwhile, the Women's Subcommittee established training camps to instruct volunteers in rendering aid.[39] In Bengal and Assam, Congress worked with the Burma Indian Association, the Federation of Indian Chambers of Commerce and Industry and the Muslim League in the Indian Evacuees' Relief Committees.[40] When the flow of refugees reached epic proportions, local Congress organizations had difficulty coping with the numbers. Sachi Mohan Chowdhuri, the Special Congress Worker for Burma refugees in Chittagong, wrote to the District Congress Committee on March 6, 1942:

> The question of the Burma refugee is an All-India problem. So All-India Congress Committee should take the matter in his hand [and dispatch more volunteers]... The Chittagong congress committee is in need of fund[s] for relief work and [the entire burden] has fallen upon it. So we hope you kindly try to help with fund[s].

It will be noted that this appeal was not addressed to the government. Little wonder, when the government was asking for aid from the Congress. The Special Worker went on to report that, in the expected evacuation of some 40,000 people from Chittagong Port, the government expected Congress to help. And further: 'we have been requested by...special evacuation officer, overseas department, Government of India, to send some Congress volunteers to different halting stations in Burma.'[41] A month later, the Bengal Provincial Congress Committee was able to report that it had been able to give aid to thousands of evacuees from Burma, Malaya and Singapore.

> In this work the congress has received ungrudging support of other organizations like the Marwari Relief Society, Bajrung Parishad, Nababidhan Samiti, etc. Even Anglo-Indians and Muslim relief associations are working in collaboration with the Congress. To cope with this work a regular volunteer corps has been organized and several centres have been opened.[42]

Even if it had been conducted in the most apolitical and disinterested way, this work by the Congress and its volunteers would have had a considerable effect. But it was neither apolitical nor disinterested. Congress was pursuing a political strategy by providing the aid and relief that the British either could or would not.[43] The British were aware of their problem. The Chief Secretary of Bengal reported in April:

> Congress has also taken the opportunity afforded by the acceptance of their assistance in dealing with evacuees from Burma to propagate with considerable success amongst those assisted the view that they owe nothing whatever to Government...and that it is the Congress which has assisted them on their way through Calcutta and provided them with the means of reaching their homes.[44]

As the war drew nearer, Congress would challenge many other aspects of British authority. When the government started setting up Air Raid Precaution (ARP) groups, the Congress was inclined to dismiss them as unnecessary and a sign of panic. There were also accusations that they were only there for the protection of 'Englishmen, Government officials and the rich'. On the other hand, the Congress Chairman of the Allahabad Municipal Board declared that he should control the ARP in that city.[45] Later, when Congress was establishing its volunteer organizations they tended to take over ARP duties. When the ARP set up first aid posts in Calcutta, the Bengal Congress set up no less than fourteen of its own first aid centres. In this, it had the enthusiastic support of the *Amrita Bazar Patrika*: 'the public are advised to get in touch with, and ask for help from, the Congress organizations as well as the official ones in case of difficulties.'[46]

The Bengal Congress formed a Civil Protection Committee in Calcutta in early 1942 at a meeting chaired by Maulana Azad.[47] The meeting divided the city into thirty-two districts and hoped to form a Civil Protection Committee in each. Out of the thirty-two districts, committees were formed in twenty six of them.[48] Azad (who took credit for this scheme) wrote later:

> The scheme I had in view was that as soon as the Japanese army reached Bengal and the British army withdrew towards Bihar, the Congress should step in and take over the control of the country. With the aid of our volunteers, we should capture power in the interregnum before the Japanese could establish themselves.[49]

In the meantime, the Civil Protection Committees would continue and extend the work with evacuees, ARP duties and first aid centres. Each Committee would form its own volunteer organization. A series of public meetings was to be held to mobilise the people.[50] Committees were reported being formed in Calcutta by the South Calcutta, Entally and North Calcutta District Committees and at

The Foundations of Quit India ♦ 161

Shraddhananda Park.[51] At Entally, the Committee was formed at a large public meeting at which speakers pointed out 'the defects and draw backs of the present A.R.P. and Civic Guard Organizations and emphasised the necessity of the adoption of a liberal policy by the Government regarding acceptance of the co-operation of all non-official and public organizations.'[52] The Superintendent of Police reported that a non-official Civil Defence Corps had been formed in the provincial town of Pabna. Similarly, a Civil Defence organization was organized in Bogra. In Khulna, 'The Khulna Congress Committee has been taking steps to organize a Civil Defence Committee...as a rival to the A.R.P. and Civil Guards organization.' Khulna students (under the influence of the Communist Party) formed a Student Defence Corps. In Jessore, a Municipal Volunteers Corps was raised.[53]

Outside Bengal, similar committees and volunteer corps were established in Karachi (in which the Muslim League initially participated), in Ahmedabad (which spread to other towns and districts in Gujarat through training camps), in Bihar and in the Central Provinces (where, at a meeting, 'Several speakers expressed doubts regarding the ability of Government to defend India').[54] Similar organizations were set up in Karnataka, Sindh and Assam.[55] All the district and city committees were asked to report to the Congress centre on their work in training, propaganda, volunteers, communal unity, spinning and training women.[56]

Probably the most impressive example of voluntary organization was in Bombay province where the Congress set up a 'People's Volunteer Brigade' in the last week of January 1942. The Congress general secretary reiterated that this organization was open to all, regardless of political affiliation, requiring only an adherence to non-violent methods. The Bombay Provincial Congress Committee reported that ten thousand volunteers had enrolled by March. Affiliated brigades in other towns and cities had appeared. The British were suitably impressed (or taken aback). They reported that in 'National Week' (April 6-13):

> ...a procession of the People's Volunteer Brigade, which was the main item on the programme of the "Week", was organized by the Bombay Provincial Congress Committee, in which 12,000 volunteers, who are said to have been enrolled in the Brigade, including 300 women, took part. Bullock carts carrying First Aid, Fire-fighting, A.R.P. and other equipment formed part of the procession.[57]

In rural areas, committees and volunteer corps were also organized. Azad considered the Congress organizations to be filling a gap in the countryside because 'the Congress agency would for example concentrate on rural areas which the official agency would probably leave untouched.'[58] In Assam, volunteer organizations undertook a number of roles. An All-India Congress Committee inspector reported from there that rural Congress committees were enrolling and training volunteers. Another report describes volunteers being organized into lathi-wielding squads (that would later be used in attacks on British communications in the Quit India campaign). The inspector noted that potential dangers arose not just from the British and the Japanese. 'There is real apprehension that if the British army have to evacuate from the province as a result of enemy pressure, the hill tribes from the northern hills may be bold enough [to] sweep down on the valley people.' He suggested that the volunteers might not be able to respond to such an attack non-violently.[59] The Orissa Provincial Congress Committee started a 'mass contact' campaign in the villages in 1942, explaining the problems associated with British flight and Japanese invasion. In preparation for social breakdown, landlords were advised to live harmoniously with the smaller farmers. The Committee advised the latter to store grain, grow cotton, spin and wear khadi and to organize Congress volunteers. Such actions, contends Palil, 'would transform the villages into invincible forts.'[60]

In the villages, more advanced plans could be laid for replacing

British authority. Gandhi was in favour of moving ahead with this scheme at full speed. In July he urged villages to make themselves into 'independent republics'—'independent of its neighbours for its own vital wants and yet interdependent for many others in which dependence is a necessity.' The village republics would work on a co-operative basis, abolish caste and make non-violence their rule. A village militia would have a rotating membership and a governing council would be 'annually elected by the adult villagers male and female.' The village masses should take advantage of the current confusion:

> Any village can become such a republic today without much interference even from the present Government whose sole effective connection to the villages is the exaction of the village revenue.[61]

Further suggestions on 'villager swaraj' were made by Congress activist Kishorelal Mashruwala in correspondence with *Harijan*. Villagers, he said, should assemble and declare that:

> From this day on, this village ends its relations with the British Government and forms its own Swaraj until a new Swaraj Government recommended by Gandhiji is established in the country.

After that, no rent or tax would be paid to British officials, local British authorities would be dissolved and a Swaraj Sabha (assembly) would be elected by all those over eighteen. Mashruwala was careful to note 'the British Government is hereby renounced nor will any foreign government be accepted, but every attempt will be made to resist it.'[62]

Gandhi continued to emphasise the non-violent nature of a future campaign. He told two US journalists in June:

> ...we have no weapons... We have then to depend on what strength we have. We have no army, no military resources,

no military skill either, worth the name, and non-violence is the only thing we can fall back upon.[63]

With this came the decidedly non-martial nature of Congress strategy, despite its being aimed at British withdrawal. The United Provinces Congress Committee, having discussed the voluntary organization, declared:

> This organization is meant to train our people in public service and to make them more efficient and disciplined citizens... The [Committee], therefore, disapproves of high-sounding military titles in our volunteer organization.[64]

A further portent for the coming campaign was the attitude of communal organizations (most prominently the Muslim League and the Hindu Mahasabha) to Congress' ongoing efforts. When asked whether Congress volunteers should work with these groups, Gandhi answered, 'you will tender your help to Muslim League or Hindu Sabha volunteers in putting out fire or tending the wounded. You will also invite their help in such matters.'[65] Discussions about co-operation in voluntary organization between Congress and the Muslim League were noted by the British in Karnataka, Ahmedabad and Karachi.[66] But these attempts (and those elsewhere) rarely bore fruit. In Bombay, despite the mass appeal of the People's Volunteer Brigade, both the League and the Mahasabha decided to set up their own organizations in competition with it.[67] The League eventually stayed away from Congress organizations in Ahmedabad and Surat.[68] But for the moment, the Congress leaders could perhaps take some comfort from reports like this one in the *Amrita Bazar Patrika*, from Mymensingh in eastern Bengal:

> More than ten thousand volunteers have enrolled in the 'Janarksha Bahinis' of the Congress in this district... The communal organizations of both the Hindus and the Muslims are finding no favour anywhere in view of the

common danger... Congress workers are touring throughout the district and report that everywhere they are getting spontaneous support.[69]

Congress built its own organization as well as that of the volunteers. Reports from District Committees to the Centre in March 1942 indicate that, as well as enrolling volunteers, the Congress organizations had distributed seventy thousand Congress membership forms.[70] The following month, the President of the Bengal Provincial Congress Committee urged his listeners not to lose sight of 'the right of self-determination': 'Every work in which they might engage themselves was but a means to the attainment of that great goal.'[71]

In these years and months before the Quit India campaign, it was becoming clearer what a huge task the Congress had set itself in contesting the dominant colonial hegemony at this time. Nehru wrote later:

> For some months previously we had been organizing, often in the face of stiff opposition, food committees and self-defence units in towns and villages... We made these vast plans and in a small measure gave effect to them, but it was obvious that we were only scratching the surface of the tremendous problem which confronted us.[72]

BRITISH REACTION

Congress made no secret of the intentions that lay behind the establishment of defence committees and volunteer organizations. Indications are that the colonial authorities eventually grasped the dangers inherent in the Congress plan. At first, however, the British appeared not to take the threat very seriously. The Chief Secretary of Bengal noted 'a demand that political organizations should be allowed to set up parallel services' in February 1942.[73] When it was discovered (by the Intelligence Branch in Bengal) that Communist Party members were organizing a 'Civil Defence Conference' in Hooghly to conduct 'constructive criticism' of Government ARP and Civil Defence and to establish a Citizens' Defence Committee, the Deputy Inspector General of Police simply remarked that 'The citizens should be encouraged to join Govt. organizations and not some parallel organization that would become a party concern.'[74] A.W. Ibbotson, the Government of India's secretary for civil defence, told all the Chief Secretaries, Chief Commissioners and Governors' secretaries:

> So far as information has been received to date there are no indications of such powerful parallel organizations being really built up as to constitute a serious danger to the administration. The matter still needs careful watching and reports from time to time on this subject will be welcomed. It is felt that Government servants should not join these unofficial organizations.[75]

From Sind, the authorities reported that a 'Civil Defence Committee' had been formed in Karachi, 'including representatives of the Congress, the Muslim League and other organizations': 'It will be allowed to organize volunteers as long as there is no attempt to run a parallel A.R.P. organization.'[76] However, at a national level, the European group of representatives felt the question important enough to be debated in the Central Legislative Assembly. There, the joint secretary for civil defence stated:

> The Government of India do not read any of the public utterances made in this connection as indicating any desire or intention to set up rival organizations which would function side by side and in competition with the official organizations. If, therefore, large organized sections of the community prefer to undertake specific and agreed portions of the task without losing their identity, the Government of India will be the last to object.[77]

There was also the hope that these efforts would fade of their own accord. The Madras Chief Secretary said in early February 1942, 'it is doubtful how far [Congress] efforts will be successful.' And later that month, 'The Congress is continuing to make efforts for the formation of the Defence Volunteer Corps but the response appears to have been poor.'[78] As we have seen above, this hope was not borne out.

When it became clear that the voluntary organizations were proceeding apace and that they were competing with official bodies as 'parallel' organizations, the Government's attitude hardened. Delhi reported:

> The Congress appears to be toying with the idea of a parallel civil defence organization of their own or at least making their cooperation in civil defence subject to conditions which would give the various A.R.P. services a "nationalist" quality.[79]

Ibbotson told provincial officers that 'any attempt to set up a parallel administration has to be guarded against'—and if it appeared, 'this would have to be resisted.'[80] All governments decided that Congress activities in this area had to be carefully watched.[81] The Governor of Bombay told the Viceroy that the real purpose of the organizations was 'to re-establish Congress' hold and prestige, and to take advantage of any weakening of authority which may result from war developments.'[82] The Viceroy told the Governors in February:

> It may be necessary to put some brake on the activities of so-called voluntary organizations which, under cover of helping civil defence, are probably seeking to establish the nucleus of a parallel organization competing with the authority of Government and spreading defeatist ideas.[83]

But the Congress was not 'spreading defeatist ideas'. In fact, in setting up these committees and voluntary organizations, Congress, far from envisaging defeat, was contesting the road to victory. That road ran through the uplift of the Indian people. The Governor of the United Provinces reported to Delhi that Nehru had given a speech in late January 'based on the assumption that the Government is entirely incompetent...and that therefore it is necessary to set up a parallel government.'[84] The real content of Asaf Ali's speeches on the subject of air raids was transparent to the local Delhi authorities:

> ...it is clear that his interest is less in the subject itself than in the opportunities afforded by it to make capital out of the alleged neglect of India's defences by the Government and to improve the standing of the Congress by getting the masses to look to it for help rather than to the authorities.[85]

The Intelligence Branch said in March that, through its constructive programme and volunteer corps, Congress was working towards a situation in which, should the administration break down, 'people will turn to them for help and guidance rather than to Government.'[86] Mirabehn was quite blunt in her interview with the Governor of Orissa when the subject of volunteer organizations came up: when the British military withdrew in the face of the Japanese, she said, 'in that event the Congress would "step into the vacuum" when the Government officials left and take charge of the situation.'[87]

The Congress Annual Report for 1942 argued that 'The more efficiency and discipline the volunteer organizations showed, the less the Government liked them'—and therefore imposed 'all manner of restrictions in most parts of the country.'[88] In Bengal, the Governor took action when Gandhi's agents started appearing in the province (see above). 'We think it better to precipitate conflict with Gandhi than to permit his envoys [to] spread dissatisfaction,' said the Governor. It was decided that those coming from other provinces would be ordered to leave Bengal; those from Bengal 'externed' from districts not their own; and locals restricted or prosecuted.[89] Widespread action was taken by local authorities to either place volunteer organizations under government control or liquidate them.[90]

The Bengal government tried to recapture some of the ground lost by setting up its own organizations. Back in May 1940, the Government of India had authorized the creation of Defence Committees at the district level (renamed 'War Committees' in June).[91] But by 1942, the Government of Bengal was still meeting with political leaders in order 'to consider how best to form some committee for the discussion of War and Civil Defence problems.'[92] The Civic Guards were created by the government in Bengali cities to protect the people, enforce order and assist in air raids (in collaboration with the police and the ARP). Their duties came to include promoting communal harmony, preventing false rumours and circulating accurate news of the war. Mukherjee says that, once the Guards started being paid, the organization was reasonably successful, numbering perhaps five thousand in Calcutta.[93]

In a further response to the flowering of Congress-sponsored voluntary organizations, the Bengal government organized the Bengal Home Guards in the countryside.[94] Like their urban counterparts, their purpose was to preserve order, raise morale and combat rumours—but also to aid evacuees, watch the coast and maintain food supply.[95] Some success in these endeavours was reported.[96] The Government felt that the Home Guards had cut the ground of legitimacy out from under the unofficial volunteer groups. It told the District Officers in May, 'no scope can now be reasonably alleged to exist for any sectional organization for "civil defence" outside that indicated by the Hon'ble Minister for Civil Defence Coordination' and enjoined them 'to watch carefully developments in your district.'[97]

British progress on this score ran into problems. The greatest of these, of course, was British reluctance to fully mobilise the Indian population—which would have required war aims very different from the ones they were prosecuting. In his letter of resignation as Bengali Finance Minister to the Governor in

November 1942, Syama Prasad Mookerjee wrote:

> The scheme for popularising the Home Guard was rejected by you in spite of unanimous advice of all the Ministers simply because you and your officials were afraid of trusting the people.[98]

A further difficulty was the impression that the Government was trying to catch up with Congress while simultaneously trying to sideline its efforts. When the formation of the Home Guards was announced, the *Amrita Bazar Patrika* pointed out that:

> The Congress, without waiting to see what steps the Government would adopt, has since January last set about the organization throughout India of rural defence parties independent of, but intended to assist the Government on matters relating to the maintenance of internal tranquillity... most people will think that the present decision of the Bengal Government is a belated adaptation of the Congress scheme...'[99]

A month earlier (just after the bombing of Colombo), the newspaper had called on District Officers to co-operate with the voluntary organizations. It warned:

> The Government and the public alike must begin to accustom themselves to new ways of life and the old bureaucratic isolation, born of a false sense of prestige or superiority, must be a thing of the past.[100]

But clearly, it was not. The colonial state had to proceed with 'voluntary' organizations under its own control; just as Congress had to resist them. Congress boycotted the District War Committees, the Civic Guards and the Home Guards.[101] After a tour of inspection of West Bengal, the Deputy Inspector-General (Civic Guards) had to report that 'his impressions are not very encouraging... Enthusiasm is in any case difficult to maintain and unfortunately in some cases withers with the approach of danger.'[102] There were difficulties recruiting ARP Wardens.[103] A hand-written note on the Government's 'Volunteer Organization' file, surveying the period from August to October 1942, concludes gloomily 'The work did not progress much... The progress achieved during the period was inconsiderable owing to Congress inspired disturbances.'[104] Krishnan notes 'the existence of local networks and the emergence of ad hoc organizations led by influential Congress leaders' and declares that, despite British efforts, 'the local leadership could not be wiped out, and it played a crucial role in many of the spontaneous mass actions in the rural areas.'[105] It is to the mass actions that we shall now turn.

Notes

1. Antonio Gramsci, Note 16, Third Notebook (1930) in *Prison Notebooks. Volume II*, ed. and trans. Joseph A. Buttigieg (New York: Columbia University Press, 1996), 23.
2. Louis Fischer, *The Life of Mahatma Gandhi* (New York: Harper & Brothers Publishers, 1950), 382.
3. Bhagwan Josh, *Struggle for Hegemony in India 1920–1947: The Colonial State, the Left and the National Movement. Volume II: 1934–41* (New Delhi: Sage Publications, 1992), 309.
4. M.K. Gandhi, 'Why?' *Harijan* 18 January 1942 in Mohandas K. Gandhi, *The Collected Works of Mahatma Gandhi*, Chief Editor: Shri R.P. Dhasmana (Delhi: Publications Division, Ministry of Information and Broadcasting, 1958–1994) (henceforward Gandhi, Collected Works) Volume 81, 421.
5. Press conference 12 April 1942 in Jawaharlal Nehru, *Nehru: The First Sixty Years, Volume Two*, ed. Dorothy Norman (London: The Bodley Head, 1965), 89.
6. See Gowher Rizvi, 'The Congress Revolt of 1942: A Historical Revision,' *Indo-British Review* XI (1) December 1984: 33.
7. Bipan Chandra et al, *India's Struggle for Independence, 1857–1947* (New Delhi: Penguin, 1989), 458.
8. Statement to the press 7 January 1942, Gandhi, Collected Works Volume 81, 410.

9   CWC Instructions in *Harijan* 25 January 1942. Appendix III, Gandhi, Collected Works Volume 81, 511.
10 A.M. and S.G. Zaidi (eds.), *The Encyclopaedia of the Indian National Congress. Volume Twelve: A Fight to the Finish* (New Delhi: S. Chand & Company, 1981) (henceforward Congress Encyclopaedia XII), 567–8.
11 Bhupen Qanungo, 'Preparations for Civil Disobedience, January-September 1940', in *A Centenary History of the Indian National Congress. Volume Three: 1935–1947* ed. M.N. Das (New Delhi: All-India Congress Committee (I), 1985), 306.
12 Nehru speech at the AICC 15 January 1942 in Bipan Chandra and Salil Misra (eds.), *Towards Freedom: Documents on the Movement for Independence in India, 1942* (New Delhi: Oxford University Press, 2016) (henceforward Towards Freedom 1942), 20.
13 CWC 17–21 June 1940, Congress Encyclopaedia XII, 428.
14 CWC Instructions in *Harijan* 25 January 1942. Appendix III, Gandhi, Collected Works Volume 81, 511.
15 'Peace Organization' *Harijan* 18 January 1942 in Gandhi, Collected Works Volume 81 420.
16 Fortnightly Report (FNR) Central Provinces and Berar 2nd half May 1942 in Towards Freedom 1942, 820.
17 Report on a speech by Nehru by the District Magistrate, Cawnpore in Towards Freedom 1942, 100; Speech by Nehru at public meeting 24 April 1942 in Towards Freedom 1942, 243.
18 Nehru to Howrah District Congress Committee 19 April 1942 in Towards Freedom 1942, 757.
19 'Desirability of Exodus', *Harijan* 15 March 1942 in Gandhi, Collected Works Volume 82, 113; 'Question Box: Evacuation', *Harijan* 3 May 1942 in Gandhi, Collected Works Volume 82, 237. He had also remarked in January 1942 that 'The age of cities is thus coming to an end' (Speech at Khadi Vidyalaya, 8 January 1942, Gandhi, Collected Works, Volume 81, 414).
20 UP Chief Secretary's analysis of Nehru's speech late January 1942, Nicholas Mansergh (ed.), *The Transfer of Power 1942–7. Volume 1: The Cripps Mission, January-April 1942* (London: Her Majesty's Stationery Office, 1970) (henceforward Transfer of Power I), 203–4.
21 Azad speech in Punjab 18 February 1942, Towards Freedom 1942, 45.
22 AICC draft resolution 29 April 1942 in Towards Freedom 1942, 795. See also Arun Chandra Bhuyan, *The Quit India Movement: The Second World War and Indian Nationalism* (New Delhi: Manas Publications), 1975, 21.

23 See Note from Special Branch, Orissa 25 May 1942 in *Towards Freedom 1942*, 831 & 836; Sudata Debchaudhury, *Japanese Imperialism and the Indian Nationalist Movement: A Study of the Political and Psychological Impact of Possible Invasion and Actual Occupation, 1939–1945* (Ph.D. Dissertation, University of Illinois-Urbana, 1992), 180; Chopra, British Secret Report, 23–4. Hutchins says that 'hundreds' of agents were sent into eastern India (Francis G. Hutchins, *Spontaneous Revolution: The Quit India Movement* (Delhi: Manohar Book Service, 1971), 240).
24 MK Gandhi, 'Our Ordered Anarchy', *Harijan* IX (26) 12 July 1942.
25 Governor of Orissa to Viceroy 25 May 1942 in *Towards Freedom 1942*, 830–831.
26 Mirabehn's report to Gandhi late May 1942, in *Towards Freedom 1942*, 831.
27 Gandhi to Mirabehn 31 May 1942 in *Towards Freedom 1942*, 833–4. See also Gandhi, Collected Works Volume 82, 352–3. Mirabehn raised the practical question of what to do with small arms left in the wake of a Japanese invasion. True to her non-violent principles, she suggested throwing them into the sea. Gandhi was not so hasty; 'I would not rule out the idea of worthy people finding them and storing them in a safe place if they can'.
28 Nariaki Nakazato, 'The Role of Colonial Administration, "Riot Systems" and Local Networks during the Calcutta Disturbances of August 1946', in *Calcutta: The Stormy Decades*, ed. Tanika Sarkar and Sekhar Bandyopadhyay (New Delhi: Social Science Press, 2015), 284. Subhas Chandra Bose added a somewhat comic-opera element to Congress efforts when he was placed in charge of organizing the Congress Volunteers for the Calcutta session in 1928. Mihir Bose writes: 'Characteristically, he gave the operation a thoroughly military look. 2,000 volunteers were organized; all of them received a certain amount of military training and half of them wore uniforms, with specially designed steel-chained epaulettes for the officers.' Gandhi described the effect as that of 'a Bertram Mills Circus' (Mihir Bose. *The Lost Hero: A Biography of Subhas Bose*, (London: Quartet Books, 1982), 65–6). Bose's uniform, as 'General-Officer-Commanding' was made by a well-known British tailor in Calcutta and is today prominently displayed in the museum at Netaji Bhavan in Kolkata.
29 Bidyut Chakrabarty, 'Political Mobilization in the Localities: The 1942 Quit India Movement in Midnapur', *Modern Asian Studies* 26 (4) 1992: 802 & 813. Chakrabarty points out that while the Non-Co-Operation campaign in the district began with leadership from 'the jotedar-rich-

peasant section' it gave rise to the emergence of 'the lower peasantry as a political power.' (802)

30 This information comes from *Amar Kutir* literature and from its museum in Bolpur, West Bengal. I am most grateful for the invaluable assistance of Julfikar Alam (University of Gour Banga, West Bengal) in carrying out the research on *Amar Kutir*.

31 Satish Chandra Samanta, Syamadas Bhattacharyya, Ananga Mohan Das & Prahlad Kumar Pramanik, *August Revolution and Two Years' National Government in Midnapore* (Calcutta: Orient Book Company, 1946), 5.

32 Nakazato, Calcutta Disturbances, 285–6.

33 Sarvepalli Gopal, *Jawaharlal Nehru: A Biography. Volume One: 1889–1947* (Cambridge (Mass.), Harvard University Press, 1976), 266.

34 Despite the relatively low-key nature of the campaign, the training camps attracted considerable numbers. Qanungo puts forward the following figures: United Provinces: 30,178; Bombay Province: 2635; Central Provinces: 1027; Bengal: 1540; Malabar: 2500; NWFP (Red Shirts): 15,940 (Qanungo, Preparations, Congress History III, 340).

35 Nakazato, Calcutta Disturbances, 286.

36 CWC Instructions in *Harijan* 25 January 1942. Appendix III, Gandhi, Collected Works Volume 81, 511.

37 CWC Instructions regarding Future Course of Action, 7 January 1942 in Towards Freedom 1942, 41–2; UP Provincial Congress Committee instruction 5 February 1942 in Towards Freedom 1942, 68–70; Volunteer Corps—Second Circular 25 March 1942 in P.N. Chopra, *Quit India Movement: British Secret Report* (Faridabad: Thomson Press (India)), 1976, 67.

38 AICC Circular No. 8 24 March a942 in Towards Freedom 1942, 735. See also Resolutions of the United Provinces Congress Committee 9 January 1942, in Towards Freedom 1942, 43; 2nd Circular on Volunteer Corps 25 March 1942 in Chopra, British Secret Report, 67.

39 'Relief of Evacuees', *Amrita Bazar Patrika* (henceforward ABP) 16 February 1942, 3.

40 Yasmin Khan, *India at War: The Subcontinent and the Second World War* (Oxford: Oxford University Press, 2015), 106. Congress volunteers also supplied food to evacuees passing through Purnea in Bihar—'an enterprise in which the local Muslim League also has been cooperating.' (FNR Bihar 2nd half April 1942 in Towards Freedom 1942, 87.)

41 Letter from Special Worker for Refugees, Chittagong to District Congress Committee 6 March 1942 in Towards Freedom 1942, 704–705. Bayly and Harper comment on these 'halting stations' that 'Indians believed

that the Congress Party was sending workers to help them, but none came.' Three pages later, however, they report that Congress volunteers did turn up (Christopher Bayly & Tim Harper, *Forgotten Armies: Britain's Asian Empire and the War with Japan* (London, Penguin, 2005), 183 & 186).

42 Bengal Provincial Congress Committee Report 10 April 1942 in Towards Freedom 1942, 84. As well as in Calcutta, Evacuation Relief Centres were organized by Congress in Chittagong and Faridpur. Meanwhile, the Lucknow District Congress Committee was organizing traffic the other way: helping people who wanted to evacuate the city settle in the countryside (Towards Freedom 1942, 743).

43 Khan comments: 'And among the refugees, the idea of Congress as a protector had taken root... The faith in the Congress to provide protection where the British state had failed to do so is a telling insight into the loss of faith in the Raj.' (Khan, India at War, 105.)

44 Chief Secretary Report 1st half April 1942. British Library: India Office Records (henceforward IOR): Fortnightly Reports of Governors, Chief Commissioners and Chief Secretaries (1937–1948). L/PJ/5/149.

45 Fortnightly Report, UP 1st half March 1942 in Towards Freedom 1942, 721.

46 Editorial, ABP 6 April 1942, 4.

47 The Bengal Provincial Congress Committee reports this as taking place on 5 February (Bengal Provincial Congress Committee Report, 10 April 1942 in Towards Freedom 1942, 84. The ABP reports it as 2 March (ABP 2 March 1942, 3).

48 Bengal Provincial Congress Committee report, 10 April 1942 in Towards Freedom 1942, 84.

49 Maulana Abul Kalam Azad, *India Wins Freedom: An Autobiographical Narrative* (Bombay: Orient Longmans, 1959), 73.

50 'Central Calcutta D.C.C.' ABP 4 March, 5. The Bengal Congress was split at this time between the followers of the Bose brothers and those of the central leadership. The volunteer organization of the former was called the National Service Corps; that of the latter, the Civil Defence Volunteer Corps (Chief Secretary Report, 1st half March 1942. IOR: Fortnightly Reports of Governors, Chief Commissioners and Chief Secretaries (1937–1948). L/PJ/5/149.

51 ABP 16 February 1942, 3; 2 March 1942, 3; 15 June 1942, 3. *Hindustan Standard* 28 February 1942. West Bengal State Archive (henceforward WBSA) W–145/42 Formation of volunteer parties for civil defence work.

52 ABP 2 March 1942, 3.

53 Superintendent of Police, Pabna Report 7 January 1942. WBSA: W–145/42 Volunteers; WBSA: W–375/42 Record of war activity. Voluntary organizations and unofficial activities; FNR Presidency Division 1st half February 1942. WBSA: W–145/42 Volunteers; Superintendent of Police Khulna Report 7 February 1942 and letter to the Minister of Civil Defence, Government of Bengal 11 March 1942. WBSA W–145/42 Volunteers.
54 FNR Sindh 2nd half March 1942; District Officer Karachi to Chief Secretary, Bengal 30 April 194. WBSA: W–145/42 Volunteers; Note on work of Gujarat Provincial Congress Committee (undated) in Towards Freedom 1942, 70; FNR Bihar 2nd half June 1942 in Towards Freedom 1942, 55; FNR Central Provinces & Berar 2nd half April 1942 in Towards Freedom, 1942, 93.
55 Towards Freedom 1942, 54 & 57; Chopra, British Secret Report, 67.
56 Bhupen Qanungo, 'The Quit India Movement, 1942' in *A Centenary History of the Indian National Congress. Volume Three: 1935–1947* ed. M.N. Das (New Delhi: All-India Congress Committee (I), 1985), 480.
57 FNR Bombay 1st half April 1942 in Towards Freedom 1942, 92.
58 Azad in ABP 10 February 1942. WBSA W–145/42 Volunteers.
59 Chopra, British Secret Report, 187; Inspection Report, Assam Provincial Congress committee 8 June 1942 in Chopra, British Secret Report, 370.
60 Biswamoy Pati, 'The Climax of Popular Protest: The Quit India Movement in Orissa,' *Indian Economic and Social History Review* 29 (1) 1992: 10–11.
61 MK Gandhi, 'Village Swaraj,' *Harijan* 20 July 1942, Gandhi, Collected Works Volume 83, 113–114.
62 K.G. Mashruwala, 'Village Swaraj,' *Harijan* IX (32) 23 August 1942.
63 M.K. Gandhi, 'An Important Interview,' *Harijan* IX (22) 14 June 1942.
64 The Committee changed the name of the organization from *Karmi Sena* (workers' or volunteer army) to *Karmi Seva Dal* (Volunteer Service Organization) and abolished the post of *Senapati* (military commander) (ABP 13 April 1939, 6).
65 Question Box, *Harijan* IX (3) 1 February 1942.
66 Towards Freedom 1942, 53–54.
67 Bombay Provincial Congress Committee report 16 March 1942, Towards Freedom 1942, 81.
68 Gujarat Provincial Congress Committee report 29 June 1942, Towards Freedom 1942, 55.
69 'Congress CD,' ABP 16 June 1942, 4.
70 Towards Freedom 1942, 82–83.

71 'Celebration of National Week,' ABP 7 April 1942, 3.
72 Jawaharlal Nehru, *The Discovery of India*. London: Meridian Books Limited, 1947, 400–401.
73 Specifically by Congress (Bose wing) and the Forward Bloc. Chief Secretary Report 2nd half February 1942. IOR: Fortnightly Reports of Governors, Chief Commissioners and Chief Secretaries (1937–1948). L/PJ/5/149.
74 Deputy Inspector General of Police, Intelligence Branch 9 April 1942. WBSA: W–145/42 Volunteers.
75 AW Ibbotson to Chief Secretaries, Chief Commissioners and Governors' secretaries, n.d. WBSA: W–145/42 Volunteers.
76 FNR Sind 2nd half March 1942 in Towards Freedom 1942, 727.
77 Speech by N.V.H. Symons (Joint Secretary, Civil Defence department) in Central Legislative Assembly, 10 March 1942. WBSA: W–145/42 Volunteers.
78 Madras Chief Secretary Report 1st half February 1942; Madras CS Report 2nd half February 1942. IOR: Fortnightly Reports of Governors, Chief Commissioners and Chief Secretaries (1937–1948). L/PJ/5/149. Such doubts were not confined to the British. Prantik Samiti, a Congress worker in Gujarat reported on volunteer organization on 29 June 1942: 'there is considerable flagging of interest. We are finding it difficult to enroll new volunteers and to keep up the enthusiasm of the enrolled ones. Firstly, there is no exciting day to day work in which we can engage the volunteers ... Secondly, an impression was gathering amongst the people that the war-danger has receded and there was no need of such an alert.' (Report from Prantik Samiti (Secretary, Congress office Gujarat) 29 June 1942 in Towards Freedom 1942, 859–860.)
79 Delhi FNR 2nd half January 1942 in Towards Freedom, 1942, 59.
80 AW Ibbotson to all Provincial Governors and Chief Commissioners 14 February 1942. WBSA: W–145/42 Volunteers.
81 For example, 'The plans for drill of a military nature' in Assam (FNR Assam 1st half April 1942, Towards Freedom 1942, 83–4).
82 Sir Roger Lumley to Viceroy 21 January 1942, Transfer of Power I, 51.
83 Viceroy to Governors 17 February 1942, Transfer of Power I, 192.
84 Sir Maurice Hallett to Viceroy 17 February 1942, Transfer of Power I, 200.
85 FNR Delhi 2nd half February 1942, Towards Freedom 1942, 72.
86 Intelligence Summary 4 March 1942 Chief Secretary: Intelligence Summary files. IOR: R/20/B/2340–2376 1941–1952. At almost the same time (and in almost the same words), the Governor of Bombay told the

Viceroy that Congress 'wants to pose as the controlling body, to which everyone will look for help and guidance.' (Sir Roger Lumley to Viceroy 5 March 1942, Towards Freedom 1942, 52.)

87 FNR Orissa 5 June 1942, Towards Freedom 1942, 835. One further threat to the colonial authorities was posed by the volunteer organizations: 'Bombay Police argued that the People's Volunteer Brigade provided a well-knit organization for any scheme of mass civil disobedience Gandhi might have in mind.' (Special Branch, Bombay Review 12 June 1942 in K.K. Chaudhari, *Quit India Revolution: The Ethos of its Central Direction* (Mumbai: Popular Prakashan Pvt. Ltd., 1996), 40.

88 Annual Report 1940–1945, Congress Encyclopaedia XII, 569.

89 See Towards Freedom 1942, 836–839.

90 See reports from Jessore, Murshidabad, Pabna and Bogra (WBSA: W–145/42 Volunteers; WBSA: 362- (22)/42) Conference of Commissioners of Divisions held in July 1942. Proceedings). Action extended to the Hindustan Scout Association in Bengal which was banned from practicing military drill (WBSA: W–220/41 Policy to be adopted towards volunteer organizations).

91 Governor Report 2nd half May 1940; Chief Secretary Report 1st half June 1940. IOR: Fortnightly Reports of Governors, Chief Commissioners and Chief Secretaries (1937–1948). L/PJ/5/146.

92 WBSA: W–375/42 Volunteer Organizations.

93 Janam Mukherjee, *Hungry Bengal: War, Famine, Riots and the End of Empire* (Noida (India): Harper Collins, 2015), 33–34.

94 Memorandum for Bengal Cabinet preparing formation of Bengal Home Guards 26 March 1942; A.D. Gordon Memorandum on duties and structure of Home Guards 23 March 1942. WBSA: W–145/42 Volunteers.

95 Mukherjee, Hungry Bengal, 35–36.

96 See report from Murshidabad district. WBSA: W–375/42 Volunteer Organizations.

97 Additional Secretary to the Government of Bengal to all District Officers and Commissioners of Police 23 May 1942. WBSA: W–145/42 Volunteers.

98 Syama Prasad Mookerjee, Letter of Resignation, 16 November 1942 in Devadas Gandhi, *India Unreconciled: A documented history of Indian political events from the crisis of August 1942 to February 1944* (New Delhi: The Hindustan Times, 1944), 104.

99 Editorial, ABP 1 May 1942, 4.

100 Editorial, ABP 7 April 1942, 4.

101 Bhuyan, Quit India Movement, 13. As did the Communist Party which declared in March 1942: 'All Party Members and sympathisers must join the Peoples' Volunteer Brigade (P.V.B.) and on no account the Civic Guards' (CPI Party Letter II (4) 7 March 1942 in Towards Freedom 1942, 482). The Muslim League also officially boycotted the War Committees—but the Chief Secretary reported in June 1940 that 'many Muslim Leaguers have joined the War Committees' (Governor Report 1st half June 1940; Chief Secretary Report 2nd half June 1940. IOR: Fortnightly Reports of Governors, Chief Commissioners and Chief Secretaries (1937–1948). L/PJ/5/146.

102 Chief Secretary Report 2nd half January 1942. IOR: Fortnightly Reports of Governors, Chief Commissioners and Chief Secretaries (1937–1948). L/PJ/5/149.

103 Governor Report 2nd half January 1942. IOR: Fortnightly Reports of Governors, Chief Commissioners and Chief Secretaries (1937–1948). L/PJ/5/149; Khan, India at War, 111.

104 WBSA: W–375–42 Volunteer Organizations.

105 Shri Krishan, 'Crowd Vigour and Social Identity: The Quit India Movement in western India,' *Indian Economic and Social History Review* 33 (4) 1996: 479.

7

QUIT INDIA!

> About 15.00 hours, a crowd of about 1,000 people appeared from the west (that is on the roads from Ghosi and Dohrighat). Many were armed with lathis and spears. As we learnt later, some also carried plough-shares, hammers and spades... With this contingent came two elephants with people on each... Three emissaries now approached us... They explained that they had not come to fight their Indian brethren; but Swaraj had now been attained; and they only wished to place the Congress flag on the thana [police station]. Combined with this, was the demand for all official papers.
>
> —Robert H. Niblett, *The Congress Rebellion in Azamgarh*, August–September, 1942.[1]

The *Amrita Bazar Patrika* reported the arrests of the Congress leadership in its late morning edition of Sunday, August 9, 1942. The next day the paper editorialised that 'The arrest of the Congress leaders does not show the Government's strength... It is not sportsmanship either.'[2] The headlines over the next few days revealed an escalating campaign of mass demonstrations in the cities and increasingly desperate government attempts to suppress them. On Tuesday, August 11:

> 'Police Firing on Lucknow and Poona Students'
> 'Bombay Trouble Assumes Very Serious Proportions'
> 'Hartal in Calcutta. Congress Organizations in Bengal Banned.'

Wednesday, August 12:

> 'Police Open Fire a Dozen Times on Bombay Crowds'
> 'Lathi Charges... Firing at Delhi, Patna, Agra, Cawnpore, Wardha and Madura'

The edition also reported attacks on railway stations and police stations and an attempt to storm the Patna Secretariat. In Bombay, the textile mills, markets, schools and colleges were closed. Bonfires of hats, ties 'and other types of European costumes' were set alight. 'The Government of Bombay have introduced whipping as punishment for rioters,' the paper noted.

Thursday, August 13:

> 'Police Firing on Procession at Delhi'
> 'All Approaches to New Delhi Being Guarded by Armed Police and Troops'
> 'Firing at Allahabad'
> 'Karachi Order: Death for Arson and Whipping for Rioting'
> 'Student strikes and demonstrations in Calcutta'

It is not my intention in this chapter to cover the events of the Quit India movement in any detail. Such accounts exist elsewhere. My main preoccupation here is with the attempts (especially in the countryside) to displace British authority in the course of the movement. Before doing so and in order to place this in context, I will consider the Congress plan for the campaign, the measure of support it received from Indians and the British reaction to it.

As we saw in Chapter Five, Gandhi's plans for the campaign were by no means fully thought through by early August.[3]

Congress did not expect immediate arrests. Azad wrote later:

> Gandhiji held that the British would regard his move for an organized mass movement as a warning and not take any precipitate action. He would therefore have time to work out the details of the movement and develop its tempo according to his plans.[4]

Gandhi was prepared to negotiate, on the basis of this 'warning', and would kick off the movement only if negotiation failed. The British, on the other hand, believed that the campaign would start as soon as the All-India Congress Committee voted for it and therefore moved against the Congress leadership with as much speed as they could muster.[5] Back in June, Gandhi had some advice on how to prepare for this circumstance:

> Question: But what happens to your movement if you are arrested... Would not the movement go to pieces?
>
> No, not if we have worked among the people. Our arrests would work up the movement, they would stir everyone in India to do his little bit.[6]

As a start, he advised the Committee in August that from the moment the resolution was passed they should consider themselves free men and women—'no longer under the heel of imperialism... The bond of the slave is snapped the moment he considers himself to be a free being.' They should therefore act accordingly. He called on Government servants, soldiers and students to declare their allegiance to Congress.[7] Das argues that it was the intention of the Congress leadership to spread the movement beyond the Congress 'parameter' and that this was a further reason why no rigid plan of action was fashioned beforehand.[8]

Before the arrests, Gandhi had drafted a set of 'Instructions for Civil Resisters'. These were discussed by the Congress Working Committee on August 8, and were due to be finalised the following day, but British action intervened. The Instructions envisaged negotiations for 'at least three weeks'. If they failed, there would be a twenty-four hour *hartal* which at this stage would not involve government officials. However, officials ordered to perpetrate excesses would resign at once. All students would come out and not return until independence was achieved. Farms and homes would not be vacated for military purposes without compensation. Land tax was not to be paid to the government—and further, 'if a zamindar wants to side with the Government, no tax should be paid to him.'[9] After Gandhi's arrest, a meeting of All-India Congress Committee members and other leaders still at large agreed on a twelve-point programme for the movement in similar terms. Campaigners in Gujarat issued guidelines calling for complete non-co-operation with authorities. Police were to be persuaded to disobey orders and Government servants to resign. Villages should declare themselves 'Azad' (free) and ignore local officials.[10]

The initial stages of the campaign then, were to have been characterised by moderate civil disobedience, the most important aim of which was to encourage an *atmosphere* of Indian freedom and detachment from British rule. British reaction (which I shall come to in a moment) made this difficult. Gandhi, however, had left a considerable opening for more militant action if things did not go according to plan. If the leaders are arrested he said, 'every Indian will consider himself a leader and will sacrifice himself, and will not worry if his action results in anarchy.'[11] He had stated in July, 'I don't want rioting as a direct result. If in spite of all precautions rioting does take place, it cannot be helped'; in any case, 'My intention is to make the thing as short and swift as possible.'[12] At that time Mirabehn had told the Viceroy's Private Secretary:

> On this occasion, he [Gandhi] would do his very utmost to ensure non-violence. But he would not feel justified in calling [the] movement off merely because cases of violence

occurred. He could not do so without doing greater violence to the ideals for which he was working.[13]

The spread of the movement was spectacular. Hutchins says that it dominated Bihar, the United Provinces and Bombay; it was significant in Madras, Assam, Bengal, Orissa, Delhi and the Central Provinces; it was strong in the North West Frontier province—but not in Punjab and Sind.[14] Niblett (quoted at the beginning of this chapter) wrote: 'rebellion it certainly was. It overwhelmed Behar and rolled westward. Though checked in the eastern confines of the United Provinces, hardly a part of India escaped sporadic outbursts.'[15] In the affected areas, according to Harcourt, 'British administrative control...broke down completely. Nearly a month elapsed before it could be reasserted and even then only partially.' He continues, 'all lines of communication between upper India and the Bengal-Assam area were severed during the month of August.'[16]

In addition to geographical spread, there was evidence of widespread social support for the campaign. The Governor of Bengal told a government conference in December that he had been 'disappointed at the lack of antagonism to the recent movement'—which he ascribed to distrust of the British and the desire to be on good terms with a future Congress government.[17] The All-India Congress Committee successfully appealed to students not only to leave their schools and colleges but to go to the villages and encourage farmers to boycott the economy and set up *panchayats* (local councils).[18] Following August 9, there was a significant increase in strikes and labour militancy in the cities and towns of Bengal.[19]

Support from students and workers was to be expected, but it also came from unpredictable quarters. Many of the major Indian businessmen supported the campaign—though it was not the brainchild of the capitalist class and they did not dominate it, as the British sometimes supposed.[20] The Intelligence Bureau reported that there was 'no room for doubt that the Congress movement, both overt and underground, has received substantial support from Indian "Big Business".'[21] As the campaign continued and repression mounted, the Federation of Indian Chambers of Commerce and Industry said that it led to a 'growing conviction that Britain did not desire to give up her imperialistic domination over India.'[22] The Intelligence Bureau was convinced that some industrialists—including the Calcutta and Ahmedabad mill owners, the Birla brothers and Tata—were financing strikes by their own workers in support of Quit India. It was also widely rumoured that, when sections of the movement were driven underground, the bourgeoisie supported them in continuing the struggle.[23]

In the countryside of the United Provinces and Bihar, Chandra tells us that smaller landlords participated in the campaign, while the bigger ones 'maintained a stance of neutrality and refused to assist the British in crushing the rebellion.' Furthermore, 'A significant feature of the pattern of peasant activity was its total concentration on attacking symbols of British authority and a total lack of any incidents of anti-zamindar violence.'[24]

Support of various kinds also expressed itself in unexpected ways. Reporting on a British-sponsored meeting to support the war effort in Bihar, the Assistant Magistrate, J.W. Orr, wrote:

> But the bombshell which really woke up the meeting…was a speech by a 30-year-old Indian Christian who advocated a massive [military] recruitment, not so much to win the war as to obtain the necessary training for the inevitable war of the future between the whites and the non-whites.[25]

It was reported to New Delhi in December 1942 that Boy Scouts in various parts of Bengal 'shouted objectionable slogans during the recent disturbances' and in a couple of instances 'observed "Hartal" in pursuance of the recent Congress policy.'[26]

In the months before the campaign began, the British, in Bengal at least, were inclined to dismiss its prospects of success.

At a July Conference of Divisional Commissioners:

> Mr [H.P.V.] Townsend [Presidency Division] considered that the proposals for a movement by Mr Gandhi had fallen flat: at least they have not been mentioned as being important in any district. He doubted whether any movement of the kind thought of would catch on in Bengal, where the people were too close to the Japanese and had been refugees from Burma, etc., and had heard the stories.

Likewise, A.J. Dash (Rajshahi Division) said that in his area 'there was nothing favourable for such a campaign as 99 per cent of the population seemed to be apathetic and the remainder well disposed.'[27] By August, however, the Viceroy had to admit that India was seething when he advised the Secretary of State not to expose Congress plans (in an attempt to unmask subversion) since 'publication in this country must spread all sorts of ideas as to possible action against ourselves which may not have occurred to individuals.'[28] By the end of the month, he was telling Churchill that the movement was 'by far the most serious rebellion since that of 1857', the depths of which they were concealing from the public.[29]

British repression, therefore, was eventually fierce—along the lines suggested by Sir Reginald Maxwell (Home Member) back in April 1940: 'not merely to reduce Congress to a condition in which they will be prepared to make terms but to crush the Congress finally as a political organization.'[30] The Viceroy told the Governors at that time:

> I feel very strongly that the only possible answer to a 'declaration of war' by any section of Congress in the present circumstances must be the declared determination to crush the organization as a whole.[31]

In August 1942, this necessitated, as a starter, the arrest of the Congress leadership. It had been felt that the further afield the Congress leaders could be moved, the less successful the movement would be. Thus suggestions for their exile in Uganda, Aden and Nyasaland were made before the idea was eventually dropped.[32] Other aspects of the crackdown were more serious. Prasad says that during the movement, '31 battalions of the Field Army besides internal security troops' had to be deployed against it.[33] In Bengal and elsewhere, whipping was instituted as a punishment for rioting. The Viceroy telegrammed the Governor to acknowledge the 'deterrent effect [of] knowledge that these penalties exist, and [the] fact also that on occasion they may be of great value.' But he pointed out that the British Cabinet was 'sensitive' on the question and suggested 'it would be well, given Cabinet feeling, to close down publicity or public references to whipping as much as possible.'[34]

When the campaign moved on to sabotage of communications, the Viceroy authorized the machine-gunning of saboteurs from the air. He told the Secretary of State:

> We shall, I fear...have to resort to this weapon in other areas also, if attack on communications develops on a serious scale, as now beginning to seem possible. But I have given instructions that any reference to this if at all possible must be kept out of statements to the press.

Amery, in reply, noted 'with approval the measures you have authorized against saboteurs' and promised 'full support.'[35] With the prospect of machine gunning being raised in Parliament, the Viceroy suggested to Amery 'it may be worthwhile mentioning that in many cases this action was taken against mobs engaged in tearing up lines on vital strategic railways.' He added, however: 'But this is not true of all cases in which firing occurred from aircraft.'[36]

Stories of British misbehaviour were so widespread that the underground Congress Radio took up the question of how to respond to attempted rape by British soldiers:

> Without hesitation we answer, do all that you can. You should, of course, try to prevent acts of rape as any other by non-violent resistance, but if you are free and still alive, then kill or get killed. Rape is outside politics.[37]

The violence of the British response was due partly to their conviction that the movement was part of a Japanese offensive against India, for which Congress and its supporters were the 'Fifth Column'. Churchill told Parliament in September:

> It may well be that these activities by the Congress Party have been aided by Japanese fifth-column work on a widely extended scale... It is noteworthy, for instance, that communications of the Indian forces defending Bengal on the Assam frontier have been specially attacked.[38]

Linlithgow said that in 1942 Congress believed 'that the Japanese had [a] good deal more than a sporting chance' and therefore 'the rebellion was timed very much with an eye on developments in the eastern theatre of war.'[39] General Slim wrote later:

> We...had to bear in mind the possibility that the rebellion was concerted with the Japanese and that an invasion might be attempted simultaneously.[40]

The British had little evidence on which to base such accusations. The notion of Japanese control was rejected by their own reports whenever the question was seriously examined.[41] Congress, of course, rejected the suggestion out of hand. The Congress Radio pointed out that the Japanese would hardly have been pleased by the Quit India upsurge:

> They are astute enough to see what the British are lazy enough to disregard: the inherent strength of the India people which is now expressing itself.[42]

The possibility of a more militant campaign, left open by Gandhi, has been noted above. Once the Congress leaders were arrested, that possibility was acted upon. As Omvedt puts it, 'what was remembered by an aroused people...were basically two points: *karenge ya marenge* [do or die], and "let everyone be his own leader".'[43] Demonstrations, strikes and parades developed into physical attacks on communications systems and attempts to take over or destroy government institutions—police stations, post offices and administrative centres. Congress Radio broadcast to its listeners:

> Remember this is a revolution and the British government is a usurper government and we are out to set up the free state of India. As such, there is no property in India that may not be destroyed by us so that its use may be denied to the usurpers.[44]

In the initial stages of the campaign, these were mass attacks, not guerrilla actions. In the Bengali districts of Bardhaman and Birbhum, they were led by the *Amar Kutir* organization (see previous chapter) and its secretary, Manoranjam Dutta:

> In 1942, he led a large mob (that included a contingent of local *santhals*) [indigenous people] to the Bolpur Railway Station and blockaded the military transportation of food grains. The blockade resulted in a violent skirmish between the military and the mob led by Dutta.[45]

At the beginning of the chapter we noted Robert Niblett's defence of the Madhuban police station against a crowd of some five thousand. Despite holding off this attack, Niblett advised withdrawing from the affected areas: 'We were obviously in the midst of a rebellion and the administration had lost its prestige.' His advice was eventually accepted. He concluded: 'the people, though unarmed, had now realized their strength.'[46]

Mass militancy and, later on, individual sabotage had evident public support. A government report noted 'There is little disposition on the part of the general public to regard saboteurs and bandits as anti-social and criminal elements of society.'[47]

ALTERNATIVE GOVERNMENTS

The replacement of the British administrative structure by alternative structures soon came into play. Hiteshranjan Sanyal says that when the All-India Congress Committee's Twelve-Point Programme was distributed, the setting up of parallel government was 'a note which was invariably added to the programme.'[48] A Committee instruction to farmers in Bengal told them to declare their villages free and 'to establish a panchayat [village council] in your village. The panchayat will be your Government.'[49] The formation of alternative governments came to be seen as the next stage after mass demonstrations. 'The anger of the people,' said the Gujarat Provincial Congress Committee, 'must be channelled into building up strength to remove foreign rule and should not be confined to acts of destruction.' Villages should proclaim their independence from the British government, make their own laws and collect their own revenue.[50] In late September or early October, Ram Manohar Lohia (a leading socialist in the Congress) declared:

> The programme before the masses so far was a negative one, but we should now give them something concrete to do... We should now establish preliminary governments in villages, towns, cities, tehsils, districts and provinces...'[51]

The British police reported the same message from Lucknow, Bombay, the Central Provinces and Behar. The Intelligence Branch in Calcutta discovered Congress bulletins advocating a similar programme for Bengal. The British had a firm grasp of what was happening. The Assistant Inspector-General of Police (CID) in the United Provinces told his superintendents at this time:

> The general plan appears to be still the capture of the rural areas and includes the establishment of the rule of

the masses, the removal of all signs of the existence of government, the winning over by persuasion, intimidation or social boycott of police, other officials and of all who assist government, the rendering of police stations useless and the seizure of police arms, the stoppage of recruitment, a no-rent campaign, regular hartals, the prevention of schools and colleges from functioning and the systematic tampering with the means of communication generally.[52]

The Bengal Chief Secretary reported that Congress 'declares that the movement has been successful in expelling British civil administration from a considerable part of rural India.'[53] Niblett noted the existence of 'areas, where the power of Government had ceased.'[54] While an extensive network of Congress organizations and volunteers had been established in the cities, the parallel governments were concentrated in the countryside. More or less effective urban administration and, consequently, effective repression, made it difficult to take and maintain the next step in the cities.[55] In Ahmedabad, however, an attempt was made to establish an 'Azad Government' which divided the city into administrative districts, organized demonstrations, levied taxes, issued bulletins, gathered intelligence and punished notorious policemen.[56] In another urban setting, students at the Benares Hindu University declared the campus free Indian soil and proceeded to raise the Congress flag, take out processions and commence military training. But ten days later the university was occupied by British and Australian troops and student resistance was defeated.[57]

Progress in rural areas was a good deal more promising. I will attempt to sketch out the extent of the movement before examining what the alternative governments actually did. The events in Midnapore will be treated in a separate section.

In **Bengal**, parallel governments were concentrated in the Midnapore district, especially in the Contai, Sadar, Mahisadal and Tamluk sub-divisions. Sarkar points out that Tamluk and the districts around it 'were old Gandhian bases with a tradition of sustained constructive work.' The movement there was better organized and less 'elemental and violent' than elsewhere.[58] In Contai, Sadal and Mahisadal the British reported 'So-called "criminal and civil courts"...being run by the Congress...and Congress camps are springing up.'[59] No revenue and no rent campaigns emerged in Birbhum, Malda and Dacca districts.[60]

In **Bihar and east United Provinces**, from mid-August 'most villages threw off the authority of the Government, coercing village officials where necessary.'[61] Police were withdrawn and Congress organizations began administering justice and collecting land revenue.[62] In Ballia (in east Azamgarh district) the Quit India campaign was initiated by student demonstrations which were attacked by the police. Thereupon, railway stations, police stations and post offices were attacked and burned, as was any paper currency the insurgents could get hold of. From August 16 there were pitched battles around the raising of the Congress flag leading to police firing, arrests and casualties. The demand for 'panchayat raj' was raised. Fifty thousand demonstrators marched on the gaol to free those arrested. At this, the District Magistrate (an Indian) tried to extract a deal from the leading activist, Chittu Pandey, to restrain the demonstrators. Having little success in this regard, he released those in gaol. Popular organs of self-government were already forming and Ballia declared its independence on August 20. However, the army re-occupied Ballia on the night of August 22–23 and Ballia's independence was snuffed out with considerable brutality.[63]

In Ghazipur (in the same area), under the leadership of Baldev Pandey, a teacher, the Congress flag was raised over the police station, the railway station burned and bits of the airport were destroyed by airport workers. The police surrendered, as did the *tehsil* office, from which the records were burned. After that, 'the whole district of Ghazipur remained under the people's raj for full ten days. Police stations, courts, and every other department of government passed from the hands of the government officials into those of the people's representatives.' Once again, the people's rule was suppressed by British military force.[64]

In **Bombay province**, the movement was concentrated in Satara, a district south of Poona. According to Omvedt, in Satara 'they fought not only with the idea that they were free to use all means, including violent ones, but also that in some form or another they would take their future in their own hands and set up their own government.'[65] At first, there were attempts to seize power through mass marches on government centres. As one participant put it:

> Our idea was to gather thousands, go to the *kacheri* [court], bring down the Union Jack and raise the national flag, put Gandhi topi on the *mamledar* [tax collector] and *faujdar* [policeman] and come home!'[66]

In the process, some two-thousand people were arrested. But the struggle continued into 1943. A *Prati Sarkar* (parallel government) was set up which in turn established *nyanya mandals* (people's courts). The new government imposed prohibition, authorized 'Gandhi marriages' and established libraries and educational institutions. It managed to continue functioning at some level until 1945. One reason for its longevity was evidently the support it received from the tiny princely state of Aundh (situated in the Satara district) and its ruler, Raja Bala Sahib. The state provided a place of refuge and shelter for independence activists.[67]

In **Orissa**, after the initial stages of demonstration, picket and boycott, the area between Kansabausa and Gomei became an independent zone from which all British authority disappeared. (As Nanda points out, this was helped by the fact that the area was inaccessible during the monsoon.)[68] Biswamoy Pati relates that in the zone 'a parallel government with its administrative parashad, court, jail and secretariat was set up.' A *Santi Sena*

[Peace Corps] was established. In late September these structures were suppressed by the police, leaving twenty-six dead and forty-six injured.[69] In the Dhenkanal area of the province also, 'The Panchayat system of administration was set up at places.'[70]

The parallel administrations were not just the result of the spread of Congress ideas. They also came into existence to deal with concrete necessities. As we saw in the previous chapter, Congress had long forecast a collapse of British authority and the new structures were aimed at preventing social disorder. In Ballia, for example, Mitra argues that the formation of an alternative government 'would never have taken place without the collapse of the administration in the surrounding countryside.'[71] Omvedt tells us:

> ...some ideas of building an alternate power were there from the beginning, though they were brought into action only as activists at the village level responded to the dilemmas and pressures brought on by the needs of the movement.[72]

One thing that had to be taken in hand very quickly (especially in Bengal) was food supply. In Midnapore district, faced with the Government's 'uncertain and vacillating policy in regard to paddy and rice', the Congress organizations imposed 'a policy of stopping all exports and encouraging imports of paddy and rice for the people.'[73] Administrative arrangements for food, trade and transport had to follow.

Another aspect of self-sufficiency, particularly in view of the looming food shortages in Bengal, was the preservation of grain stocks in the villages. The 'War Council' organizer of the United Provinces Congress advised villagers not to send their grain to market—both to preserve their stocks and to prevent it being used by the military.[74] Satish Chandra Samanta, a Congress leader from Midnapore, wrote shortly afterwards:

> Our workers appealed to the people to be fearless and to organize themselves for resisting all sorts of oppression, and

> advised them to grow more food, to produce necessaries as far as possible, to use only indigenous article[s] and to preserve food grains inside the Sub-division and not to allow them to be exported.[75]

Villages that were 'independent' had to defend themselves against the British and against bandits. As far as the former were concerned, their agents had to be caught, their guilt or innocence established and punishment decided. Thus the people's courts were established.[76] The counter-hegemonic bodies did not (as in 1857) look back to any pre-British models. According to Harcourt, they hoped to establish 'a kind of modern government either in place of the Raj's local administration...or alongside it as a "parallel government".' The rebel governments therefore often had departments of justice, health, agriculture, education, propaganda, war and so on.[77]

At the level of the village economy, the aim of Congress, as we have seen, was to make the villages self-sufficient, thus wresting them from the economic control of the British and providing a basis for them to resist the Japanese. One way of doing this was to boycott the paper currency. Congress Radio advised villagers not to touch British currency, but instead to set up a barter economy. In a further broadcast, it reported the All-India Congress Committee's call for a boycott of paper currency.

> Do not keep money with you. It is a fraud. Soon it will lose all value and buy nothing. Convert money into goods while there is yet time.[78]

Attitudes towards the payment of rent in the liberated zones seem to have varied. Niblett reports that villagers were asked to make a political distinction in this regard: 'they were also advised...to pay their rents to all zamindars who did not actively oppose the movement.'[79] The All-India Congress Committee 'Instruction to the Peasants of India' was more specific:

Pay the landlord who is with you just enough rent to maintain himself and his family. Pay nothing to the landlord who is an ally of the Government.[80]

However, in Patkania village (in eastern United Provinces), and no doubt elsewhere, there were attempts to launch a campaign for the non-payment of rent, apparently regardless of the political sympathies of those extracting it.[81]

This radical programme of political and economic decentralization was combined with a vision that united and co-ordinated the movement across regions, demonstrating (according to Harcourt) 'a supra-local awareness uncharacteristic of purely traditional peasant insurgents.'[82] The All-India Congress Committee pointed out in an appeal to students:

> The strength that can consciously break up a vast country into its numberless villages can also put them together into a new symphony of health and beauty.[83]

MIDNAPORE

In the district of Midnapore in Bengal, Congress workers had for some time carried out the constructive programme and had led mass struggles in the area. There was 'a good network of Congress organization in these areas [particularly around the towns of Contai and Tamluk] which yielded results... The popularity of the Congress caused alarm to the district administration.'[84] During the individual *satyagraha* movement (from October 1940), thirty six participants in the area were arrested and imprisoned. The movement was, according to Satish Chandra Samanta, 'a source of encouragement and inspiration to the people.'[85] When it began, the Quit India movement was led by left Congress elements and the Forward Bloc.[86]

From the middle of 1942, Congress campaigned against denial

policies and especially against grain exports from the region. Samanta relates that Congress activists had calculated that 1941 would be a food deficit year for the region around Tamluk. They approached the District Magistrate and advised stopping exports of paddy and rice and importing paddy from outside—'but the bureaucratic head of the District did not condescend to listen to our advice.'[87]

Once the Quit India movement started, mass demonstrations erupted across Midnapore in which 'Hindu and Mahomedan processionists' participated. Villages declared themselves independent and 'at war.' At Mahishadal, 'a band of nationalist volunteers in uniform used to lead the processions.' Twenty thousand gathered at the police station to declare independence. The Sub-Division Officer, Mr Shaikh, ordered a lathi-charge. 'The constables, however, did not move and Mr Shaikh, dumbfounded, withdrew rapidly with his constables.'[88]

On September 8, over two thousand villagers turned out to stop the export of rice from Danipur, which the rice mill owners were carrying out under police protection. When the police opened fire, three were killed. Forty Congress volunteers then led a demonstration to the rice mill. 'The mill owners expressed regret for having exported paddy and promised not to do so in the future.'[89]

At this point, on October 16, a fierce typhoon, followed by a tidal wave, devastated the Tamluk and Contai sub-districts of Midnapore.[90] Locals estimated that there were ten thousand dead and three-quarters of the cattle destroyed.[91] Once again, the British seemed incapable of rising to this occasion. Rescues were made very difficult due to the seizure of all the river transport under the denial policy. Eventually, some Government relief centres were organized. But, says Samanta, 'These centres, run by unsympathetic Government servants, failed naturally to serve the interests of the people.' Congress workers were quick to step into the breach: 'Workers at once stopped revolutionary activities and took up relief work.'[92] A contemporary report tells us, 'Congress volunteers are giving first relief to the distressed of the affected areas up to this time,' despite being 'violently interfered with by the local officials and police.'[93]

Plans were afoot to create alternative governments in Midnapore district once the Quit India campaign began. They were put into effect in Khejuri, Bhagabanpur and Patipur in September and in Kanthi in November. The most important of them was set up by Congress workers in Tamluk sub-division in the wake of the cyclone. There, the 'Tamluk War Council', which had been leading the campaign, transformed itself into the Jatiya Sarkar, a revolutionary administration, on December 17, 1942. Its first leader was Samanta himself. 'It was intended,' he wrote later, 'to be incorporated into the body of the Great Indian Federation when the latter would be formed.' Similar governments were set up in Nandigram and Mahishadal.[94]

A system of courts was established which, it was claimed, tried over 1,600 cases.[95] Relief work for victims of the cyclone continued and there were attempts to reclaim waterlogged land. Funds were provided for health and education. A postal system was set up and the new Ministry for Publicity started producing *Biplabi* (Revolutionary), a regular Government news bulletin. Some work was done to distribute surplus paddy from the rich to the poor.[96] In order to defend themselves, the alternative government formed militias—*Vidyut Bahinis* (Lightning Armies). The *Vidyut Bahinis* of Sutahita and Mahishadal consisted of five thousand volunteers, including fifty women. Training camps were set up in the various sub-districts. In Sutahita, the *Bhagiri Sena Sibir* (Sisters' Army Camp) trained women volunteers.[97]

The eventual repression of the alternative governments in Midnapore was predictably harsh. In his letter of resignation from the Bengal Government in November 1942, Syama Prasad Mookerjee accused the British of carrying out a campaign of looting and burning in the district (which was unabated by the

Quit India! ♦ 199

cyclone in October), comparing it to 'the activities of Germans in occupied territories as advertised by British agencies.'[98] The alternative administrations were driven underground where, despite the repression, parts were still functioning in 1943.[99] This, says Chakrabarty, 'demonstrates the ability of the local Congress organizers to sustain popular zeal in the face of inhuman torture unleashed by the British to control the movement.'[100] It also changed the nature of the movement, as we shall see below. In July 1944, Gandhi requested that underground work should cease. Through the press, he told those still functioning underground:

> If you share my conviction that underground activity is not conducive to the growth of the spirit of active non-violence, you will discover yourselves [i.e. give yourselves up] and take the risk of being imprisoned, believing that imprisonment thus undergone, itself helps the freedom movement.[101]

Putting a brave face on this, Samanta wrote later that Gandhi's statements 'gave the [Tamluk] sub-division workers a new light.' The *Jatiya Sarkar* and the *Vidyut Bahini* were formally dissolved on August 8. At the end of September, 150 of its workers surrendered to the government.[102]

INSURRECTIONISM

Why did Gandhi make this call? The British counter-attack in the urban centres was swift and overwhelming. This phase of the movement came to an end quite quickly. Chakrabarty suggests that it was over 'within a week after its formal declaration'—but this, surely, is an exaggeration. Muni estimates that 'by 21 September [1942] the Government found itself in a comfortable state.'[103] At the time, the British were not so sure. The Governor of Bengal reported in early October:

> I am not at all satisfied that we have seen the last of the Congress movement, or its repercussions in Bengal at any

rate. I have the feeling that the movement so far has been a "sighting shot".[104]

Hardiman considers that in Gujarat 'the agitation began to wane by early 1943 and was dead by the middle of the year.'[105]

The alternative governments in the rural areas held on a while longer, into 1943 and even 1944. As we have seen, they were subject to intense British attack. This forced them to make defence their number one priority. In Midnapore, writes Sanyal,

> The parallel governments operated under conditions of great stress and were mostly occupied with the task of fighting the government forces and of protecting the people after the cyclone and during the famine.

Defence came to dominate everything else.

> The operation of the [Vidyut] Bahini had overshadowed all other activities of the Jatiya Sarkar... The national courts and the jails of the Jatiya Sarkar had practically become parts of the Bahini's structure.[106]

Within the parallel governments then, there was a steady rise in the importance of militarism—which would be exacerbated by the turn to sabotage and guerrilla warfare by the remnants of the movement underground.

This was reflected in the leadership of the movement. Once the central Congress leadership had been arrested in August, the organization of the movement fell to an informal leadership of All-India Congress Committee members and local Congress leaders who remained at large. A prominent political force in this group was the Congress Socialist Party, led by Jayaprakash Narayan. In February 1943, Gandhi began a fast in gaol to protest against British repression. At about this time, a serious division arose in the Quit India leadership between those who were in favour of continuing an open, non-violent movement against the British (which was being repressed) and those who felt it was time to go underground and prosecute the struggle through sabotage and guerrilla warfare. The former organized themselves into the All-India Satya Council, while the latter became the Central Directorate, a body closely associated with the Congress Socialist Party.[107] The Central Directorate abandoned the counter-hegemonic strategy of Congress in favour of precisely that which Gandhi had tried to avoid: a frontal assault on the institutions of the British state. Through guerrilla warfare, it aimed to bring about a mass (presumably armed) uprising and the seizure of power. It declared:

> It is no longer true that armed revolt against the usurper administration is entirely unpractical. British arms have become a term of derision and there is just a chance that roving guerrillas in all parts of the country may succeed against them.

This would have been difficult however, since the Central Directorate's plan involved cutting *all* communications: 'India can overthrow the British usurpers, if she *atomises* herself.'[108] Thus the Central Directorate urged Indians to keep on fighting even during what Jayaprakash Narayan himself described as 'an ebb period'. It was decided to organize, train and arm a 'Freedom Brigade' in Nepal which would then start the process of a guerrilla war in India.[109] According to Asok Kumar Dutt, a student from Bengal, Narayan also envisaged a link-up between his guerrillas and sections of the military which could bring about a military coup.[110]

This attempt at armed struggle against the British state was not successful. In the wake of his fast, Gandhi—while quite circumspect on the question of violence in the Quit India campaign in general—was nevertheless clear that he did not approve of 'secret methods', let alone guerrilla war.[111] He issued his call for the underground to 'discover themselves', which the majority of underground activists obeyed, and the Quit India campaign came to an end.

A BALANCE SHEET

The Quit India campaign can certainly be seen as a partially successful revolutionary movement, but only if it is situated in the context of the counter-hegemonic strategy and not fashioned into an attempt at armed insurrection to overthrow the colonial state. An expectation of the latter kind can only lead to an analysis of disappointment, as we shall see below. Harcourt contends:

> The overall picture then, is of a *kisan* [peasant or small farmer] revolt, led and loosely coordinated by a modernist elite, partly drawn from the village population, and partly from the urban areas.[112]

The role of the Congress, both centrally and at the local level, should not be underestimated. Das, for example, stresses the role of 'local Congressmen' in the peasant insurgencies he studies in Bengal.[113] The movement had an ongoing significance for the Congress. David Hardiman concludes from Gujarat:

> Although the agitation began to wane by 1943 and was dead by the middle of that year, this failure did not bring in its wake a decline in Congress popularity...the popularity of the Congress was enhanced.[114]

But the importance of Congress is not universally accepted. Christopher Bayly seems to imply that there was no political leadership at all. 'Ultimately,' he writes, 'what happened was not decided by the politicians at all but by ordinary people in the streets and villages of eastern India.' The movement 'broke out' and crowds 'began to attack' government buildings.[115] Omvedt too is at pains to deny a role to the Congress in her study of Satara. There, the main leader of the movement, Nana Patil, was not a Congress member. She argues that while the Congress leaders in the region claimed the movement as their own, in fact they 'remained in permanent opposition'.[116] Undoubtedly, there were instances of pure spontaneity and of conservative Congress hesitation. But overall, both these views ignore the huge foundational work put in by central and local Congress organizations in the years leading up to Quit India on which its successes rested.[117]

The movement certainly had its weaknesses, the chief of which was the lack of organized Muslim participation. Congress Radio bridled at the very suggestion of such an absence.

> The greatest lie that has been spoken is that the demand for freedom is being made only by a few people and that nine crores of Mohamadens are against the independence of India. Such a lie can never be spoken over the surface of the world except by the British.[118]

But it was a fact that organized Muslim participation was weak and that the Congress leadership was not especially active around the issue. This reflected both the rising tide of communalism and the fact that the Congress leadership tended to underestimate its danger. It should be noted, however, that during the Quit India movement, there were no significant outbreaks of communal violence.[119]

Historians who judge the Quit India movement outside the framework of the counter-hegemonic strategy are apt to regard it as relatively unimportant, or disappointingly lacking in radicalism, or a failure because it did not produce socialism. Thus Sarkar is frankly dismissive of the 'brief national governments':

> Petty 'national governments' tucked away in a corner of the rather isolated district of Midnapur, for instance, did not seriously bother Calcutta or upset communications with the Arakan or Assam fronts.[120]

The level of British repression might make one think otherwise. Chakrabarty is disappointed that the movement did not produce 'a mass peasant uprising drawing on the age-old rift between the landlord and the peasantry.' Although he then (correctly) suggests, 'This is possibly due to the intensity of anti-British feeling which prevailed over other contradictions.'[121] Hardiman goes a little further, regretting that 'We cannot therefore describe the movement in Gujarat as being "revolutionary" in a socialist sense.'[122] Omvedt argues that, despite having at its base 'particular classes and political forces which were beginning to articulate themselves as demanding...a "worker-peasant" state,' due to the lack of revolutionary leadership, the movement did not go forward 'in an anti-capitalist direction.'[123]

There was a reason for the movement not rising to these heights and it did not lie with the leadership. Defending his kisans, Harcourt points out 'it is autonomous small-holder peasants like these that have, under the leadership of a disaffected intelligentsia, made the great revolutions of our time.'[124] He could have added that these 'great revolutions' (from the eighteenth to the twentieth centuries) were bourgeois revolutions, not socialist ones.

Thus too it was in India. The struggle for freedom was not some open-ended, free-flowing process which, regardless of material conditions and even with the proper Left or 'working class' leadership, fortitude and zeal could have pushed on to 'socialism'—whatever that might have meant in India in 1942. Bemoaning reality does not make it any less real. The Indian independence movement and its victory in 1947 represented the opening shots of the bourgeois revolution in India. That revolution laid the basis for an independent state and for capitalism in India. It carried forward (for a time) the interests of the Congress, business, workers, peasants and the smaller landlords. 'Socialism' it could not produce—but it is wrong to belittle the Quit India movement for its absence.[125]

At the end of the Quit India movement, Congress stood defeated—but counter-hegemonic in its defeat. It had shown up the inadequacy, irresolution and viciousness of the British state. It had, in certain places and at certain times, pushed that state aside and rendered its rule impossible. The hegemony of the colonial State had been irreparably damaged. We will next examine how that damage infected colonial State institutions: the radio, the armed forces and the civil service.

Notes

1. Robert H. Niblett, *The Congress Rebellion in Azamgarh, August-September 1942* (Allahabad: Superintendent, Printing and Stationery, Uttar Pradesh, 1957), 13. Niblett was the District Magistrate and Collector in Azamgarh (United Provinces). According to Commissioner H.S. Ross (Gorakhpur), who wrote the Foreword, 'This book is a lasting record of this officer's lone and in many cases unsuccessful struggle to approach the problem [the Quit India disturbances] in a rational and humane manner' (ii).
2. *Amrita Bazar Patrika* (henceforward ABP) 9 August 1942, 1; 10 August 1942, 4. For an account of Gandhi's arrest, see *Harijan* IX (31) 16 August 1942.
3. Thus while the campaign was in full flight, Congress was still running training camps for Quit India volunteers in Bengal (despite Government attempts to burn and destroy them). (Satish Chandra Samanta, Syamadas Bhattacharyya, Ananga Mohan Das & Prahlad Kumar Pramanik, *August Revolution and Two Years' National Government in Midnapore* (Calcutta: Orient Book Company, 1946), 16.)
4. Azad says that he believed that the leadership would all be immediately arrested (Maulana Abul Kalam Azad, *India Wins Freedom: An Autobiographical Narrative* Bombay: Orient Longmans, 1959, 74).
5. S.D. Muni, 'The Quit India Movement', *International Studies* XVI (1) January-March 1977: 164.
6. 'An Important Interview', *Harijan* IX (22) 14 June 1942.
7. M.K. Gandhi, Speech to the AICC, 8 August 1942 in Mohandas K. Gandhi, *The Collected Works of Mahatma Gandhi*, Volume 83, Chief Ed: Shri R.P. Dhasmana (Delhi: Publications Division, Ministry of Information and Broadcasting, 1958–1994)—henceforward, Gandhi, Collected Works—Volume 83, 196 & 199–200.
8. Das, Nationalism Consciousness Bengal, 59.
9. M.K. Gandhi, 'Draft Instructions for Civil Resisters', 4 or 7 August 1942

in Gandhi, Collected Works, Volume 83, 169–172.
10. David Hardiman, 'The Quit India Movement in Gujarat,' in *The Indian Nation in 1942*, ed. Gyanendra Pandey Calcutta: K.P. Bagchi & Company, 1988), 109–121.
11. 'Question Box,' Gandhi, Collected Works Volume 83, 23.
12. M.K. Gandhi, Interview to the Press, 14 July 1942, Gandhi, Collected Works Volume 83, 99.
13. Mirabehn to Viceroy's Private Secretary, 18 July 1942 in Nicholas Mansergh (ed.), *The Transfer of Power 1942–7. Volume 2: 'Quit India', 30 April–21 September 1942* (London: Her Majesty's Stationery Office, 1971)—henceforward Transfer of Power II—408.
14. Francis G. Hutchins, *Spontaneous Revolution: The Quit India Movement* (Delhi: Manohar Book Service, 1971), 286.
15. Niblett, Congress Rebellion, 55.
16. Max Harcourt, 'Kisan populism and revolution in rural India: the 1942 disturbances in Bihar and east United Provinces,' in *Congress and the Raj: Facets of the Indian Struggle 1917–47*, ed. D.A. Low (London: Heinemann, 1977), 315 & 320. For descriptions of the unfolding of the campaign, from the British point of view, in Bihar, eastern UP, Benares and Ballia see Philip Woodruff [Philip Mason], *The Men Who Ruled India. Volume II: The Guardians* (London: Jonathan Cape, 1965), 308–312.
17. West Bengal State Archive (henceforward WBSA): Proceedings of the Conference of Commissioners, and Heads of Depts held in November 1942. File 616 (C)/42 (Proceedings).
18. Congress Radio (Part 4). www.gandhimedia.org/ImageFolio43_files/playlists/AURPEN0010/01.Part4of4.mp3
19. Suranjan Das, 'Nationalism and Popular Consciousness: Bengal 1942,' *Social Scientist* 23 (4/6) April-June 1995: 61; Milan Hauner, *India in Axis Strategy: Germany, Japan and Indian Nationalists in the Second World War* (Stuttgart: Klett-Cotta, 1981), 534.
20. Sir Henry Twynan (Governor of Central Provinces) wrote to the Viceroy (25 May 1942) that the 'new line' of opposition to the war and renewed civil disobedience was 'developed by Gandhi's capitalist friends' (Mansergh, Transfer of Power II, 119).
21. Intelligence Bureau, Government of India, 'Congress and "Big Business"', 28 February 1944. British Library: India Office Records (henceforward IOR): L/PJ/8/618A.
22. FICCI Executive Committee meeting 12 September 1942 in Federation of Indian Chambers of Commerce and Industry, *Report of the Proceedings*

of the Executive Committee for the year 1942–43 (New Delhi: India Print Works, 1943), 67.
23 Intelligence Bureau Report, 17 September 1942. IOR: L/PJ/8/618A.
24 Bipan Chandra et al, *India's Struggle for Independence, 1857–1947* (New Delhi: Penguin, 1989), 467.
25 Roland Hunt and John Harrison, *The District Officer in India, 1930–1947* (London: Scholar Press, 1982), 212.
26 WBSA: Question as to the extent to which students belonging to the Boy Scouts and Girl Guide organizations in the country affected by or took part in the recent disturbances. File: 565/42.
27 Conference of Commissioners of Divisions held in July 1942. Proceedings. West Bengal State Archive (henceforward WBSA): File 362–42 (22).
28 Viceroy to Amery, 8 August 1942 in Mansergh, Transfer of Power II, 619.
29 Viceroy to Churchill, 31 August 1942, Mansergh, Transfer of Power II, 853.
30 Maxwell made these remarks in connection with the introduction of a 'Revolutionary Movement Ordnance' by the Government of India. (Gowher Rizvi, 'The Congress Revolt of 1942: A Historical Revision,' *Indo-British Review* XI (1) December 1984: 39.)
31 Viceroy to Governors, 8 August 1940 in Rizvi, Congress Revolt, 39.
32 Mansergh, Transfer of Power II, 438, 481, 494–5, 517.
33 Bisheshwar Prasad, *Official History of the Indian Armed Forces in the Second World War, 1939–45: Volume Twelve, Defence of India—Policy and Plans* (Kanpur: Combined Inter-Services Historical Section (India and Pakistan)), 1963, 199.
34 Viceroy to Governor of Bengal, 30 August 1942. WBSA: Report regarding whippings in the province of Bengal in pursuance of ordnance III of 1942. File W–790/42.
35 Viceroy to Secretary of State and reply, 15 August 1942. IOR: Situation Reports from Viceroy (August-December 1942). L/PJ/8/603.
36 Viceroy to Secretary of State, 4 October 1942 in P.N. Chopra, *Quit India Movement: British Secret Report* (Faridabad: Thomson Press (India), 1976), 13.
37 Gautam Chatterjee, 'Quit India Movement and "illegal" Congress Radio,' *Mainstream* 12 August 1989: 16.
38 Churchill speech, 10 September 1942 in Devadas Gandhi, *India Unreconciled: A documented history of Indian political events from the crisis of August 1942 to February 1944* (New Delhi: The Hindustan Times, 1944), 42. See also Hauner, India in Axis Strategy, 539–540.

39 Viceroy to Secretary of State, 26 January 1943 in Chopra, British Secret Report, 5.
40 William Slim, *Defeat into Victory* (London: Cassell and Company Ltd., 1956), 137.
41 See 'Brief note on subversive activity in the United Provinces for the fortnight ending Sept. 14, 1942' in Chopra, British Secret Report, 158. The idea was rejected by Justice Wickenden, contracted to prove that Quit India was a *Congress* conspiracy (Chopra, British Secret Report, 14).
42 Congress Radio (Part 4). (www.gandhimedia.org/ImageFolio43_files/playlists/AURPEN0010/01.Part 4 of 4.mp3.
43 Gail Omvedt, 'The Sartara Prati Sarkar,' in *The Indian Nation in 1942*, ed. Gyanendra Pandey (Calcutta: K.P. Bagchi & Company, 1988), 237. Nehru himself was able to set something of an early example here. When the train taking him to prison stopped at Poona, crowds gathered on the platform to demonstrate support. F.E. Sharp, a Deputy Inspector-General of Police reported: 'Hardly had I alighted on the platform when to my surprise I saw Nehru with remarkable agility climbing through the corridor window on to the platform. He was about ten yards from me and rushing straight towards the crowd. I got in his way and asked him to stop, but he made no attempt to do so and hence I was constrained to stop him with outstretched arms. He struggled violently with me... He is a big man and was having a fair share of the struggle with me. At this moment a Sub-Inspector caught him round the waist and with help of two other constables he was then overpowered.' (Hutchins, Spontaneous Revolution, 268).
44 Congress Radio Part 4.
45 Amar Kutir museum, Bolpur, West Bengal. Dutta was arrested the following year.
46 Niblett, 31 & 34. Mitra makes the same point concerning the murder of several RAF officers during the campaign. The murders, he writes, showed that 'the conviction of the collapse of British rule was total ... they also suggest the widespread conviction that the Raj had ceased to exist.' (Chandan Mitra, 'Popular Uprising in 1942: The Case of Ballia,' in *The Indian Nation in 1942*, ed. Gyanendra Pandey (Calcutta: K.P. Bagchi & Company, 1988), 167).
47 Government of India Fortnightly Report (FNR) (not dated or placed) in Rizvi, Congress Revolt, 43. The saboteurs did their best to link their actions with the mainstream Congress movement. Seized Congress materials in Delhi revealed 'significant names which the bomb-makers had invented for their products—such as "Subhas blasting jelly", "Jawahar

grenade", and "Gandhi blasting stick". ('Indian Journalist', *Some Facts about the Disturbances in India, 1942–43. Compiled by an Indian Journalist from Material Supplied by Government* (Delhi: n.p. 1943), 8.)
48 Hitesranjan Sanyal, 'The Quit India Movement in Medinipur District', in *The Indian Nation in 1942*, ed. Gyanendra Pandey (Calcutta: K.P. Bagchi & Company, 1988), 20–21.
49 AICC Instruction Number 7, Bengal PCC Council of Action, 13 September 1942 in Hutchins, Spontaneous Revolution, 274.
50 Hardiman, Quit India in Gujarat, 116.
51 Lohia reported in a memorandum by the Deputy Director, Intelligence Branch, Government of India, 7 October 1942 in Chopra, British Secret Report, 220.
52 Assistant Inspector-General of Police (CID) UP to all UP superintendents of police, 5 October 1942 in Chopra, British Secret Report, 210.
53 Chief Secretary Report, 1st half December 1942. IOR: Fortnightly Reports of Governors, Chief Commissioners and Chief Secretaries (1937–1948). L/PJ/5/149.
54 Niblett, Rebellion, 43.
55 It should also be noted that in Bengal the villages were not political backwaters. The 1935 Government of India Act, by locating a large majority of General ('Hindu') and Muslim Assembly seats in rural areas, had moved the focus of Bengali politics to the countryside. 'Now, suddenly, it was rural Bengal that mattered and any party or faction intending to achieve power in the provincial assembly had to win over the countryside' (Joya Chatterji, *Bengal Divided: Hindu communalism and partition, 1932–47* (Cambridge: Cambridge University Press, 1994), 68).
56 Hardiman, Quit India in Gujarat, 102–3. Hardiman adds that 'the leadership was in the hands of young Congress socialists'—but that they were not able to sustain a prolonged strike in the mills.
57 Hutchins, Spontaneous Revolution, 292–3.
58 Sumit Sarkar, *Modern India: 1885–1947* (Madras: Macmillan India Ltd., 1986), 400.
59 Chief Secretary Report, 2nd half, December 1942. IOR: Fortnightly Reports of Governors, Chief Commissioners and Chief Secretaries (1937–1948). L/PJ/5/149.
60 Das, Nationalism and Popular Consciousness, 60.
61 Max Harcourt, 'Kisan populism and revolution in rural India: the 1942 disturbances in Bihar and east United Provinces', in *Congress and the Raj: Facets of the Indian Struggle 1917–47*, ed. D.A. Low (London:

Heinemann, 1977), 318.
62 Arun Chandra Bhuyan, *The Quit India Movement: The Second World War and Indian Nationalism*, (New Delhi: Manas Publications, 1975), 72.
63 Mitra, Ballia 165–184; Hutchins, Spontaneous Revolution, 323; Chandra, India's Struggle, 466.
64 Chopra, British Secret Report, 274–7.
65 Omvedt, Sartara Prati Sarkar, 224.
66 Omvedt, Sartara Prati Sarkar, 238.
67 Chandra, Indian Struggle, 466–7; Omvedt, Sartara Prati Sarkar, 247.
68 Chandi Prasad Nanda, *Vocalizing Silence: Political Protests in Orissa 1930–1942* (New Delhi: Sage, 2008), 333.
69 Biswamoy Pati, 'The Climax of Popular Protest: The Quit India Movement in Orissa', *Indian Economic and Social History Review* 29 (1) 1992: 19–21.
70 Chopra, British Secret Report, 100.
71 Mitra, Ballia, 179; Samanta, August Revolution, 8–9.
72 Omvedt, Sartara Prati Sarkar, 238.
73 Samanta, August Revolution, 12. See also Sarkar on Balasore district in Orissa (Sakar, Modern India, 401).
74 Circular from War Council organizer, UP Congress in Hutchins, Spontaneous Revolution, 275.
75 Samanta, August Revolution, 9.
76 In Satara for example; see Omvedt, Sartara Prati Sarkar, 239–240 & 246.
77 Harcourt, Kisan Populism, 321–2. He adds that, despite this, they often functioned as 'petty rajahdoms or dacoit bands under the authoritarian rule of a local strong arm man.' This seems a little harsh, especially considering he provides no examples or sources to confirm this assertion.
78 Congress Radio Part 1 & Part 2 ((www.gandhimedia.org/ImageFolio43_files/playlists/AURPEN0010/01.Parts1–4 of 4.mp3). See also Hutchins, Spontaneous Revolution, 274–5.
79 Niblett, Rebellion, 28.
80 AICC Instruction Number 12 to the Peasants of India (not dated) in Hutchins, Spontaneous Revoilution, 274.
81 Gyanendra Pandey, 'The Revolt of August 1942 in Eastern UP and Bihar', in *The Indian Nation in 1942*, ed. Gyanendra Pandey (Calcutta: K.P. Bagchi & Company, 1988), 133–4.
82 Harcourt, Kisan Populism, 322.
83 Hutchins, Spontaneous Revolution, 275.

84 Bidyut Chakrabarty, 'Political Mobilization in the Localities: The 1942 Quit India Movement in Midnapur,' *Modern Asian Studies* 26 (4) 1992: 805. See also Chandra, India's Struggle, 466.
85 Samanta, August Revolution, 6. My examination of the movement in Midnapore will draw heavily on Samanta's account.
86 Hitesranjan Sanyal, 'The Quit India Movement in Medinipur District,' in *The Indian Nation in 1942*, ed. Gyanendra Pandey Calcutta: K.P. Bagchi & Company, 1988, 44 & 45. Sanyal notes that 'For all practical purposes...the Forward Bloc merged with the Congress.'
87 Samanta, August Revolution, 10. See also Sanyal, Medinipur, 40.
88 Samanta, August Revolution, 14–15.
89 Samanta, August Revolution, 10–12. See also Sarkar, Modern India, 401.
90 'The Congress workers were making preparations for keeping law and order and establish[ing] a National Government in the villages, when the cyclone swept over the district and made their task enormously more difficult.' (Samanta, August Revolution, 9)
91 According to the Sub-District Officer at Tamluk, the toll was: 3,837 dead; 1072 injured; 68,193 cattle killed; 1,10,346 houses totally destroyed; 76,958 houses damaged (Samanta, August Revolution 30).
92 Samanta, August Revolution, 32–3.
93 'Free India,' *India Ravaged: Being an account of atrocities committed under British Aegis over the whole sub-continent of India in the latter part of 1942* (No place or publisher: 1943), 83–84. The inadequacy of British efforts may have been deliberate. Samanta says that after the cyclone 'The District Officer reported that in view of the misdeeds of the "rebels" of Midnapore the district must be made to suffer.' He adds that this allegation was confirmed by Dr S.P Mukherjee in the Bengal Legislative Assembly on 12 February 1943 (August Revolution, 31–2).
94 Samanta, August Revolution, 33; Sanyal, Medinipur, 1942, 54–6; Sakar, Modern India, 400.
95 Chief Secretary Report 1st half January 1943. IOR: Fortnightly Reports of Governors, Chief Commissioners and Chief Secretaries (1937–1948). L/PJ/5/150; Sarkar, Modern India, 401.
96 Sanyal, Medinipur, 54; Samanta, August Revolution, 16; Chakrabarty, Quit India in Midnapur, 806; Sarkar, Modern India, 401; Chandra, India's Struggle, 466.
97 Samanta, August Revolution, 9 & 34. See also Sanyal, Medinipur, 45–6.
98 Syama Prasad Mookerjee, Minister of Finance (Bengal) 16 November 1942 in Devedas Gandhi, India Unreconciled, 105. According to

Bhatia, when the British forces marched into Ballia, under the orders of Commissioner Fletcher, some 130 leaders of the movement were hanged. Others were bayoneted or gaoled, and a number starved to death in prison. (Shyam Bhatia, 'Seven Days of Swaraj,' *Outlook* 24 August 2015).

99 Sanyal, Medinipur, 54.
100 Chakrabarty, Quit India in Midnapur, 792.
101 Statement to the Press, 28 July 1944, Gandhi, Collected Works Volume 84, 244. Gandhi made a similar statement on 5 August (269–70).
102 Samanta, August Revolution, 36.
103 Chakrabarty, Quit India in Midnapur, 795; S.D. Muni, 'The Quit India Movement,' *International Studies* XVI (1) January-March 1977: 167.
104 Governor Report, 1st half October 1942. IOR: Fortnightly Reports of Governors, Chief Commissioners and Chief Secretaries (1937–1948). L/PJ/5/149
105 Hardiman, Quit India inGujarat 1942, 103.
106 Sanyal, Medinipur, 58 & 60–61.
107 Bhuyan, QI, 138. The Bengal Government had foreseen a switch to tactics 'designed to dissipate and impose an incessant and exasperating strain upon the forces of law and order.' (Governor Report 1st half October 1942).
108 Bhuyan, Quit India Movement, 105–106.
109 Bhuyan, Quit India Movement, 105–6; 117–119. Sarkar describes the training camp in Nepal as 'the Nepal frontier-based provisional government of Jayaprakesh Narayan and Ramanohar Lohia' (Sarkar, Modern India, 400).
110 Chopra, British Secret Report I, 386–92.
111 Gandhi to Sadiq Ali in Bhuyan, Quit India Movement, 134.
112 Harcourt, Kisan Populism, 325.
113 Das, Nationalism and Popular Consciousness, 63.
114 Hardiman, Quit India in Gujarat, 103–4.
115 Christopher Bayly & Tim Harper, *Forgotten Armies: Britain's Asian Empire and the War with Japan* (London: Penguin, 2005), 247.
116 Omvedt, Sartara Prati Sarkar, 225 & 236. Das makes the same sort of case for Bengal (Das, Nationalism and Popular Consciousness, 59–64).
117 Omvedt herself acknowledges: 'But it was also a revolution that, with all its violence, was in many ways initiated if not led by Gandhi himself.' (Omvedt, Sartara Prati Sarkar, 237).
118 Congress Radio in Gautam Chatterjee, 'Quit India Movement and "illegal" Congress Radio,' *Mainstream*, 12 August 1989: 16.

119 Hutchins, Spontaneous Revolution, 288.
120 Sarkar, Modern India, 395 & 400.
121 Chakrabarty, Quit India in Midnapur, 792.
122 Hardiman, Quit India in Gujarat, 103. Exactly what 'socialism' would have looked like in rural Gujarat at this time however, beggars the imagination.
123 Omvedt, Sartara Prati Sarkar, 224–5, 256. My comment in the previous footnote applies.
124 Harcourt, Kisan Populism, 325.
125 For a longer version of this argument, see David Lockwood, *The Indian Bourgeoisie: A Political History of the Indian Capitalist Class in the Early Twentieth Century* (London: IB Tauris, 2012).

8

WAR ON THE AIR

You will be surprised to hear that I have never listened to a radio, nor have I ever been to a cinema... I do not care to have news from all corners of the globe within the space of half an hour. It leaves one little time to think. And why must one have news from all quarters of the globe every half an hour or so?

—M.K. Gandhi in *Harijan*, May 3, 1942.

Gandhi's views on this subject were not widely held. Radio news and radio broadcasts in general were listened to intensely by those Indians and Europeans who had access to radio sets. The *Indian Listener* (the magazine of All-India Radio) advertised radio sets for sale in January 1936, ranging in price from ₹100 (the 'Hetro') to ₹650 (the PYE 'Empire').[1] In Calcutta in 1940, HMV radios were selling for ₹400, while Pilot Radios ('All-Wave—All World') retailed at ₹550.[2] Two years later, prices had dropped somewhat. The GEC All-India Midget could be purchased for ₹230.[3] All radio sets were imported and there was a 50 per cent duty on each set.[4] Given that the minimum pay of government clerks in Calcutta was ₹60 a month, a radio remained beyond the means of many average city folk, let alone those in the countryside.[5] Despite this, in 1940 All-India Radio estimated that 1,20,000 people in British India owned radio licenses.[6] This rose to 1,25,347 licences by the end of March 1941; and to 1,55,131 by the end of March 1942.[7] These were tiny numbers in a population of some 389 million (according to the 1941 census). Nevertheless, if Zivin's figure of one domestic listener in 350 is approximately correct, this still gives a listening audience of well over a million.[8] The phenomena of collective listening and the spread of news (and rumour) gathered from the radio should not be discounted.

Gramsci identified broadcasting as one method of bolstering hegemonic rule. '[T]he State,' he wrote, 'when it wants to initiate an unpopular action or policy, creates in advance a suitable or appropriate public opinion.' One way of doing this was through the press and the radio, 'which may or may not,' according to Femia, 'have *direct* ties with the government.'[9] British state hegemony in India was contested on the air as in other areas. It competed with the hostile state broadcasters of the Axis powers.[10] It was also challenged by non-state broadcasters: Subhas Chandra Bose's Azad Hind Radio (from Berlin and then from Tokyo) and the illegal Congress Radio from 'somewhere in India' during the Quit India movement. The British and their competitors all regarded radio as an important means of communication and each in their own way attempted to use, if not dominate it. In this chapter, I will consider the efforts in this regard of the British, the Congress and the Axis (including both Berlin and Tokyo, and the efforts of Subhas Chandra Bose from both locations).

ALL INDIA RADIO

In the inter-war period, there had been amateur attempts at local radio broadcasting. A joint venture between the *Times of India* and the Department of Posts and Telegraphs was set up in Bombay and there were other private initiatives in Calcutta and Madras. The Indian Broadcasting Company was formed in 1928 with the permission of the Government and started broadcasting from July 1927, from Calcutta and Bombay. Unable to survive financially, the Company went into liquidation in early 1930. From this experience it appeared that only the resources of the state could undertake and maintain viable broadcasting. This conclusion was reached at a time when the Government had started to regard radio as a useful addition to its powers.[11] Caution had to be exercised in this respect though, since (as Singh pointed out) at that time 'anything coming from the Government—however well-meaning—is viewed with extreme, often quite unreasonable, mistrust and suspicion.'[12]

In April 1930, the Indian State Broadcasting Service was inaugurated with Government support and under the guidance of the Department of Industries and Commerce. It was a wobbly start. The following October it was announced that the Service would close down due to Government cutbacks. This produced agitation, especially in Bengal. In May 1932, the Government of India decided to continue the Service (which would be renamed All India Radio (AIR) in June 1936) under state management.[13] At this time there were proposals to make broadcasting a *mass* phenomenon—setting up radio receivers 'in the village square or headman's court' to hear the message of the Government. But by the end of the interwar period, 'wide-scale broadcasting to village India...was tacitly acknowledged to be an unmanageable project.'[14] This kind of scheme, however, would resurface (at least in Bengal) during the next war.

With broadcasting now in its hands, how was the Government of India going to use it? There were different views in London and New Delhi on this score. When the Indian Broadcasting Company started in 1926, the Secretary of State Lord Birkenhead told the Viceroy that the radio could be used to control and combat dangerous rumours—an overtly political approach. The Government of India did not agree. With the advent of the Indian State Broadcasting System, the Government pledged itself not to use the broadcaster for its own political ends.[15] This was not altruistic liberalism. The Government reasoned that if the radio disseminated official views it would be seen as a propaganda machine, which would undermine its usefulness. The only way of combating this would be to accommodate the views of its critics—particularly the Congress—which it was not disposed to do.[16] The result was that AIR was used as a means of maintaining the official (and convenient) fiction that India was virtually free from any politics at all, whether British or nationalist. As Zivin puts it, 'an AIR listener would have heard no acknowledgement that there were any political parties at all in India.' Broadcasts by Government officials were covered by special rules to avoid any hint of political propaganda.[17] The radio was not used by the Government during the civil disobedience movement in 1930–31 and there was a total ban on political broadcasting during the 1937 election.[18] In the turbulent pre-war years, Pinkerton argues that the Government of India 'were unable, unprepared, or unwilling to utilise radio in either the service of empire or in the service of the Indian public.'[19]

AIR was dedicated to creating a non-political picture of India through music, literature, poetry and (strictly delineated) news bulletins. For this, it attracted the services of the Indian intelligentsia, many of whom had nationalist sympathies. They became a veritable 'enemy within' AIR. 'By the Second World War the rapidly expanding Department of Information and Broadcasting was not inaccurately known as a hotbed of British leftists and Indian nationalists.'[20] These people simply refused to make programmes critical of Indian nationalism. This could co-exist with the Government of India's 'non-political' approach until the outbreak of war—but after that, as we shall see, it became a problem.

One of these British leftists was the newly-imported Controller of Broadcasting, Lionel Fielden. A known supporter of Indian freedom, an embittered veteran of the Great War and a traitor to his upper-class origins, Fielden was appointed in August 1935 for reasons which are still somewhat obscure but which may have been a lack of suitable Indian candidates and a desire to remove him from the BBC. On his arrival, he unsurprisingly alienated himself from Anglo-Indian society by not living in official housing, avoiding the annual retreat to Simla and refusing European club membership, bridge parties and dinner invitations. In 1936, when asked who should broadcast from India for the Christmas Day Special Empire Programme, he suggested the Reverend Verrier Elwin—a well-known supporter of Gandhi.[21] Fielden was anxious to make contact with the Congress leadership, which he did, becoming friends with Gandhi, Nehru and Sarojini Naidu—but he was forbidden from putting them on the radio as he had intended. Fielden believed the radio should be a place for political debate. He unsuccessfully requested that AIR should cover the 1937 elections. In late 1936, the Home Department petitioned the Government with an accusatory list of speakers that Fielden had engaged for 'Talks' on various subjects—Congress members, communists, socialists and trade unionists prominent among them—though all of them spoke on non-political topics in which they had some expertise. Fielden gave in. From that point, 'Talks' were confined to harmless speakers on harmless subjects. 'No politics' continued to be the rule.[22]

At the outbreak of the war, the Government of India attempted to extinguish any remaining unofficial broadcasting. All amateur radio licences were suspended for the duration of the war (this applied to the Empire as a whole). There were less than fifty of these in India, mostly belonging to members of the colonial administration. Those holding licences were ordered to hand over any transmitting equipment to the government as a contribution to the war effort and to prevent it falling into enemy hands.[23]

War brought some changes to the official radio scene. Transmission hours were extended, news bulletins increased and (friendly) foreign language news services started. In April 1942, AIR announced additional services in Burmese, Thai and

Mandarin. AIR was placed under the Regulation for the Control of Broadcasting during War. The Controller remained its chief censor.[24] All AIR stations were directed to:

- Explain the Allied cause
- Denounce the evils of Nazism and Fascism
- Encourage army recruitment
- Conduct ARP education
- Encourage less consumption
- Counter enemy propaganda

Radio silence on Indian politics remained. In May 1942, Stafford Cripps suggested from London that (in the words of the Secretary of State) 'it would be a good plan for Indian representative speakers such as Nehru, Jinnah, &c., to be given each five minutes on All India Radio with a neutral summing up at the end. He feels that this might have good propaganda results.' Amery strongly encouraged the Viceroy (who needed no persuading) against this idea: 'the less interested we now appear in Indian politics the better.'[25] In the absence of domestic current events, alternatives had to be found. The Indian Princes were encouraged to broadcast, perhaps, Luthra suggests, 'in the belief that with "popular" leaders unwilling to associate themselves with the war, the average Indian's sense of feudal loyalty to the Rajas and Nawabs could thus be exploited to good effect.' Stations were asked to produce programmes on the historical exploits of the Indian Army. Difficulties arose here since those exploits were largely to do with expanding British domination. Broadcasts by outsiders had to avoid Indian affairs. When Calcutta AIR wanted to broadcast talks by visiting members of the American Technical Mission, Sir Frederick Puckle (secretary of the Department of Communications) warned that, since Americans 'are amazingly ill-informed, very sentimental and inclined to think India is inhabited entirely by Hindus,' the Calcutta station director 'should be well advised to confine the Americans to talks on the war as it affects their own country.'[26]

While the Government resisted politics, the AIR programmers and broadcasters resisted the war effort. The British, having insisted on a 'non-political' AIR, had made a rod for their own backs. When they wanted to use the radio for wartime purposes, they met resistance within AIR on the very basis of their 'non-political' arguments.[27] The Controller who succeeded Fielden, A.S. Bokhari, persuaded the Government that any idea of placing AIR under more direct British control would arouse opposition among Indian listeners and thus hinder the war effort. Further, he pleaded that 'propaganda through broadcasting...must strictly avoid violence, crudity and tiresomeness.' This was for the sake of broadcasting in the *post*-war world.[28] AIR broadcasts did not criticise prominent Indians for an anti-war or anti-British stance. The attitude of AIR staff to the war was unspoken (and certainly un-broadcast) but noticeable. Nirad Chaudhury, who had been broadcasting on international affairs at the Calcutta station since 1937, was most dissatisfied with AIR's coverage of the war. 'What lay behind the inefficiency,' he concluded, 'was the lack of conviction of its Indian staff.'[29] Some resistance was more overt. Sir George Cunningham, Governor of the North West Frontier Province, complained to the Viceroy in July 1942:

> One or two leading citizens of Peshawar have asked me with some resentment why All-India Radio should assist Congress by broadcasting extracts from *Harijan*, thus announcing to many thousands what would otherwise be read only by a few hundreds.[30]

The idea of mass broadcasting re-emerged in Bengal at this time. At a Commissioners' Conference in June, 'the provision of public new broadcasting sets with loudspeakers at least in all District and Sub-divisional Headquarters' was suggested. Bengal's Publicity Department was rather lukewarm about the idea, given the cost and difficulties with maintenance. The most the Conference could manage was one radio set per Division (two for Dacca) as an experiment. The scheme languished.³¹ But a similar scheme was simultaneously forthcoming from the army. At a meeting in May which included representatives of the local army, the police and civilian officials:

> Captain Calvert stressed the importance of adequate propaganda to combat rumours, and suggested that loud speakers should be placed on all trains travelling throughout Bengal. News could be disseminated by the train staff at every halt... It was further suggested that in all villages occupied by [army?] units, communiques translated in vernacular should be issued from the wireless news.³²

The proposal for using radio for mass propaganda was again dismissed, this time by the Railway Board. It would, said the Board, be 'quite impossible to equip all trains travelling throughout Bengal with loudspeakers and to provide the staff for operating them.' Railway staff 'are fully occupied in attending to their railway duties.' Perhaps some slogans could be broadcast at railway termini—'where the Railway Administration concerned considers that this can be done without detriment to railway working.'³³ Perhaps the most pertinent comment on mass broadcasting (concerning content rather than technical difficulties) came from the Inspector-General of the Bengal Police at the Commissioners' Conference:

> The Inspector-General suggested that, if the proposal [to broadcast in trains and stations] were accepted, action would have to be taken to improve the programmes of All-India Radio which were at present hardly satisfactory. He emphasized the necessity of commentaries.³⁴

THE BBC

In general then, AIR was not proving to be the most effective, or pliable, medium for British propaganda in the war. The Indian service also resisted rebroadcasting material broadcast in Britain—in order to encourage local talent, according to its management.[35] With the increasing effectiveness and popularity of broadcasts from Berlin and Tokyo (see below), the British had to launch some kind of counter-propaganda. Happily for them, there was at hand a ready-made broadcasting system for this very purpose: the BBC. Through the BBC they could beam short-wave broadcasts into India to counter those of Germany and Japan—and also those of Subhas Chandra Bose. The broadcasts were to consist of news bulletins, news commentary and other talks. The purpose of these broadcasts was clear from the start. A memorandum from R.A. Rendall (Assistant Controller of Overseas Programmes) in February 1942 stated: 'The primary purpose of news commentaries is propaganda... The use of Dominion speakers increases the confidence felt by the audience.'[36] Michael Barkway (Chief News Editor, Empire News Department) said in the summer of 1942, 'We want to keep up a persistent propaganda about India' and he urged broadcasters to emphasise:

- The sincerity of Britain's pledge on Indian independence after the war
- The importance of the defence of India to the Allies
- That yielding to Congress demands would cause that defence to collapse
- The unrepresentativeness of Congress.[37]

George Orwell, who broadcast BBC news commentaries to India, described them as 'an opportunity to do a bit of anti-Fascist propaganda.'[38] Sir Frederick Puckle urged a remarkably subtle approach to this propaganda (before, we should note, Japan's entry into the war):

> Our audience will not react favourably to shouts that the British are the paragons of all the virtues nor will they enthuse over the benefits, material or other, which the British connection has brought to India.[39]

Others less so. The Secretary of State had told the Viceroy in October 1940:

> It is only by sheer unadulterated boasting of ourselves...and equally frank denunciation of all who oppose us, whether Nazis or Congress, that we shall really effect the masses.[40]

Later the Viceroy still advocated a blanket ban on any publicity for Congress. If mention of the Congress could not be avoided, then it 'should be subjected to the closest scrutiny and that the minimum of publicity should be accorded to it.'[41]

The 'Hindustani Service' of the BBC was to redress the propaganda balance—and to do so firmly under the control of the British government. Its controlling committee contained representatives of the Ministry of Information and of the India Office. It first head, Sir Malcolm Darling (ex-Indian Civil Service), called for 'firm political control of the service'.[42] This was duly exercised in the following years. At one point in 1942, the India Office strongly criticised 'the presentation and content of the Hindustani bulletins'. On the other hand, in 1943 the BBC staff complained of insufficient guidance from the India Office on how to handle the Bengal Famine—guidance which it clearly expected to be forthcoming.[43] Generally speaking, the propaganda was clear enough—enough to elicit this complaint from Rajkumari Amrit Kaur to Nehru in July:

> The propaganda down the B.B.C. against us is iniquitous. I wish someone like you would contradict it whenever possible. It is the misrepresentation that is so cruel. And then 'we fight for freedom' every morning makes me really sick.[44]

The Hindustani Service of the BBC started on May 11, 1940, initially with short daily broadcasts to India in English and Hindustani. Soon, in response to the Axis threat, the BBC also started broadcasts in Bengali, Gujarati, Tamil, Marathi and Sinhalese. Puckle hoped the service would provide 'something

we can't get out here, something fresh, authentic and arresting...
I want it to be a quarter-of-an-hour to which every Indian will
feel he must tune in.'[45] It was headed by Sir Malcolm Darling,
aided by Lionel Fielden (hotfoot from his riotous career in AIR)
and another AIR operative, Z.A. Bokhari (who was a close friend
of Fielden's).[46] Within three months, Fielden and Bokhari had
fallen out with Darling over 'differences of thought and feeling'—
almost certainly the intensity and tone of British propaganda
to be broadcast. Fielden left the BBC for good.[47] Bokhari and
Darling continued to spar until the Hindustani Service became
part of the BBC's Eastern Service under Rushbrook Williams
in September 1941.[48]

The Eastern Service's English news bulletins were read by
Indians.[49] They were certainly appreciated by a section of Indian
listeners. The sub-editor of the *Sunday Standard* in Bombay wrote
to the *New Statesman* in August 1941:

> ...the Indian listener to-day wants news, just as it is, without
> any superfluous sugar-coating...exactly what he gets from
> the Hindustani Service of the BBC... I still remember how
> people in a metropolis like Bombay and a small town like
> Dehra Dun eagerly await to hear the announcer begin his
> bulletin with "London salutes India".[50]

But despite its loyalist enthusiasts, there were doubts within the
BBC about the service's effectiveness. From outside, Kingsley
Martin (editor of the *New Statesman*) asserted that it was inferior
to its German competitor: 'the Germans, who have made a special
study of India, well understand how to meet Indian tastes and
susceptibilities.'[51] Fielden, in the same publication, demanded the
wholesale reorganization of British propaganda.[52]

On the inside, George Orwell—a prominent writer and
broadcaster for the Eastern Service—had his faith in the
effectiveness of its 'anti-Fascist propaganda' tested. He wrote to
George Woodcock:

In any case, there is no question of getting to the Indian *masses* with any sort of broadcast, because they don't possess radios, certainly not shortwave sets. In our outfit we are really only broadcasting for the students, who, however won't listen to anything except news & perhaps music while the political situation is what it is.[53]

Some months later he was even more pessimistic, declaring that these students ('a small hostile audience...a few thousand at most'), who reviled British propaganda, would only listen to 'literary broadcasts'.[54] Orwell was disinclined to disseminate official British views on the Indian situation. On the eve of the Quit India campaign (August 8, 1942), he told his listeners 'It is not our place to comment on India's internal politics.'[55] His masters were not so circumspect. Once Quit India was underway, a 'policy handout' was distributed informing BBC workers that everything was 'under control'. Orwell wrote in his 'War-time Diary', 'Almost everyone [was] utterly disgusted. Some of the Indians [at the Eastern Service] when they hear this kind of stuff turn quite pale, a strange sight.'[56] He felt that the British strategy through the BBC was hopelessly contradictory: 'Our radio strategy is useless, or slightly more than useless. Our radio strategy is even more hopeless than our military strategy.'[57]

The BBC was constantly preoccupied with who listened to its broadcasts to India and what effect they had. In April 1940, Laurence Brander, the Intelligence Officer at the Eastern Service, was dispatched to India to investigate. After some six months, the results he reported were hardly encouraging. In reply to a questionnaire about the programmes, Brander received a 4 per cent return from Europeans, 60 per cent from Army personnel ('fresh from England mostly and wireless minded' according to Brander)—and none at all from Indians.[58] After talking with Brander on his return, Orwell wrote 'our broadcasts are utterly useless because nobody listens to them.' While Indians seemed to think that the BBC news was more truthful than Axis broadcasts, Brander told him 'that we should broadcast news and music and nothing else. This is what I have been saying for some time past.'[59] This, of course, was what AIR was doing—but it did not represent what the Governments of India and Britain wanted from the radio in India.

CONGRESS RADIO

The Congress Radio, as an explicitly political station, dedicated to the destruction of British rule, was clearly a challenge to British hegemony. It was set up illegally by Congress activists during the Quit India movement. It was on the air, mostly from Bombay, from late August to mid-November 1942, again during Gandhi's fast from February to March 1943 and then finally for a week in January 1944. The activists involved included Achyat Patwardhan (a Congress Socialist Party (CSP) member closely associated with the Sartara parallel government), Purshottam Trikandas (another CSP member), Usha Mehta (a Gandhian Congress member) and Ram Mohan Lohia (one of the leaders of the CSP).[60] Usha Mehta was an established student activist and had edited *Harijan* for a period in the late 1930s. Her father was a judge and she was studying for an MA. Nevertheless, she gathered together a group of like-minded students interested in an underground radio station.[61] Mehta and her comrades were in need of technicians. B.M. ('Bob') Tanna was a 'ham' radio operator who had not turned in his transmitting equipment at the beginning of the war. In 1940, he had been arrested for using it to transmit news about cotton futures.[62] Turning to more patriotic pursuits, he began broadcasting 'Azad Hind Radio' in the same year, 'from his former Ham shack, loading his wife's clothesline as an antenna.'[63] He was arrested again and his equipment was seized. By this time he had made contact with Mehta's students. The students also approached Nariman Abarbad Printer, a trained wireless and radio engineer, to construct a transmitter. It would appear that Printer was not altogether dedicated to the cause. At the trial of the Congress Radio activists, the Home Department testified:

> This accused [Printer] has no sympathy for the Congress as such. He is, however, an unscrupulous individual, and will not hesitate to engage in unlawful activities for the sake of profit if he thinks he can get away with it.[64]

Despite this, Printer repaired an old transmitter—and sold it to the Congress activists.[65] Congress Radio started broadcasting on August 13, 1942 with Usha Mehta announcing: 'This is the Congress Radio calling on 42.34 metres from somewhere in India.'[66] The first broadcast went out from a rented flat in the Sea View building in central Bombay. Thereafter, broadcasts were made at 8.30 a.m. in English and 8.45 p.m. in Hindi. After Mehta's introduction, the song 'Sare Jahan Se Acha Hindustan Hamara' ('Anthem of the People of India') by Muhammad Iqbal was played. Recorded speeches and the news followed. The programme closed with 'Bande Mataram'. Apart from Usha Mehta's contribution, the broadcasts were not live. To enhance security, programmes were recorded onto 78 rpm records at a separate recording studio and then transported to the broadcast centre.[67] Despite Bombay being the only working station of Congress Radio—Lohia tried to set up a station in Calcutta but failed due to the non-availability of batteries—it is claimed that it could be heard in many parts of India.[68] In one of his own broadcasts on Azad Hind Radio, Subhas Chandra Bose indicated that he was receiving reports of Congress Radio broadcasts in Germany.[69] The station was financed from a variety of sources. Usha Mehta relates that private donations—for example from the sale of supporters' jewellery—were important. Elsewhere it is claimed that Lohia 'took up the financial responsibilities of running the stations'. Chaudhuri maintains that it was financed principally by 'cotton merchants, grain dealers, share market men, business houses and trade associations in Bombay'.[70]

The British took the threat represented by Congress Radio very seriously, from the moment its broadcasts were announced in a bulletin published by the underground Congress organization in Bombay. At first they assumed that the broadcasts were coming either from Bose's Azad Hind Radio in Berlin or from Kabul. When they worked out that the station was operating from Indian soil, the authorities set out to discover it and close it down. Military Intelligence and the Bombay Special Branch were put on the case. The broadcasts were monitored from October 8 (and stenographic records kept) to track down the source and to monitor the content. However, monitoring ceased in early November 'as it was more depressing than rewarding.'[71] In November, the police raided almost all the radio shops in Bombay trying to discover the source of Congress Radio's equipment. In order to thwart these plans, the Congress activists frequently moved both broadcasting and recording studios to avoid detection. During the broadcasting period from August to November 1942, the station was moved at least six times. On these occasions, the equipment would be piled into a car. Chaudhuri continues: 'in order to give them the appearance of bona fide travellers, they had purchased...bedding with a hold-all, a hat box, two suit cases and a water bottle to be taken in the car in which the transmitter was taken from place to place.'[72]

As well as songs and speeches by national leaders (which were supplied by Lohia), Congress Radio also broadcast its own version of the news. It told its listeners:

> The entire world is aware that a ban has been laid on the publication of news nowadays. All the news coming from outside into India and also sent out of India are censored. Even the provinces in India are ignorant about the news in neighbouring provinces... The newspapers are nowadays suppressing the truth and are spreading falsehood. You should not read such newspapers.[73]

The station sent reporters out to make on-the-spot reports during the Quit India movement. Reports came in on collective fines imposed by the British on Muzaffapur (Bihar), the humiliation of Indian women by police in Surat (Bombay) and British excesses in Chimur (Central Provinces).[74] In May 1942, the station announced that it had captured a secret circular issued by the District Magistrate in the 24 Parganas district entitled 'Instructions regarding the withdrawal of officers and offices in the event of enemy invasion'. After noting that this revealed Britain's real intentions, the announcer read out the entire circular.[75] Congress Radio was the first to broadcast news of the bombing raids on Chittagong and of the uprising in Ballia.[76]

Gandhi's appeal to Indian soldiers was broadcast on October 27, in which he advised them to tell their officers, 'Your just orders we shall carry out but the order to fire on our own people we shall never obey.' The radio also reported on mutinous action by over three hundred soldiers in Meerut, some of whom may have been executed.[77]

As the radio station was strongly influenced by leaders of the CSP, it tended to reflect the leftist line of the organization.

> The free India will be of the workers and peasants. The effective weapon to open the gate of freedom and break the chains of slavery is *hartal*. The workers in factories and mines would have to cease work, as their work would further enchain and enslave them and would be instrumental in killing thousands of their fighting brothers in different parts of India.[78]

The Viceroy was firmly of the opinion that the station—and indeed most nationalist activity—was part of the Japanese Fifth Column. However, as Congress Radio itself pointed out, British investigation failed to uncover any evidence of this.[79] The Congress broadcasters also rejected any idea (again from Linlithgow) that they were the tools of big business. 'Big Business,' said an announcer, 'is too much an appendage of British interests to strike out independently'; it would be 'well-advised' to 'fall in line' with the national movement.[80]

By November, the British were closing in. On November 11, Tanna was arrested on suspicion but released for lack of evidence. The following day, Printer was arrested. For a number of possible reasons—his financial indebtedness, the threat of serious fraud charges connected with his management of the Bombay Technical Institute and perhaps physical duress—he agreed to co-operate and gave the British the current locations of both the recording studio and the transmitting station.[81] That night, the police forced their way into the station as the broadcast was concluding with the strains of 'Bande Mataram'. According to Mehta, she ordered them to stand to attention until the anthem was finished—which they did. The activists were taken into custody and after a six-month investigation; five of them were charged and tried in a special court. Mehta and two others were sentenced to four years' 'rigorous imprisonment'.[82]

During the Quit India movement the illegal Congress Radio, firstly, provided news, information and some semblance of leadership to a forcibly decentralised campaign in which one of the main problems was the increasing isolation of the areas of resistance. Secondly, it should be pointed out that the radio station was not a 'guerrilla' or hit-and-run action, despite the enforced mobility of the transmitting and recording equipment. It was a sustained attempt to create an alternative narrative of events to that of the Government and to challenge the British state's monopoly of the airwaves.

AXIS BROADCASTS

The airwaves in India were also subject to the attentions of rival states—once war broke out, particularly those of Germany and Japan. An early project of the German government was the station

'Shanghai Calling', sending short-wave broadcasts of anti-British propaganda in Hindustani into India from Japanese-occupied Shanghai.[83] For some years before the war, German broadcasts were advertised in *The Indian Listener* (magazine of All-India Radio). In 1936, listeners could tune into 'Folk Song Singing by the Hitler Youth' and 'Music by the Reichswehr Band' among other programmes.[84] In May 1941, the Broadcasting Section of the German Foreign Office reported that there were 1,20,000 radio sets in India (which was fairly accurate), 30,000 of which could receive short-wave broadcasts. German broadcasting to India started seriously at this point, beaming in programmes in Bengali, Hindustani, Telugu and Tamil.[85] Lionel Fielden wrote later:

> The Germans had a beautiful and easy target. They could make common cause with the Nationalists, laugh at the "freedom" which we failed to give, caricature the Viceroy and the Government, make fun of the top heavy bureaucracy and point to all the muddles of Mr Chamberlain. The effect in India was instantaneous and smashing. Indian quite naturally found German rudeness (and, I must say, German music) much more entertaining than what All-India Radio could provide.[86]

Chaudhuri, in Calcutta in 1940, wrote 'Everybody who had a wireless set tuned in to Berlin radio.'[87] These efforts were boosted by the establishment of the Free India Centre in Berlin in the summer of 1942 by Subhas Chandra Bose (of whom, more below). At its height the Centre boasted three radio stations, putting out regular three-hour broadcasts which concentrated on talks and Indian music.[88] 'Indians,' says Hutchins, 'listened eagerly to the regular broadcasts in Hindi from Berlin at eight each evening'— while Zivin notes 'the common practice of group listening to German broadcasts in shops and restaurants.'[89]

Once the war in Asia started, broadcasts from Japan (and Japanese-occupied countries) surpassed those from Germany in frequency and popularity. The Government of India commented 'It [Japan] is now endeavouring to undermine morale generally by fostering the impression that our troops have not fought hard in the Far East and have been deserting to the Japanese armies.'[90] The state-run Japan Broadcasting Corporation (*Nippon Hoso Kyokai*—NHK) had started daily short-wave broadcasts from June 1935 to China, Indochina, Malaya, India and the East Indies.[91] Broadcasts aimed at Malaya (now from a station in Formosa) had taken a subversive turn in early 1941: for example, 'they reported unrest among Indian troops based near the Malay-Thai border, stating that Indians resented their treatment by British officers.'[92] Japan's entry into the war opened up a new front on the air for the Japanese. When Penang fell in December 1941, the Broadcasting Station there was immediately taken over by the Japanese.

> From 24th December regular broadcasts in Malay, Hindustani, Chinese and English have been given, of a most violent pan-Asiatic and anti-British kind. Every device of German propaganda methods [which the Japanese were apparently copying] is used unceasingly to reach and subvert our Indian and Malay troops, and to undermine the morale and loyalty of the several Asiatic communities in unoccupied Malaya.[93]

The Japanese built a radio station in Singapore within a month of the island's surrender and others were added in Malaya, Sumatra and Saigon. These stations were aimed at India, Burma, unoccupied China, Australia and the South Pacific islands. In Rangoon, despite the destruction of the radio station during the fighting, it was reconstructed and started broadcasting to Burma and India in July 1942.[94] In February 1943, an official of the Japanese Board of Information (the controlling body of overseas broadcasting) told a House of Representatives committee that Japanese radio stations were broadcasting seventy-seven times per day to 'enemy peoples'. The same official told Japan's ruling party that India, Java and America were listening to Japan.[95] 'Radio is playing an amazing part in the Greater East Asian War,' said another high-ranking Japanese official. 'It is serving as a bomb to crush the basic thought and ideas of enemy countries.'[96]

Rolo concluded that 'In its propaganda to India too, Japan has been successful to some degree.'[97] This was probably something of an understatement. Japanese broadcasts could be received quite clearly in Bengal and Bihar. According to the Bengal Chief Secretary's report in late January 1942, 'these are eagerly listened to and are the most fruitful source from which mischievous rumours emanate.'[98] A further report in May said that 'an increasing number of people now rely on broadcasts from Tokyo for news rather than on the All India Radio.'[99] Further afield, the Central Provinces related that 'The Tokyo radio is reported to be popular', while the United Provinces said that 'increased attention is being paid to the Japanese broadcasts.'[100] Mr Larkin, Commissioner for Dacca, explained to a Bengal Commissioners' conference in November 1942:

> With regard to propaganda done by the All-India Radio, Mr Larkin observed that it was not of much use. People were more anxious to listen to [the Japanese station in] Saigon and foreign stations than to the All-India Radio because the foreign stations provided more exciting news.[101]

Japanese broadcasts also warned of impending attacks. In Burma, for example:

> Japanese propaganda broadcasts from Bangkok and Tokyo... had the precocity to warn the bazaars to go into the jungle on certain days as they proposed to bomb the area. Frequently the Japanese bombers would arrive exactly on time to carry out their pre-announced plan, and once it was known that stock could be placed on this impudent advice, it was only necessary for the rumour to be circularized in the bazaar for the entire population, including Government servants, to vacate the town, sometimes for several days.[102]

Japanese radio revealed that 'they were aware of the troop movements in Chota Nagpur [Bihar] and knew even the names of the officers in command.'[103] The bombing of Chittagong in April 1942 was reported by Tokyo radio two days before it was officially announced.[104]

However, Japanese broadcasting overseas was not a seamless story of success. Ryo relates that many of the broadcasters were 'liberals'. Unlike at All India Radio, 'The war overwhelmed us all... and the feeling of patriotism that gripped the nation drove us into a desperate war effort.' Views on war broadcasts differed somewhat. The Cabinet Information Bureau (a co-ordinating body containing representatives of various broadcasting agencies and of which Ryo was a member) wanted the Japanese message to concentrate on 'the self-determination of peoples and the independence of oppressed nations.' Ryo was ordered to write scripts to this effect. The Imperial General Headquarters (the Army and Navy supreme command) was of the view that Japanese military victories and the spread of the empire was the main thing. Japanese defeats were not suitable subjects for the radio. Ryo and his fellow-broadcasters therefore also 'had to maintain the fictional achievements of the Japanese army and navy and the pressures on NHK's overseas broadcasting became stronger than ever to cover over the real course of events.'[105]

German and Japanese state-sponsored broadcasts to India were joined in 1942 by those of Subhas Chandra Bose, operating from their soil. As we noted in Chapter 3, having escaped the British in Calcutta, Bose reached Germany in April 1941. He remained there until February 1943. Once Japan entered the war, Bose considered that the prospects of support for the Indian cause would be better in Tokyo than in Berlin and he made a series of requests to the German government to be transported there.[106] In the meantime, the German government helped him establish the Azad Hind radio station to beam shortwave broadcasts into India. The first of these went out on January 19, 1942. The announcer declared:

> [O]ur transmissions will be by Indians and for Indians. To most of the Indian people the only channel of information is British, and thus they imbibe unconsciously the British propaganda, and live in an unreal world.[107]

Bose made several broadcasts under his pseudonym, 'Orlando Mazzotta'. On the day that Singapore surrendered, he broadcast for the first time under his own name.[108] Broadcasts continued through 1942 and into 1943. Pre-recorded speeches by Bose were played even after he had departed for Japan.[109] His broadcasts, naturally, attacked the British. 'Let imperialism based on tanks and machine guns rule in India so that the Indian people may see for themselves what British imperialism really is,' he said in December 1942. He was also at pains to explain his current strategy.

> Once again I assure you that my co-operation with other Powers [Germany and Japan] has been, and always will be, on the basis of a complete and unconditional independence of India.[110]

The broadcasts contained advice for the Congress and the national movement. Sometimes they were timed to coincide with important Congress meetings—thus broadcasts were intensified at the time of the Allahabad Congress Working Committee meeting in April 1942. At that time, Bose assured his listeners:

> My secret agents, who are operating throughout India, are regularly getting their orders over the radio in secret codes... When the overseas Indians advance, lakhs and lakhs of Indians who are operating behind enemy lines will join them. Therefore, my friends, you need not think that you are alone or without support in this struggle.[111]

During the Quit India movement, through Azad Hind Radio, Bose called on Muslims and Sikhs to join the struggle and for the armed forces to mutiny.[112] As the movement began to ebb, he broadcast a warning to Congress:

> [T]here may be a gradual weakening of our forces from within, after some months, owing to a feeling that non-violent resistance cannot prevail against guns and bombs... in such a psychological moment, the agents of British imperialism may again put forward an offer or a compromise, and some of you may then be inclined to accept it as a lesser evil than failure.[113]

Like the Japanese, Azad Hind Radio also broadcast useful information for Indians—for example, warning the residents of Bombay that their city would be bombed on April 18 and 24.[114]

Bose and his supporters always denied that the broadcasts were controlled by the German or Japanese states. The question was raised at the Indian National Army trials that followed the war. There, the Azad Hind Government Minister for Propaganda maintained that Azad Hind's four broadcasting stations functioned independently. He said:

> The broadcasts were not controlled by the Japanese. Officers of the I.N.A. were not made to broadcast, but they voluntarily offered to broadcast. I deny that I.N.A. officers were made to broadcast on plans laid down by the Japanese.[115]

If this were the case (and there seems little evidence to suggest otherwise), then Azad Hind Radio was an example of Indians (albeit with external support) broadcasting to Indians—bypassing and defying the hegemony of the colonial state over the airwaves.

The broadcasts were certainly listened to. Congress President Azad wrote to Nehru from Calcutta in March 1942:

> Four or five days ago, a statement of Subhas Babu was broadcast from Berlin, and the next day it was announced that it might be heard in his own voice which had been recorded. I heard it. It was the voice of Subhas Babu.[116]

Mitra suggests that 'radio broadcasts from Tokyo and Berlin... were listened to with great avidity' and that they 'focused on the activities, real or imaginary, of Subhas Chandra Bose.'[117] Sanyal tells us that 'Subash [sic] Bose's speeches broadcast from Germany proved to be particularly effective in expanding sympathy and support for his venture.'[118] Prisoners in the Punjab heard the broadcasts in gaol, while a journalist told Gandhi in July, 'People are happy when Subhas Babu says on the radio that there are no differences between him and you.'[119]

The British initially shrugged off the impact of Azad Hind Radio, simply noting in early March that 'The so-called "Free Hindusthan" radio in Germany broadcast early in the month what purported to be a speech by Subhas Chandra Bose.' The Viceroy wrote to Viscount Halifax:

> Bose's broadcasts have excited more curiosity than interest in India and except in Bengal have not had much effect. There were suggestions that it was not really Bose's voice.[120]

But a District Officer in Bihar was less sanguine. He noted the prominence given by German radio to Bose's intention to set up a free Indian government when the Japanese invaded. He concluded:

> There is now a very great danger of the people [becoming] demoralised and the broadcasts from Germany and Japan help to aggravate the panic.[121]

Orissa reported in March that 'the public now pay closer attention to broadcasts from Tokyo and Berlin than to those from England and India.'[122] The Governor of the United Provinces told the Viceroy that the prevalent atmosphere of 'alarm despondency and defeatism' was in part due 'to enemy broadcasts which are increasingly popular.'[123] 'Axis broadcasts are freely listened to everywhere,' noted the Bihar Intelligence Department in September 1942, 'and have played an appreciable part in fomenting unrest and prolonging resistance.'[124] Just as disturbing was the report by a BBC official resulting from four months' investigation of radio in India. He reported:

> The enemy wireless rapidly took advantage of the situation... It spread rumours and lies of a kind that only an oriental appetite could swallow... It gave hints on sabotage; from Saigon it gave orders and directions, and next day would announce that the orders and directions of the previous day had been obeyed with the following results... The usual question when an Indian buys a wireless set, I was told by big dealers in Bombay, is "Can I hear Germany and Japan on this"... Nine large stations batter at India every night... Against this, there are only A.I.R. and the BBC.[125]

In the face of their popularity, the British attitude towards hostile broadcasts soon stiffened. In May 1942 the Government of India granted the power to Provincial Governments 'to call in wireless receiving sets in an area immediately threatened with enemy attack'. This was, it said, 'to make it impossible for the enemy to unsettle the population of the area by false or tendentious propaganda or to communicate instructions to fifth columnists.' However, the Government declared it had 'no intention of imposing a general ban on listening to enemy broadcasts by private individuals.'[126] Later, the Government decided to prosecute radio licence holders who were giving public performances of Axis broadcasts and in October it authorized Provincial Governments to confiscate radio sets being used primarily to listen to the Japanese.[127] These actions probably did not dramatically reduce the numbers of people listening to Berlin, Tokyo, Saigon or Subhas Chandra Bose.

COMMON SENSE

In the *Prison Notebooks*, Gramsci used the term 'common sense' to refer to 'the uncritical and largely unconscious way of perceiving and understanding the world that has become "common" in any given epoch.'[128] He wrote:

> Common sense is not something rigid and immobile, but is continually transforming itself, enriching itself with scientific ideas and with philosophical opinions which have entered ordinary life.[129]

For ruling groups, a suitably well-accepted 'common sense' that (among other things) justifies their rule is essential for the exercise of their hegemony. For those interested in subverting it, the transformation of existing common sense into a new one is an essential part of a counter-hegemonic strategy.[130]

Gramsci emphasised,

> ...the necessity for new popular beliefs, that is to say a new common sense and with it a new culture and a new philosophy which will be rooted in the popular consciousness with the same solidity and imperative quality as traditional beliefs.[131]

In the inter-war period, the radio came to be seen as a key contributor to the making of 'common sense', especially in countries where the state exercised a monopoly over broadcasting. A relatively gentle version of the process took place in Britain, but this would soon be joined by more direct forms of radio propaganda in the Soviet, Fascist and Nazi regimes.[132] The use of radio to advance the nation's cause was well underway when war broke out and would expand as the war continued.

But not for the colonial state in India. True, there was the problem of a restricted listening audience. Yet as we have seen, an audience of many tens of thousands did exist and the influence of radio broadcasts extended well beyond them. In reality, neither New Delhi nor London ever really entered the fray—or entered it too late—in terms of using radio to preserve and promote the common sense of British colonial hegemony. The Government of

India abandoned the idea of mass broadcasting twice—once in 1930 and once during the war. They refused to engage politically through AIR on the grounds that their nationalist opponents might demand (or take) equal time. They were then blocked from using AIR for the war effort. Their last resort was to counter Axis and Azad Hind broadcasts through the BBC Eastern Service, concentrating on general war and anti-fascist commentary. But as we have seen, even this was wracked with self-doubt. In any case, effective propaganda would have been hobbled by the general problem with the war effort: as Briggs points out: 'In Europe it was possible to speak with the voice of liberators: in Asia it was impossible to avoid the entanglement with Empire.'[133] British radio sometimes seemed to have the opposite of its intended effect. In April 1942, Assam was moved to report:

> The ubiquitous radio by which a great many persons pick up enemy announcements as well as the material put out by the B.B.C. and all-India Radio has had a deleterious effect upon morale, including that of the European population.[134]

What of the rival 'common senses' on offer? Zivin suggests:

> The most potent weapon the Axis wielded in India was likely its propaganda soliciting anti-British feeling, and in this regard the radio was its most impressive war technology. State broadcasting in India was woefully unprepared to match the assault.[135]

The problem for the Axis stations, particularly those sponsored by Japan, was that the alternative they offered was based on an invasion. In 1942, this seemed a likely prospect—but, given the experience of Japanese-occupied territories to that point, not a particularly attractive one. Japanese stations could deliver a steady diet of anti-British propaganda and news broadcasts that were in marked contrast to the British offerings. But they could not build up a vision of a future society—apart from a 'Co-Prosperity Sphere' under Japanese tutelage. As the invasion became less likely, so did the Japanese alternative. Bose's Azad Hind Radio was also inhibited from projecting a new society in India until Bose turned to the Japanese for help. Thus, for all of 1942 (while Bose remained in Germany) his broadcasts were confined to offering commentary on events and advice to the Congress leadership. When he too became dependent on a Japanese invasion, the idea of a new India, based on the Indian National Army, rose and fell with the military fortunes of the Japanese forces.

Only the illegal Congress Radio, though on the air for such a short period, had the sense of an alternative hegemony around it. It was produced by the Quit India movement and became a voice, an organizer and a demonstration that the movement still existed. It had a genuine counter-hegemonic message to put across, against British hegemony and Japanese invasion. It was not the desperate rear-guard action of a faltering state, nor the voice of an outside force.

Notes

1. *Indian Listener* I (2), 7 January 1936.
2. *Amrita Bazar Patrika* (henceforward ABP), 20 March 1940, 6 & 7.
3. ABP 15 February 1942, 4.
4. Lionel Fielden, *The Natural Bent* (London: Andre Deutsch, 1960), 187.
5. Government advertisement, ABP, 16 February 1942, 7.
6. Zulfikar A. Bokhari (a future luminary in the BBC Eastern Service) considered this to be 'a gross understatement' (Asa Briggs, *The History of Broadcasting in the United Kingdom. Volume III: The War of Words* (London: Oxford University Press, 1970), 508).
7. George Orwell, *The Complete Works of George Orwell. Volume Thirteen: All Propaganda is Lies, 1941–1942*, ed. Peter Davison (London: Secker and Warburg, 1998)—henceforward Orwell XIII—90; ABP 8 May 1942, 6.
8. Joselyn Zivin, '"Bent": A Colonial Subversive and Indian Broadcasting,' *Past and Present* 162 (1), February 1999: 196.
9. Both quotes from Joseph V. Femia, *Gramsci's Political Thought: Hegemony,*

Consciousness and the Revolutionary Process (Oxford: Clarendon Press, 1987), 27.
10 By late 1942, nine state radio stations (not all hostile) were beaming into Bengal, including those of Japan, Germany, the Voice of America and Radio Moscow (Joselyn A. Zivin, *The Projection of India: Imperial Propaganda, the British State and Nationalist India, 1930–47* (Department of History, Duke University: PhD Dissertation, 1994), 184).
11 Pradip N. Thomas, *The Political Economy of Communications in India: the good, the bad and the ugly* (New Delhi: Sage Publications, 2010), 46; I.G.P. Singh, 'Broadcasting in India', *The Spectator* 23 August 1935: 286–7.
12 Singh, Broadcasting, 286.
13 H.R. Luthra, *Indian Broadcasting* (New Delhi: Publications Division, Ministry of Information and Broadcasting, Government of India, 1986), 64–5. For the renaming, see Fielden, Natural Bent, 192–3.
14 Joselyn Zivin, 'The Imagined Reign of the Iron Lecturer: Village Broadcasting in Colonial India', *Modern Asian Studies* 32 (3) July 1998: 717; Zivin, Projection of India, 152. Clement Attlee claimed in November 1945 that '15 years ago he had advocated the setting up of wireless receivers on the village greens of India' (Notes on Chequers discussion, 27 November 1945 in Robin J. Moore, *Escape from Empire: The Attlee Government and the Indian Problem* (Oxford: Clarendon Press, 1983), 43).
15 Luthra, Indian Broadcasting, 100. Thomas suggests that AIR was 'an indispensable medium for propaganda, information gathering and dissemination' which the Government used against the Axis and Congress (Political Economy, 46). The Government's actions suggest otherwise.
16 See E.M. Jenkins (Secretary of the Department of Industries and Commerce) to Hugh Macgregor (Information Officer at the India Office), probably 1936, in Luthra, Indian Broadcasting, 99–100. Jenkins also asked (in a Note for the Executive Committee, 13 January 1936) if the opening of the Legislative Assembly was broadcast, then why not the opening of the annual Congress session?
17 Luthra, Indian Broadcasting, 111.
18 Alasdair Pinkerton, 'Radio and the Raj: Broadcasting in British India', *Journal of the Royal Asiatic Society* Series 3 18 (2) 2008: 176 & 189; Zivin, Bent, 214.
19 Pinkerton, Radio and the Raj, 178.
20 Zivin, Projection of India, 37; see also 59 & 154.

21 Luthra, Indian Broadcasting 149. According to Luthra, Fielden was reprimanded by BBC authorities for the suggestion. However, *The Indian Listener* reveals that Elwin did broadcast on Christmas Day and his (rather innocuous) message was reprinted in its pages. ('Mr Verrier Elwin's Christmas Day Broadcast from the Bombay Studio,' *Indian Listener* I (2), 7 January 1936: 71).
22 Fielden, Natural Bent, 154–204. See also Luthra, Indian Broadcasting, 149–151; Zivin, Bent, 195–215.
23 Owen Williamson, 'The Mahatma's Hams,' accessed at www.oocities.org/sadaqathullah/mahatma.html 10 October 2016; Gandhimedia.org, 'The Story of the Secret Congress Radio,' www.gandhimedia.org.
24 Luthra, Indian Broadcasting, 127–7; ABP, 9 April 1942, 6.
25 Amery to Viceroy 6 May 1942, in Nicholas Mansergh (ed.), *The Transfer of Power 1942–7. Volume 2: 'Quit India', 30 April–21 September 1942* (London: Her Majesty's Stationery Office, 1971) (henceforward Transfer of Power II), 39; Viceroy's rejection, 50.
26 Luthra, Indian Broadcasting, 130–131.
27 'But while political controversy was banned from the airwaves, so too was official propaganda. In their compromised liberalism, the British denied themselves what they most needed from radio, the opportunity to defend their project of rule to Indian citizens.' (Zivin, Projection of India, 7.)
28 Luthra, Indian Broadcasting, 128–9.
29 Nirad C. Chaudhuri, *Thy Hand, Great Anarch! India: 1921–1952* (London: The Hogarth Press, 1990), 652.
30 Sir George Cunningham to Viceroy 8 July 1942, Transfer of Power II, 353.
31 West Bengal State Archive (henceforward WBSA): Conference of Commissioners of Divisions held in July 1942. Proceedings. 362/(22)/42.
32 WBSA: Minutes of the meeting held at H.Q. 15 India Corps, 26 May 1942. File on Rumours. 368/42.
33 WBSA: File on Rumours. 368/42.
34 WBSA: Conference of Commissioners of Divisions held in July 1942. Proceedings. 362/(22)/42
35 Briggs, War of Words, 509.
36 Orwell XIII, 88.
37 Orwell XIII, 410–411.
38 Ruvani Ranasinha, 'South Asian Broadcasters in Britain and the BBC: talking to India (1941–1943),' *South Asian Diaspora* 2 (1) March 2010:, 63.

39 Sir Frederick Puckle, 'A Review of War Publicity. December 1939 to February 1941' in Zivin, Projection of India, 164.
40 Amery to Viceroy, 14 October 1940 in Zivin, Projection of India, 147.
41 Viceroy to Amery, 27 June 1942 Transfer of Power II, 277.
42 Briggs, War of Words, 506–7.
43 Briggs, War of Words, 507 & 511. Other British figures of authority were also listening. Sir Stafford Cripps, listening to the service in India in March 1942, wrote to the Minister of Information: 'The comic ignorance of a confusion between a Sheikh and a Sikh does not help to build up British prestige, but merely makes us a laughing stock.' (Cripps to Minister of Information 28 March 1942, in Nicholas Mansergh (ed.), *The Transfer of Power 1942–7. Volume 1: The Cripps Mission, January-April 1942* (London: Her Majesty's Stationery Office, 1970) (henceforward Transfer of Power I), 517.)
44 Rajkumari Amrit Kaur to Nehru 25 July 1942, in Bipan Chandra and Salil Misra (eds.), *Towards Freedom: Documents on the Movement for Independence in India, 1942* (New Delhi: Oxford University Press, 2016) (henceforward, Towards Freedom 1942), 902.
45 Puckle to Director General, Ministry of Information, 18 January 1940 in Briggs, War of Words, 505.
46 Briggs, War of Words, 505.
47 Fielden, Natural Bent, 216. Darling apparently considered Fielden to be 'a real snake in the grass' (Clive Dewey, *Anglo-Indian Attitudes: The Mind of the Indian Civil Service* (London: Hambledon Press, 1993), 245, note 3).
48 Briggs, War of Words, 505.
49 Orwell, XIII 9–12; Ranasinha, South Asian Broadcasters, 61–2.
50 Briggs, War of Words, 507.
51 *New Statesman*, 5 July 1941 in Briggs, War of Words, 506. What this 'special study' was and what it reflected about 'Indian tastes and susceptibilities' was not revealed.
52 *New Statesman*, 19 July 1941 in Briggs, War of Words, 506.
53 Orwell to Woodcock, 2 December 1942, in George Orwell, *The Collected Essays, Journalism and Letters of George Orwell. Volume II: My Country Right or Left, 1940–1943*, ed. Sonia Orwell and Ian Argus (London: Secker & Warburg, 1968) (henceforward Orwell, Volume 2), 268.
54 George Orwell, 'Poetry and the Microphone,' Autumn 1943 in Orwell, Volume 2, 329.
55 George Orwell, 'News Review,' 8 August 1942 in Orwell, XIII, 455.
56 George Orwell, 'War-time Diary,' 12 August 1942 in Orwell, XIII, 472.

57 George Orwell, 'War-time Diary', 14 March 1942 in Orwell, XIII, 229. Also he wrote here: 'All propaganda is lies, even when one is telling the truth. I don't think this matters as long as one knows what one is doing and why.'
58 Briggs, War of Words, 508.
59 George Orwell, 'War-time Diary', 5 October 1942 in George Orwell, *The Complete Works of George Orwell. Volume Fourteen: Keeping Our Little Corner Clean, 1941–1942*, ed. Peter Davison (London: Secker and Warburg, 1998) (henceforward Orwell, XIV), 76.
60 K.K. Chaudhari, *Quit India Revolution: The Ethos of its Central Direction* (Mumbai: Popular Prakashan Pvt. Ltd., 1996), 245, 247 & 261. Chatterjee maintains that the initiative was taken by Lohia, who put it in the hands of Vithaldas Madhavji Khakar, a twenty-year old Gujarati to organize (Gautam Chatterjee, 'Quit India Movement and "illegal" Congress Radio,' *Mainstream* 12 August 1989: 15). Mehta herself relates that Lohia became involved after the broadcasts had started (Usha Mehta, 'On My Life and the Indian Underground Radio (Congress Radio)' (Talk with Peter Ruhe, Mumbai, 17 December 1988). www.gandhiserve.org).
61 Mehta, Congress Radio; Chaudhari, Quit India Revolution, 250.
62 Chaudhari, Quit India Revolution, 249.
63 Williamson, Hams.
64 Chatterjee, Illegal Radio, 15
65 Williamson, Hams.
66 13 August is the date given by Mehta (Mehta, Congress Radio). Chaudhari gives two dates, 27 August and 29 August (Quit India Revolution, 246 & 258), while Williamson says that broadcasts started on 2 September (Williamson, Hams).
67 Mehta, Congress Radio; Gandhimedia.org, Story of Secret Congress Radio; Williamson, Hams; Chatterjee, Illegal Radio, 15.
68 Chaudhari, Quit India Revolution, 245–6; Williamson, Hams; Gandhimedia.org, Story of Secret Congress Radion; Mehta, Congress Radio.
69 Bose broadcast, 4 September 1942 in George Orwell, *The War Commentaries*, ed. W.J. West (Harmondsworth: Penguin, 1987), 235.
70 Mehta, Congress Radio; Gandhimedia.org, Story of Secret Congress Radio; Chaudhari, Quit India Revolution, 248.
71 Chaudhari, Quit India Revolution, 258; Chatterjee, Illegal Radio, 16; Mehta, Congress Radio.
72 Chaudhari, Quit India Revolution, 262; Mehta, Congress Radio;

Gandhimedia.org, Story of Secret Congress Radio.
73 Congress Radio broadcast, 20 October 1942 in Chatterjee, Illegal Radio, 16.
74 Congress Radio broadcasts, 20 & 28 October 1942 in Chatterjee, Illegal Radio, 16.
75 Gandhimedia.org, 'Indian Underground Radio', Parts 1–4. http://www.gandhimedia.org/cgi-bin/gm/gm.cgi?action=view& link=Audio/Radio_Programs/English&image=AURPEN0010.mp3&img=&tt=mp3, Part 2.
76 Gandhimedia.org, Story of Secret Congress Radio.
77 Chatterjee, Illegal Radio, 17.
78 Chatterjee, Illegal Radio, 17.
79 Gandhimedia.org, 'Indian Underground Radio', Parts 1–4. http://www.gandhimedia.org/cgi-bin/gm/gm.cgi?action=view& link=Audio/Radio_Programs/English&image=AURPEN0010.mp3&img=&tt=mp3, Part 3. See also Chaudhari, Quit India Revolution, 269. However, a Congress Radio broadcast on landings by Japanese saboteurs on the west coast near Malabar by submarine and rubber boats did convey a sense of approval for the operations (Gandhimedia.org, 'Indian Underground Radio', Parts 1–4. http://www.gandhimedia.org/cgi-bin/gm/gm.cgi?action=view&link=Audio/Radio_Programs/English&image=AURPEN0010.mp3&img=&tt=mp3, Part 1).
80 Gandhimedia.org, 'Indian Underground Radio', Parts 1–4. http://www.gandhimedia.org/cgi-bin/gm/gm.cgi?action=view& link=Audio/Radio_Programs/English&image=AURPEN0010.mp3&img=&tt=mp3, Part 3. As most of it did—see David Lockwood, *The Indian Bourgeoisie: A Political History of the Indian Capitalist Class in the Early Twentieth Century* (London: IB Tauris, 2012).
81 Gandhimedia.org, Story of Secret Congress Radio; Williamson, Hams.
82 Mehta was released in 1946 by Morarji Desai—one of his first acts as Chief Minister of Bombay Province (Mehta, Congress Radio).
83 Charles J. Rolo, *Radio Goes to War* (London: Faber, 1943), 168.
84 *Indian Listener* I (2), 7 January 1936.
85 Mihir Bose comments: 'Radio propaganda by itself could not bring about rebellion, [German Foreign Minister] von Ribbentrop concluded, but it could foment discontent—and that was a beginning.' (Mihir Bose, *The Lost Hero: A Biography of Subhas Bose* (London: Quartet Books, 1982), 181–182.)
86 Fielden, Natural Bent, 215.
87 Chaudhuri, Anarch, 573.
88 Bose, Lost Hero, 200.

89 Francis G. Hutchins, *Spontaneous Revolution: The Quit India Movement* (Delhi: Manohar Book Service, 1971), 299; Zivin, Projection of India, 161.
90 Government of India, *The Fifth Column as a Weapon in War* (New Delhi: Government of India Press, 1942), 19.
91 Sekijiro Takagaki, *The Japan Year Book 1942–43* (Tokyo: Japan Times Press, n.d. [1943]), 523.
92 Peter Elphick, *Singapore: The Pregnable Fortress—A Study in Deception, Discord and Desertion* (London: Hodder & Stoughton, 1995), 69.
93 Government of India, Fifth Column, 19.
94 Namikawa Ryo, 'Japanese Overseas Broadcasting: A Personal View', in *Film and Radio Propaganda in World War II*, ed. Kenneth R.M. Short (London: Croom Helm, 1983), 330; Hutchins, Spontaneous Revolution, 316.
95 L.D. Meo, *Japan's Radio War on Australia, 1941–1945* (Melbourne: Melbourne University Press, 1968), 45.
96 Rolo, Radio Goes to War, 170.
97 Rolo, Radio Goes to War, 173.
98 British Library, India Office Records (henceforward IOR): Fortnightly Reports of Governors, Chief Commissioners and Chief Secretaries (1937–1948). Chief Secretary Report, 2nd half, January 1942. L/PJ/5/149.
99 Fortnightly Report Bengal, 2nd half May 1942, Towards Freedom 1942, 777.
100 Fortnightly Report Central Provinces 1st half, February 1942, Towards Freedom 1942, 708; Fortnightly Report United Provinces, 2nd half, February 1942, Towards Freedom 1942, 713.
101 A.B. Chatterjee, the Bengal Organizer of the National War Front, agreed. See WBSA: Proceedings of the Conference of Commissioners and heads of departments held in November 1942. 616 (C)/42 Proceedings.
102 WBSA: Lessons learned during Air raids. W–732/42.
103 Fortnightly Report Bihar, 2nd half, February 1942, Towards Freedom 1942, 714.
104 Fortnightly Report Bengal, 2nd half, May 1942, Towards Freedom 1942, 777.
105 Thus the Battle of the Midway in June 1942 had to be portrayed as a Japanese victory (Ryo, Japanese Overseas Broadcasting, 323, 327–8).
106 See Bose's letter to Ribbentrop, 5 December 1942 in Sisir K. Bose and Sugata Bose (eds.), *Azad Hind: Writings and Speeches, 1941–1943 by Subhas Chandra Bose* (Calcutta: Netaji Research Bureau, 2007), 170–172; Bose, Lost Hero, 195–8.

107 Transcript in Orwell, War Commentaries, 13.
108 Bose, Lost Hero, 193.
109 Subhas Chandra Bose, Azad Hind, 193.
110 Bose broadcast, 20 July 1942 in Orwell, War Commentaries, 228.
111 Bose broadcast, 25 April 1942, Towards Freedom 1942, 390.
112 Bose broadcast, 4 September 1942 in Orwell, War Commentaries, 232.
113 Bose broadcast, 4 September 1942 in Orwell, War Commentaries, 230.
114 Fortnightly Report, Bombay, 2nd half, April 1942 in Towards Freedom 1942, 756.
115 Moti Ram (ed.), *Two Historic Trials in Red Fort. An Authentic Account of the Trial by a General Court Martial of Captain Shah Nawaz Khan, Captain P.K. Sahgal and Lt. G.S. Dhillon and the Trial by A European Military Commission of Emperor Bahadur Shah* (New Delhi: Moti Ram, 1946[?]), 128 & 130. Meo suggests that the opposite may have been true before Bose's arrival. Critical of the low standard of Tokyo's broadcasts, 'Japanese intelligence in Singapore ... sent members of the Free India Army (i.e. supporters of Chandra Bose) to Tokyo to take over' (Meo, Japan's Radio War, 272).
116 Jawaharlal Nehru, *A Bunch of Old Letters* (London: Asia Publishing House, 1960), 475.
117 Chandan Mitra, 'Popular Uprising in 1942: The Case of Ballia,' in *The Indian Nation in 1942*, ed. Gyanendra Pandey (Calcutta: K.P. Bagchi & Company, 1988),169.
118 Hitesranjan Sanyal, 'The Quit India Movement in Medinipur District,' in *The Indian Nation in 1942*, ed. Gyanendra Pandey (Calcutta: K.P. Bagchi & Company, 1988), 26.
119 M.K. Gandhi, 'Interview to Journalist' (before 25 July 1942) in *Harijan* 2 August 1942, Mohandas K. Gandhi, *The Collected Works of Mahatma Gandhi*, Chief Ed. Shri R.P. Dhasmana (Delhi: Publications Division, Ministry of Information and Broadcasting, 1958–1994) Volume 83, 134.
120 Viceroy to Halifax, 27 March 1942, Transfer of Power I, 504.
121 District Officer's report contained in Fortnightly Report, Bihar 1st half March 1942, Towards Freedom 1942, 723.
122 Fortnightly Report, Orissa, 2nd half, March 1942, Towards Freedom 1942, 727.
123 Sir M. Hallett to Viceroy, 2 April 1942 in Transfer of Power II, 25.
124 Gyanendra Pandey, 'The Revolt of August 1942 in Eastern UP and Bihar,' in *The Indian Nation in 1942*, ed. Gyanendra Pandey (Calcutta: K.P. Bagchi & Company, 1988), 154. See also Hutchins, Spontaneous Revolution, 300.

125 BBC officer's memorandum forwarded by Amery to the Viceroy 3 November 1942 in Transfer of Power III, 197. This may have been the report by Laurence Brander, mentioned by Orwell above. In any case, the Viceroy described it as 'tripe' (196).
126 ABP, 10 May 1942, 4.
127 Zivin, Projection of India, 161; Viceroy to Amery, 24 October 1942 in Transfer of Power III, 154.
128 Editors' comment in Antonio Gramsci, *Selections from the Prison Notebooks of Antonio Gramsci*, ed. and trans. Quintin Hoare & Geoffrey Nowell Smith (New York: International Publishers, 1975) (henceforward SPN), 322; see also 199 & 323.
129 From 'Gli intelletuali e l'organizzazione delle cultura' cited in Gramsci, SPN 326.
130 See Guido Liguori, 'Common sense in Gramsci', in *Perspectives on Gramsci* ed. Joseph Francese (London: Routledge, 2009), 124, 128 & 130.
131 Gramsci, SPN, 424.
132 'The existence of broadcasting constitutes the main difference in propaganda between this War and the last. The principal features of this new development are the time element, the universality of the medium and the stamp of authority.' (BBC Monitoring Service, *Weekly Analysis*, 3 January 1940 in Briggs, War of Words, 1.)
133 Briggs, War of Words, 502.
134 Fortnightly Report, Assam, 1st half, April 1942, in Towards Freedom 1942, 745–6.
135 Zivin, Projection of India, 159.

9

STATE DECAY

We felt that the British Government had, on its own, cut off all the bonds that had bound us to the British Crown and relieved us of all obligations to it... We bona fide believed that the British Crown having ceased to provide any protection to us could no longer demand allegiance from us.

–Prem Sahgal

I felt like one deserted by the British in a state of utter and tragic helplessness... I felt convinced that there was no possibility of the British being able to defend or hold India against Japanese invasion.

–Gurubaksh Singh

We, the Indians were being left in the lurch. I as well as most of the other officers had a feeling of being handed over like cattle to the Japs and by the Japs to Mohan Singh.

–Shah Nawaz Khan, Statements by the accused at the first Indian National Army trial, November-December 1945.[1]

The municipal plaque that marks what remains of Farrer Park in Singapore notes that it had been used as a racecourse by the Singapore Turf Club since 1924, then as an airstrip and, after 1933, as public playing fields. The racecourse grandstand was converted into a sports club. The plaque is silent on what happened in the park in February 1942, although the government-sponsored website mentions that it was 'an assembly point for Malay and Indian prisoners-of-war.'[2] A point for assembly—and for what one British officer described as 'the parting of the ways.'[3] The events in Farrer Park on February 17, 1942 constituted the single most dramatic indication to that point of the decline of the British colonial state: the abandonment of British responsibility for units of the British Indian army and the handing over of them for use by an enemy power.

Singapore had surrendered to the Japanese on February 15. Included in that surrender were some 65,000 Indian officers and men. That night and on the following day the Indian soldiers were ordered by the Japanese (an order passed on by the British) to assemble at Farrer Park. About 40,000 did so by the next day. Major Iwaichi Fujiwara, the Japanese Army intelligence officer liaising with Indian nationalists in Southeast Asia, was in charge. He wrote later:

> We agreed that the formalities should begin at 1300 hours on the 17th when a representative of the British Army would hand over Indian POWs to us. Following the transfer, I, representing the Japanese Army, was to deliver a speech, followed by Capt. Mohan [Singh], and Pritam [two Indians working with the Japanese], in that order.[4]

At the sports club building, a platform and a microphone had been set up in the central balcony, overlooking the field.[5] The first to speak was Colonel Hunt from Malaya Command Headquarters. His exact remarks are uncertain, but their content can be gauged from the statements of the INA prisoners above. The Indians were told that they were now POWs under the command of the Japanese, to whom the British were handing them over. Next came Major Fujiwara, speaking in Japanese which was translated into English and Hindustani. Japan's proclamation of a 'war of liberation' in East Asia has been dealt with in Chapter Three. It was these sentiments that Fujiwara communicated to the POWs. They were not really prisoners, he said, but friends. The British would soon be defeated and the Co-Prosperity Sphere would come into existence, with India guarding its western flank.[6] So saying, he handed them on to Captain Mohan Singh, formerly of the British Army in Malaya. It was he who broke the news of the formation of an Indian National Army to fight the British alongside the Japanese and he invited the Indian soldiers to join. Mohan Singh's speech was, by all accounts, received very positively by those in the park. Eventually, some 40,000 Indians (including an initial 20,000 POWs) signed up for what was to be the first INA.[7] Its First Division of 16,300 men paraded on September 10, 1942.[8]

The events in Farrer Park were a very obvious indication of the weakness of the British colonial state at this time. In this instance it was an external weakness, in the face of Japanese advance and conquest. It added a crucial element to the internal weakness of the state in India. Significant sections of this book have been devoted to the positive building strategy of the Congress: the campaigns of the 1920s and 1930s, the constructive programme, the Provincial Ministries (for all their weaknesses), the eventual position on the war and the Quit India movement. As well as building a counter-hegemony, the object was also to undermine the dominant structures. This was successful to such an extent that large numbers of Indians had no faith in the ability of the British to defend them against invasion—a lack of faith that was confirmed in Farrer Park. As Khan puts it:

> Even if the Raj had never been actively *liked* in the past, at least it could be relied upon as a coherent administration,

one that would keep its inhabitants reasonably secure from military incursion and underwrite the validity of currency and savings. Now [after 1942] there was a widespread loss of faith in even the most basic functions of the imperial state.[9]

This feeling was not confined to the Indian population. Bombay reported in March 1942:

> There is evidence that in the European community beneath the surface there is a feeling of distrust of the Civil Power and of the Military Command in India.[10]

This atmosphere, together with the actions of the Congress over the past two decades that had led up to it, had an effect on the state structures themselves, particularly on the armed forces and on the civil service, which will be examined in this chapter.[11] It is perhaps ironic, but also significant, that in a period when the state powers of the Government of India and the Provincial Governments were hugely increased (as is generally the case in wartime), the two main pillars of the state, its civil and military administrations, began to wobble.

THE ARMED FORCES

Since the uprising of 1857, the relative proportions of British and Indian soldiers in the armed services had been a matter of some debate. Various exercises in 'Indianization'—that is, increasing the numbers of Indian soldiers and officers relative to the British—had been undertaken. The war threw the delicate planning involved to the winds. The Empire demanded unprecedented numbers of soldiers. With large numbers of able-bodied Britons returning home to fight there, large number of Indians—both soldiers and officers—had to be recruited. Importantly, this meant opening up the officer corps to larger numbers of Indians than ever before. Before the outbreak of war, the Indian army numbered about 1,60,000. By 1943 it stood at nearly two million. At the beginning of the war there were 577 Indian Commissioned Officers (ICOs—trained and commissioned in India), of whom 140 were medical officers. Between May 1940 and September 1941, 1,400 Indian became officers. In 1942 it was planned to increase the annual intake from 900 to 2,000. By 1945, there were 8,000 ICOs, including 220 lieutenant-colonels and four temporary or acting Brigadiers.[12]

These increases had meant that the sources of recruitment had to be expanded far wider than had been the previous British practice. To this point, recruitment had been concentrated on those Indians that the British considered the 'martial races'—mostly quite specific northern and western Indian communities that the British regarded as good fighters (either, in the past, against themselves, or against the Empire's enemies). The Simon Commission listed the 'martial races' as Punjabis, Pathans, Sikhs, Marathas and Gurkhas. It reported: 'Whereas the most virile of the so-called martial races provide fine fighting material, other communities and areas in India do not furnish a single man for the regular Army.'[13] The 'non-martial races' were, according to a Government of India statement to Parliament in 1931, 'by their physique and tradition...rendered practically incapable of resisting military aggression of any kind.'[14] But the war forced the British to cast their recruiting nets considerably more widely and the 'non-martial races' had to be included.

British military authorities continued to fret during the war at the martial abilities of the new recruits who did not come from traditional recruiting areas—especially when it became apparent 'that the new recruits treated the armed forces as a well-paid and stable source of employment' rather than an imperial vocation.[15] A further source of disquiet, particularly regarding Indian officers, was that the expansion of recruitment necessitated the inclusion of 'the educated, sometimes urban, ICOs from middle and upper class families [who] were familiar with the currents of Indian nationalism and, in many cases, with nationalist politicians themselves.'[16] Lieutenant-Colonel George Wren (of the Frontier Force Rifles) wrote to Wavell in December in December 1942, 'we have...bred a new class of officer who may be loyal to India, and perhaps to Congress, but is not necessarily loyal to us.'[17] The Secretary of State noted the problems associated with 'non-traditional' recruitment in 1943. Wavell replied that while he was confident in the army's loyalty: 'He thought however that a potential source of danger lay in the Indian Air Force, where the men enlisted were almost entirely from the politically conscious non-martial classes.'[18] An Indian officer confirmed in the same year:

> A number of people are loyal but they will only remain so as long as it suits them...every Indian (soldiers included) desires a higher political status for India...the consensus was that we should help the British defeat the Axis powers and deal with the British afterwards.[19]

These doubts persisted for the duration and were strengthened by the prospect of internal political upheaval at war's end.[20]

Two factors worked to undermine the steadfastness of the Indian army still further. The first was the racial discrimination practiced against Indians in the armed forces. Racism on the part of British officers and men against Indian soldiers was common enough. But when this treatment was extended to the increasing numbers of Indian officers, problems arose.[21] Indian Commissioned Officers were paid less than their British equivalents and their powers were more restricted. Worse off were the Viceroy's Commissioned Officers. According to the Simon Commission: 'the holder of a "Viceroy's commission," whatever his experience and length of service, is lower in rank and command than the most newly joined of British subalterns.'[22] They did not eat with British officers.[23] In general, Indian officers were excluded from the clubs, swimming pools, superior railway carriages and buses of the Raj.[24]

The second factor affecting the loyalty of Indian soldiers was political influence and infiltration. No less a person than the Commander-in-Chief in India, General Auchinleck, commented 'It is no use shutting one's eyes to the fact that any Indian officer worth his salt is a Nationalist.'[25] In the interwar period there had been various attempts to subvert soldiers and officers. In the late 1920s and early 1930s for example:

> The Kirti Lehar [Toilers' Party] group enhanced its relations with serving Indian soldiers from the Meerut cantonment and soldiers attended lectures at the Kirti Lehar Office. Later, the desertions from the army by a number of Sepoys were attributed to the insidious influence and pernicious preaching of the Kirti Lehar group.[26]

Such subversion had its effect. In 1940, a majority of the Sikh cavalry troops in the Central India Horse refused to board a ship for Egypt, under the influence of Kirti Lehar. Their leaders were court-martialled and deported to the Andaman Islands.[27] In the same year, Sikh troops in Bombay refused to participate in what they denounced as an 'imperialist war'. Four of them were executed, the rest sent to the Andamans.[28]

Military discontent was not confined to soldiers within India—in fact, it was probably more widespread among Indian soldiers stationed abroad, particularly in Southeast Asia. Again in 1940 (May), soldiers from the 4/19th Hyderabad Regiment, stationed at Tyersall Park camp in Singapore, refused to obey orders when one of their officers, Lieutenant Mohammed Zahir, was ordered home for expressing nationalist views (including the hope that Britain would lose the war) and allegedly co-habiting with a white woman. British troops were put on standby. The situation was defused when military authorities agreed to Zahir farewelling his troops before being ordered out of Singapore. The Secretary of State wrote to the Viceroy that the incident 'gives one some cause for anxiety as far as some portions at any rate of the Indian Army are concerned.'[29]

The most successful organization in this regard was the Indian Independence League (IIL), founded by the veteran Indian revolutionary, Rash Behari Bose, in his Japanese exile in 1929.[30] One of the purposes of the IIL was to convert Indian soldiers stationed outside India to the nationalist cause. In this it had the support of the Japanese government, particularly after December 1941. Elphick tells us that its work among Indian troops in Hong Kong 'was considered very serious', while in Malaya, 'The IIL's success rate in creating or nurturing nationalist feelings [among Indian officers] was high.' In one instance:

> Several officers [of the First Bahawalpur Battalion], who later rose to high positions in the ranks of the Indian National Army, were known to have had contacts with IIL agents during the pre-war months.[31]

The IIL had a branch in Bangkok led by Pritam Singh. Major Fujiwara made contact with the group in October 1941. Pritam Singh told him that 'Indian troops in the British-Indian Army harboured anti-British sentiments and were receptive to propaganda' which the IIL was endeavouring to provide. By this stage, Japan's entry into the war was widely expected, and Singh suggested that IIL agents should accompany Japanese troops into Malaya. Late that month the two agreed that the IIL, as well as agitating for Indian independence amongst Indian civilians, would strengthen its propaganda among Indian soldiers in Malaya, Burma and India. Furthermore:

> The I.I.L. shall advance, together with Japanese troops, to southern Thailand and Malaya... It shall engage in operations to win over Indian masses and Indian soldiers from British-Indian troops by instigating an anti-British sentiment amongst them and [creating] a spirit of friendly cooperation with the Japanese.[32]

On the first day of the Japanese attack on Malaya, Indian soldiers at Kota Bharu refused to defend the airfield and shot their commanding officer dead. Elphick suggests that one reason for this may have been the headlong flight of the RAAF ground staff. But he adds: 'there can be little doubt that the underlying reason was that the Hyderabads [the battalion involved] did not feel like fighting a war which had nothing to do with them, an argument often used by IIL agents.'[33]

In India itself, other political organizations—the Congress, the Forward Bloc and the Communist Party—were also engaged in political agitation in the Indian armed forces.[34] By the end of 1942, desertion was becoming a serious problem. Deshpande points out that while 'homesickness, loneliness, discontent and harsh discipline' were some of the causes, 'the influence of politics on the process cannot be ruled out...the British suspected that in the disturbed conditions of 1942 subversive influence was most probably working in the armed forces.'[35] Subhas Chandra Bose claimed in July 1942:

> It is indeed gratifying to know that, in the new Indian Army built up by the British since 1939, we have a fair percentage of friends and supporters. That percentage has to be increased still further in the days to come. This is how revolutions have been made all over the world ...[36]

As the Japanese advanced, soldiers retreating into India, wounded, defeated and demoralised, had the effect of 'making the plight of the state visible', according to Indivar Kamtekar.[37] In the months leading up to the Quit India campaign, doubts in the loyalty of the armed forces grew. The Viceroy reported a conversation with Feroz Khan Noon, the Defence Member of his Council, to Amery in July:

> ...he said quite frankly that, while they [Indian officers] might not favour the Congress policy, they, Muhammedans alike with Hindus, were very much for Gandhi as the one man

who could make the British sit up: and that he was not free from doubt as to the extent to which, if it came to firing, they would be anxious to fire on Congress supporters. He went so far [as] to affirm his doubts as to whether these officers would prove staunch in the event of a Japanese or German invasion of India.[38]

Once the Quit India campaign was underway, there were isolated, though significant incidents of disloyalty. On August 24, the First Rajindra Lancers (a unit of the Patiala State forces) refused to parade, shouting 'Inquilab Zindabad'! A number were arrested, whereupon the following day those still at large marched into Patiala under a Congress flag. A meeting was held which demanded the release of those arrested and denounced mistreatment by officers. More arrests followed and those incarcerated were court-martialled.[39] In Agra, an Indian officer, ordered to suppress demonstrations, 'ensured that his men did not have to fire by tacit agreement with the leaders of the demonstrations.'[40] In September a second lieutenant refused an order to lead his men into a city (the location of which is not indicated in the report) because they might be called upon to shoot their fellow Indians. He was given the opportunity to resign as the British believed a court-martial would produce a more serious revolt.[41] Bayly and Harper conclude 'the Indian element of the army, particularly the VCOs, was wobbling.'

Congress Radio maintained a steady focus on the armed forces during the campaign. On the one hand, it reported mutinies. In late October it reported 306 Indian soldiers shot in Meerut:

> It appears that there were skirmishes between Indian and British soldiers. Consequent upon the Indian soldiers' refusal to fire on unarmed countrymen, British soldiers are reported to have practised black treachery in disarming them and making them stand before the firing squad.[42]

On the other, the Radio appealed to soldiers to join the revolt. Gandhi's advice to soldiers to refuse orders to fire on the people was broadcast.[43] Congress Radio also suggested a more circumspect approach:

> If you cannot yet openly come over to the people, administer to yourself with proper ceremony the oath of allegiance to the free state of India that is to be. Do not suppress your own people. History will never forgive you if you do so.[44]

Congress Radio predicted that 'the loyalty of the Indian army to the British shall disappear on the day our revolution reaches its climax and we are in a position to capture power.'[45]

British anxiety over the loyalty of the armed forces continued after Quit India had been largely suppressed. In the United Provinces, an Intelligence Report in April 1943 feared that the movement had gained a hearing in the military. It suggested that ideas of a Congress government after the war should be firmly countered, that recruits should be more thoroughly checked and that soldiers on leave should be watched in case they made contact with subversive elements.[46]

By the end of the war, the seeds of discontent had been well fertilised in the armed wing of the British colonial state. Much of this work had taken place among Indian soldiers outside India where they were at their most vulnerable, disoriented and subject to racial discrimination. But there also had been considerable undermining of the steadfastness of the armed forces within India. These seeds would shortly come to fruition at the end of the war in the Naval Mutiny and the mass protests against the trials of INA officers.[47]

THE STATE BUREAUCRACY AND POLICE

Bipan Chandra argues that an important element of Congress strategy was 'to undermine the hold of the colonial state on the members of its own state apparatuses, destroy their morale, promote "rebelliousness" among them, and to neutralise or win them over to the national cause.[48] Gandhi wrote in 1937, 'Our non-violence, therefore, meant that we are out to convert the administrators of the system; their conversion may or may not be willing.'[49]

The colonial bureaucracy was divided into various sections by seniority, pay and race. The absolute bureaucratic elite consisted of the Central Services and the much larger All-India Services—commonly called the Indian Civil Service (ICS)—controlled in the former case by the Government of India and in the latter directly by the Secretary of State.[50] The elite filled the positions of District Officer (variously called Collector, Deputy Commissioner and District Magistrate), Divisional Commissioner, Commissioner and above in the Provinces and supplied members of Provincial Governments.[51] The elite occupied the 'superior posts' not only in the governmental bureaucracy but also in the Police, Forestry, Engineering, Educational, Agricultural, Veterinary and Medical services. They gained their positions through competitive examination in London and later in Allahabad.[52] They were, until the interwar years, overwhelmingly European.

Evans comments that 'There was no governing class in India—the I.C.S. monopolized the role of such a class.'[53] Dewey elaborates:

> Their monopoly of information meant that they could skew it in any way they chose. They took up issues that mattered to them; they tailored their reports to their recommendations; they retreated into a demi-official world if they thought their actions might be censured.[54]

In 1924, according to the Simon Commission, the All-India Services numbered 4,279.[55]

Below the All-India Services were the Provincial Services, generally recruited in India, appointed by Provincial Governments and occupying the middle and subordinate ranks of the bureaucracy in all the services listed above. Ewing describes them as 'a vast army of subordinate clerks and provincial staff, recruited in India to do the more humdrum tasks.' They were, of course, vital to the functioning of the machine.[56] Here, the domination of Europeans ceased to exist. Those in the Provincial Services were overwhelmingly Indian because of their large numbers at lower levels.[57]

The pattern of European preponderance in the top ranks with large numbers of Indians at the lower levels was widespread throughout the colonial bureaucracy. In 1930, as reported by the Simon Commission:

- In the ICS, out of 5,250 personnel, 3,500 were European.
- In the Police Services, there were 600 European officers and 800 European sergeants out of a total of 1,87,000 (the rest being Indian).
- In Education, there were 200 Europeans and 1,500 Indians at the higher grades and 11,000 Indians in the subordinate services.
- In the Railways, 3,500 Europeans and 7,700 Indians in the higher and intermediate staff, out of a total of 8,00,000.
- In the Judiciary, taking the Madras Presidency as an example, the Commission reported that of 800 presiding officers in courts below the level of District Magistrates, only twelve were Europeans.[58]

The Commission correctly pointed out:

> These figures show how small relatively are the numbers of Europeans in government employ. It will be realised, however, that they are, broadly speaking, employed at the top.[59]

It was also possible for Indians to be promoted from the Provincial Services into the Superior ones. But this path was fraught with difficulties. In Bombay, it was revealed in 1921 that the most senior officer in the Provincial Services had been waiting twelve years for promotion to a Senior position.[60] During and after the

First World War, due to the reduction in numbers of the Senior Services (see below), 'Indians from the Provincial Services were promoted to hold junior district posts.'[61] After the war it was suggested that those acting in these positions be made members of the Senior Services. The Viceroy blocked this, 'arguing that this might impair prestige, seriously effect *esprit de corps* and lead the members [of the Senior Services] to believe that their status was under attack.'[62]

There was some hostility between the two services. Once the Montagu-Chelmsford reforms were operating in Bengal, it was alleged that Indian Provincial ministers were using Provincial Service civil servants to collect information on which the Superior Service could be attacked. It is perhaps not surprising that hostility became racial in nature. Ewing continues: 'Racial feelings were particularly fierce in Madras and were given edge by the considerable hostility with which the provincial regarded the imperial [Superior] services.'[63]

Scions of the Indian elite were now being allowed to enter the ICS at an increasing rate. The First World War dragged many European ICS officers away to fight. Vacancies mounted until by 1918, the service was two hundred short of its required workforce. 'Indianization' was designed, at least temporarily, to fill the gap, but it became increasingly permanent as the remaining young men of Britain were reluctant to take on a career in India. Indianization of the Superior Services sat well with the 1919 reforms and was fuelled by them.[64] However, the reforms created discontent amongst the incumbent ICS officers, many of whom took early retirement, thus creating more vacancies. The Simon Commission reported:

> Recruitment in Britain for the All-India Services was suspended during the War, and the tradition that India offered a career for young men had hardly begun to revive, when it was confronted by the outspoken discontent of the

services in India and the premature retirement of many officers... It is not surprising that the sources of recruitment in this country practically dried up.[65]

In addition, it saved money: 'Retrenchment [cost-cutting] committees urged more rapid Indianization and the abolition of certain posts in a bid to balance the budget.'[66] In 1922, 17.6 per cent of the personnel in the Superior Services were Indian. By 1929 that had risen to 29 per cent; by 1939 to 49.5 per cent; and by 1946 to 54 per cent.[67] In the Superior Police Service, Indians constituted 10 per cent in 1924; 18.5 per cent in 1929; and 37 per cent in 1939.[68]

The ongoing campaign of the Congress to undermine British state institutions caused the ICS and the upper ranks of the police to suffer a decline in their authority and prestige.[69] The Simon Commission declared:

> The noncooperation movement of 1920–22 made the work of the head of the district and the police officials in some areas extraordinarily difficult. Nothing could be more depressing than the loss of the confidence of the common people...'[70]

Gupta notes the changes in attitude of parts of the bureaucracy in relation to the ebb and flow of the mass movements from this point onwards, particularly among its increasing numbers of Indian officers:

> While in periods of mass upheaval most of the Indian members of the services would play safe, in the more quiescent periods of political change (1922–29, 1932–39) their role can be shown to have been in support of liberal national points of view, whether it be over fiscal autonomy, reduction of the safeguards for British business interests, or Indianization of the officer cadre of the armed forces.[71]

The accession to power of the Congress Ministries in 1937 changed attitudes in the lower ranks of the bureaucracy while damaging the morale of the ICS. In his optimistic account of the Ministries (published in 1940), N.S. Venguswamy pointed out that the state officials 'knew that any delay or failure on the part of the Congress to go ahead with its constructive programme would be attributed to them, to their indifference or opposition.' He was confident that 'the Civil Services in India have adapted themselves to the new scheme of things and...they are functioning today as they ought to function.'[72] But the ICS found the situation difficult to accept. They now had to serve those they had tried to suppress.[73] According to the Governor of Bombay in 1938:

> ...the main difficulty lies in the accession to power of a party which has vilified and defied Government and Government officials for the previous twenty years and which now claims to be the only party in the State.[74]

At lower levels meanwhile, once Congress ministers were in office, 'There is considerable evidence to suggest a wavering of loyalties among the junior administrative staff... Many of them sympathized with the Congress to a considerable extent.'[75] Even after the resignation of the Congress Ministries in 1939 these attitudes remained. For junior officers—and even for some Indian members of the ICS—'playing safe' meant preparing for a probable return of Congress to power.[76] Sir Andrew Clow, Governor of Assam, suggested to the Viceroy in October 1942 that 'The conviction that while we may hold India for the war, we are going to leave it thereafter' had produced a tendency among officers even at higher levels to work 'with one eye on the Adviser or Governor who would act upon their notes and another on the future Ministers who might read them.'[77]

The outbreak of war in Europe and the disappearance of the Congress Ministries steadied the situation somewhat. As the Congress moved to an anti-war position, the state bureaucracy was given leave to implement firm measures against it and discipline within the services was tightened up. This, however, proved to be only temporary.[78] The Home Member maintained in 1939 'the trend of events [was]...undermining the morale of the services at breakneck speed.'[79]

Learning the lesson of the First World War and fearing further dilution of the European element, the Government of India refused leave to ICS officers to join the British forces. But the problem of recruitment remained. In 1942–3, 'no European candidate was available on account of the War.'[80] The question of ceasing European recruitment altogether arose. The Viceroy wrote to the Secretary of State in February 1942:

> One-sided recruitment will produce...an over-Indianised bloc in the Service which will not either now or on the future help much in maintaining its intended character... continued recruitment to the I.C.S [in Britain] is regarded as an indication of our intention of staying here indefinitely.[81]

In any case, as the war-time state expanded, it was forced to draw in increasing numbers of educated middle-class Indians—along with their ideas. According to Chaudhuri, in Calcutta in 1942 all the upper level Indian officials regarded themselves as indispensable and believed they would remain so under the Japanese. The lower ranks meanwhile seemed indifferent to the expected arrival of the Japanese. Writing on Burma, Prasad tells us:

> It was not to be expected that many of the lowest rank of public servants would remain steadfast. They were bound by no particular ties of patriotism and loyalty to the foreign government, and to them the coming of the Japanese meant nothing more than a change of masters.[82]

Hopes in the future of the superior services under the Japanese were dashed by the arrival of those retreating from Burma, Malaya and Singapore. The ICS was left to contemplate its fate under an occupying Japanese force.[83] In Chapter Four we noted the gloomy attitude of British officials in Bengal to the prospect of an invasion. In April, as we know, District Officers were instructed to remain in their positions and, if necessary, obey reasonable orders of the enemy commanders.[84] Before the instruction was modified, the ICS could only have interpreted it as either a death warrant or an invitation to collaborate. Neither of these interpretations was designed to improve the morale of the superior services. Congress Radio made great play of the instruction (of which it had obtained a copy) and broadcast it in full. The Radio declared:

> [Britain] wants the Indian Civil Service if needs be to serve Japanese masters... The command of the British to her officers to obey the Axis invaders shows the spirit of surrender that permeates Britain.

The order not to flee with indecent haste showed that the Government 'is very doubtful about the loyalty of its officers. The Government remembers the humiliation of Penang.'[85]

Before the Quit India campaign, there had been instances of collusion between junior Indian district officials and Congress activists.[86] During the campaign there was some support from Indian members of the ICS. Renuka Ray, a well-connected Congress activist, recalls that when collecting funds for the families of gaoled activists, 'government officials including many Indian members of the ICS and some members of the defence forces...gave us monthly donations towards this fund.' Furthermore, when the Congress leader, Aruna Asaf Ali, went underground, 'She mostly stayed at the houses of the Indian members of the ICS.'[87] But support from the ICS was not widespread. In order to encourage the loyal elements of the ICS to hold firm when the campaign began, the Viceroy raised with Amery 'the desirability of some guarantee of protection against victimisation in the interest of securing the fullest support for our present activities against Congress from the various services'—though he admitted that no such guarantee could really be given.[88]

At the lower levels, it was a somewhat different story. Congress Radio advised its listeners not to kill lower level government officials.

> Appeal to railwaymen, policemen and soldiers to cease work or at least not to do it well. Ask them to disown allegiance at least mentally to the usurper administration and to take the oath of allegiance to the free state of India that is soon to arise.[89]

Chandra argues that the behaviour of these officials underwent a 'qualitative change' at this time. 'Government officials, especially those at the lower levels of the police and administration, were generous in their assistance to the movement. They gave shelter, provided information and helped monetarily.'[90] According to a Deputy Inspector-General of Police in Patna, 'anti-British feeling is by no means confined to non-official elements but is particularly noticeable among Indian Officials.'[91] Subordinate officials lent typewriters, envelopes, and service stamps to the cause. They carried out internal sabotage in various Provincial Secretariats. Many teachers, doctors, station masters, revenue officers and even lower magistrates did not fully co-operate with British operations and helped the campaign where they could.[92] An Intelligence Report on Secretariat staff in New Delhi said that the movement had shaken their loyalty. Open and animated discussions were taking place about it. Support for the movement opened the way for complaints about treatment at work, excessive workload and restricted promotion. The report went on:

> The younger elements, those recruited for the duration of the war, are most affected by the recent Congress events. They are responsible for most of the discontent in the Secretariat and are believed to have contact with the outside agitators... This type of Government servant might commit sabotage from within should the situation deteriorate.[93]

It was no doubt a younger element who tipped off the Delhi Congress Committee about the arrest of the Congress leadership on August 9. As we know, the Congress leaders did not attempt to flee. However, the Committee was able to print posters protesting against the arrests and calling for a general strike which went up within thirty minutes of the deed.[94]

In the lower ranks of the Police Service a collapse in morale was particularly worrying for the authorities. Even General Slim admitted that 'the lot of the Indian policeman was a particularly unhappy one' in that he was being asked to repress those whom he suspected would soon return to power. Slim admitted that 'there were some mutinies in the police'.[95] *Harijan* declared that 'It is the duty of all Indian [police] officers to say to their superiors that they can no longer obey orders which compel them to arrest, sentence and imprison their own patriots'.[96] A Police Superintendent reported from Bihar:

> Wherein we have attempted to clear crowds by *lathi* charge, they [ordinary police] have done the minimum that is possible, and it is only the officers who have done all that is possible.[97]

The Governor of Bihar told the Viceroy a week later 'I have had very poor reports of the ordinary constabulary and in some places of the armed police: their hearts are not in the job.'[98] The unwillingness of sections of the police to repress the movement probably accounts for the drafting in of 55 battalions of soldiers to do it for them.[99] There were defections, resignations and desertions by the police as a result of Quit India in Bombay, United Provinces and Bihar.[100] In Bombay, Epstein claims that police morale was only just maintained by a pay increase, a pledge from the Viceroy that there would be no enquiry into excesses and heavy military backup. Even then, 'the civil administration barely succeeded in holding firm across the presidency.'[101] More seriously still, there were police strikes in Bihar, Jamshedpur and Karachi.[102] From Jamshedpur, Congress Radio reported the mass resignation of 600 police who were surrounded by British troops and threatened with death if they did not return to their posts. The death threat proved an empty one and the rebellious police were arrested instead.[103]

In 1944, the Viceroy, Field Marshal Wavell, wrote that the British element in the ICS 'might almost be described as moribund, the senior members are [so] tired and disheartened.'[104] A month later he raised 'the much wider problem of how we are to keep the I.C.S. and the Indian police going after the war' in view of retirements and junior British officials no longer finding their positions sufficiently financially attractive.[105] Wavell reported to the British Cabinet on 'the weakness and weariness of the instrument still at our disposal in the shape of the British element in the Indian Civil Service and the inability of that instrument to cope with the problems before it.'[106] Recruitment for India in Britain had dried up by 1943–4. Indian officers in the superior services (now in a dominant position) meanwhile were impatient for regime change, if not for nationalist motives then with an eye to the well-rewarded posts soon to be vacated by senior British retirees.[107] At the lower levels, it was recognised that those in the Provincial Services were strongly influenced by nationalist politics and consequently unreliable in their loyalty to the British Raj. This was a state bureaucracy that was no longer able to implement the colonial state's instructions, nor to defend it against its enemies.

Lack of British recruits, retirement of senior British officials, recruitment of Indians to the superior services and the effects of British defeat all undoubtedly contributed to the weakening of the colonial state machine. But surely the major cause was the necessity of recruiting masses of Indians at the lower levels and the effect on those masses of the Congress Ministries on the one hand, and the Quit India movement on the other. The Ministries and the Movement were integral parts of the counter-hegemonic strategy. They were made more effective by the support they received—and the support that grew—at the lower levels of the colonial state.

Notes

1. Moti Ram (ed.), *Two Historic Trials in Red Fort. An Authentic Account of the Trial by a General Court Martial of Captain Shah Nawaz Khan, Captain P.K. Sahgal and Lt. G.S. Dhillon and the Trial by A European Military Commission of Emperor Bahadur Shah* (New Delhi: Moti Ram, 1946[?]), 104–5, 113, 118.
2. https://roots.sg/Context/Places/history-sites/farrer-park.
3. Major Madum according to Shah Nawaz Khan (Ram, Two Historic Trials, 104).
4. Fujiwara Iwaichi, *F. Kikan: Japanese Army Intelligence Operations in Southeast Asia during World War II*, trans. Akashi Yoji (Hong Kong: Heinemann Asia: 1983), 183.
5. Fujiwara recalls: 'We were in agreement that our speeches to the 50,000 Indian officers and men were of extreme importance, and it was vital that we get hold of a good microphone. In order to record this historical scene, I requested photographers from the Army Propaganda Unit to attend.' (F. Kikan, 181 & 183.)
6. For the content of Fujiwara's speech, see F. Kikan, 181–2. It was translated into Hindustani by 'the most senior Indian officer in the British Army in Singapore, Colonel Gill', who agreed to the job 'without hesitation' (F. Kikan, 184).
7. Peter Ward Fay, *The Forgotten Army: India's Armed Struggle for Independence, 1942–1945* (Ann Arbor: University of Michigan Press, 1995), 76 & 81–84; Tarak Barkawi, 'Culture and Combat in the Colonies: The Indian Army in the Second World War,' *Journal of Contemporary History* 41 (2) April 2006: 339 & 343; Brian Farrell & Sandy Hunter (eds.), *Sixty Years On: The Fall of Singapore Revisited* (Singapore: Eastern Universities Press, 2002), 285.
8. The First INA however was destined only to last until December 1942. This was because of widening differences between the Indian military leaders and the Japanese. The Indian leadership (most prominently Mohan Singh) was just as keen to prevent Japanese tutelage as they were to defeat the British (Two Historic Trials, 114 & 118; Milan Hauner, *India in Axis Strategy: Germany, Japan and Indian Nationalists in the Second World War* (Stuttgart: Klett-Cotta, 1981), 595). They were pledged to gain Congress approval before any military action was taken and then only in the event of a revolutionary situation in India (Hugh Toye, 'The First Indian National Army, 1941–42,' *Journal Of Southeast Asian Studies* XV (2) September 1984: 374). Mohan Singh wanted to raise INA strength

to half a million but this was well beyond a figure that the Japanese would tolerate. Finally relations broke down over Japanese jurisdiction over Indian troops and Japan's commitment to Indian independence. Toye comments: '... when at the end of 1942 the Indian [National Army] leaders realised that they had been the victims of a Japanese confidence trick, they boldly faced their oppressors, disbanded their army, and ceased to cooperate' (Toye, First INA, 365). Having disbanded the First INA, they were either imprisoned or returned to POW camps (Toye, First INA, 377–379; Joyce C. Lebra, *Jungle Alliance: Japan and the Indian National Army* (Singapore: Asia Pacific Press Pte Ltd, 1971), 97; Hauner, India in Axis Strategy, 596–600). The INA's second coming would await the arrival of Subhas Chandra Bose in Japan in May 1943.

9   Yasmin Khan, *India at War: The Subcontinent and the Second World War* (Oxford: Oxford University Press, 2015), 121. See also Bayly & Harper: 'Quite suddenly the feeling of awe for the state ... which more than troops and police had sustained foreign rule, simply vanished' (Christopher Bayly & Tim Harper, *Forgotten Armies: Britain's Asian Empire and the War with Japan* (London: Penguin, 2005, 247).

10 Fortnightly Report Bombay 1st half March 1942 in Bipan Chandra and Salil Misra (eds.), *Towards Freedom: Documents on the Movement for Independence in India, 1942* (New Delhi: Oxford University Press, 2016)—henceforward Towards Freedom 1942–717.

11 'Each time the mass movement disturbed the earlier equilibrium to establish a new one it sapped the strength of the state to some extent, while the Congress organization and the mass movement correspondingly gained a sense of strength and power.' (Bhagwan Josh, *Struggle for Hegemony in India 1920–1947: The Colonial State, the Left and the National Movement. Volume II: 1934–41* (New Delhi: Sage Publications, 1992), 75.)

12 Kaushik Roy, 'Military Loyalty in the Colonial Context: A Case Study of the Indian Army during World War II,' *Journal of Military History* 73 April 2009: 509; Barkawi, Culture and Combat, 330–333. See also Sri Nandan Prasad, *Official History of the Indian Armed Forces in the Second World War, 1939–45: Volume 4, Expansion of the Armed Forces and Defence Organisation, 1939–45* (Calcutta: Orient Longmans, 1956), 183 & 187.

13 Indian Statutory Commission [Simons Commission], *Report of the Indian Statutory Commission: Volume I—Survey* (London: His Majesty's Stationery Office, 1930), 96–8. An accompanying map showing the numbers of Indians in the army by province in 1929 revealed that Bengal and Assam provided none. In the First World War, Punjab (population:

20 million) sent 249,000 to fight while Bengal (population: 45 million) sent 7000.

14 'India in 1929–1930' (Calcutta: Government of India, 1931) in Anirudh Deshpande, 'Hopes and Disillusionment: Recruitment, demobilisation and the emergence of discontent in the Indian armed forces after the Second World War,' *Indian Economic and Social History Review* XXXIII (2) 1996: 177.

15 Sanjoy Bhattacharya, 'British Military Information Management Techniques and the South Asian Soldier: Eastern India during the Second World War,' *Modern Asian Studies* XXXIV (2) April 2000: 496.

16 A survey of over a hundred ICOs early in the war revealed that a fifth of them 'had friends or family who were active in nationalist politics.' (Barkawi, Culture and Combat, 331.) See also Roy, Military Loyalty, 509; Bhattacharya, British Military Information, 490. Bayly & Harper add that mass recruitment in Britain also had its effect: 'many of the new British officer class in India had no natural allegiance to the Empire.' (Bayly, Armies, 73.)

17 Peter Elphick, *Singapore: The Pregnable Fortress—A Study in Deception, Discord and Desertion*. London: Hodder & Stoughton, 1995, 69. See also Sujeta Mahajan, 'British Policy, Nationalist Strategy and Popular National Upsurge, 1945–46,' in *Myth and Reality: The Struggle for Freedom in India, 1945–47* ed. Amit Kumar Gupta (New Delhi: Manohar, 1987), 61.

18 S. Woodburn Kirby et al, *The War against Japan, Volume II: India's Most Dangerous Hour* (London, HMSO 1958), 384. Gupta points out: 'The Royal Indian Navy and the Royal Indian Air Force were recruited on a wider basis and their loyalty to the Raj could not be relied upon if it came to a crisis.' (Partha Sarati Gupta, 'Imperial Strategy and the Transfer of Power, 1939–51,' in *Myth and Reality: The Struggle for Freedom in India, 1945–47* ed. Amit Kumar Gupta (New Delhi: Manohar, 1987), 6.)

19 Barkawi, Culture and Combat, 336–7.

20 See Gupta, Imperial Strategy, 6; Bhattacharya, British Military Information, 508.

21 There were three kinds of Indian officer: Indian Commissioned Officers (ICOs), trained in India at Dehra Dun; King's Commissioned Officers (KCOs), trained at Sandhurst in the UK; and Viceroy's Commissioned Officers, whose commissions were granted by the Viceroy.

22 Simon Commission I, 101.

23 Elphick, Singapore, 66.

24 Barkawi, Culture and Combat, 331–2 & 337; Bayly & Harper, Armies, 65–6; Roy, Military Loyalty, 509.

25 Cited in Barkawi, Culture and Combat, 344.
26 The Kirti Lehar were an anti-British group, founded in 1928, originating from the Ghadar movement (Bhupinder Singh, *The Anti-British Movements from Gadar Lehar to Kirti Kisan Lehar: 1913–1939.* PhD Thesis. Patiala: Faculty of Social Sciences, Punjabi University, 2011 (no page numbers).)
27 Elphick, Singapore, 68.
28 Roy, Military Loyalty, 507.
29 Lord Zetland to Linlithgow, 9 May 1940 in Elphick, Singapore, 67.
30 Toye, First INA, 371.
31 The IIL did not confine itself to work amongst Indian troops. In May 1941 it was involved in a strike of Tamil rubber estate workers in the Port Swettenham (now Klang) area (Elphick, Singapore, 66–70).
32 F. Kikan, 32, 40 & 45.
33 Elphick, Singapore, 71.
34 See for example the case of a Forward Bloc member who joined the army in Lucknow specifically 'to spread disaffection among the soldiers' (P.N. Chopra, *Quit India Movement: British Secret Report* (Faridabad: Thomson Press (India), 1976), 166). Also Hauner, India in Axis Strategy, 608.
35 Dashpande, British Military Policy, 150.
36 Bose broadcast on Azad Hind Radio, 20 July 1942 in George Orwell, *The War Commentaries* ed. W.J. West (Harmondsworth: Penguin, 1987), 228.
37 Indivar Kamtekar, 'The Shiver of 1942', *Studies in History* XVIII (1) 2002: 85.
38 Viceroy to Amery, 28 July 1942 in Nicholas Mansergh (ed.), *The Transfer of Power 1942–7. Volume 2: 'Quit India', 30 April–21 September 1942* (London: Her Majesty's Stationery Office, 1971)—henceforward Transfer of Power II—489.
39 Chopra, British Secret Report, 177.
40 Barkawi, Culture and Combat, 33.
41 See Viceroy to Amery, 1 September 1942, Transfer of Power II 873; Bayly & Harper, Armies, 248–9.
42 Congress Radio broadcast, 26 October 1942 in Gautam Chatterjee, 'Quit India Movement and "illegal" Congress Radio', *Mainstream* 12 August 1989: 17.
43 Congress Radio broadcast, 27 October 1942 in Chatterjee, Illegal Radio, 17.
44 Congress Radio (Parts 1–4) (http://www.gandhimedia.org/cgi-bin/gm/gm.cgi?action=view&link=Audio/Radio_Programs/English&image=AURPEN0010.mp3&img=0&search=congress%20

radio&cat=all&tt=mp3&bool=and) Part IV.
45 Congress Radio Part IV. It is interesting to note that those leading the Quit India movement believed that the army would be amongst the last of the British institutions to collapse, in contrast to Bose and the INA whose strategy depended on it being the first.
46 Intelligence Report, United Provinces, 26 April 1943 in Chopra, British Secret Report, 305–6.
47 By the end of the war, says Potter, 'it became clear that the undivided loyalty of the Indian armed forces could no longer be relied upon.' (David C. Potter, 'Manpower Shortage and the End of Colonialism: The Case of the Indian Civil Service,' *Modern Asian Studies* 7 (1) 1973: 68.)
48 Bipan Chandra, *The Writings of Bipan Chandra: The Making of Modern India from Marx to Gandhi* (Hyderabad: Orient Black Swan, 2012), 30.
49 MK Gandhi, 'My Meaning of Office Acceptance,' *Harijan* 4 September 1939 in Mohandas K. Gandhi. *The Collected Works of Mahatma Gandhi*. Chief Editor: Shri R.P. Dhasmana. Delhi: Publications Division, Ministry of Information and Broadcasting, 1958–1994 –henceforward Gandhi, Collected Works)—Volume 72, 190.
50 Ewing refers to this control as constituting 'a vital lever in the exercise of executive authority.' (Ann Ewing, 'The Indian Civil Service 1919–1924: Service Discontent and the Response in London and Delhi.' *Modern Asian Studies* 18 (1) 1984: 47.)
51 On the title 'District Officer' see David C. Potter, 'The Last of the Indian Civil Service,' *South Asia—Journal of South Asian Studies* II (1–2) 1979: footnote 6, 27.
52 Ann Ewing, 'Administering India: The Indian Civil Service,' *History Today* XXXII (6), June 1982: 43.
53 Hubert Evans, *Looking Back on India* (London: Frank Cass, 1988), 194.
54 Clive Dewey, *Anglo-Indian Attitudes: The Mind of the Indian Civil Service* (London: Hambledon Press, 1993), 5.
55 Simon I, 268.
56 Ewing, Administering India, 43; Arudra Burra, 'The Indian Civil Service and the nationalist movement: neutrality, politics and continuity,' *Commonwealth and Comparative Politics* 48 (4) November 2010: 407.
57 Thus, for example, in the Police Services before the First World War those in the Superior Service (part of the All-India Services), at the rank of Assistant Superintendent and above were recruited in Britain and were all Europeans. Those in the Provincial Services (constables, sergeants, Inspectors and Deputy Superintendents) were recruited in India and were by and large Indian. (Percival Griffiths, *To Guard My*

People: The History of the Indian Police (London: Ernest Benn Limited, 1971), 173 & 176.)
58 Simon I, 272. In the judiciary, 'It is clear,' said the Commission, 'that the subordinate judiciary in every province is almost wholly Indian ... they are frequently selected from the clerical staff of the District Officer.'
59 Simon I, 272.
60 Ewing, The ICS, 37.
61 Simon I, 290.
62 Ewing, The ICS, 35.
63 Ewing, The ICS, 37 & 44.
64 Ewing, Administering India, 45.
65 Simon I, 267.
66 Ewing, The ICS, 44. See also Simon Epstein, 'District Officers in Decline: The Erosion of British Authority in the Bombay Countryside, 1919 to 1947,' *Modern Asian Studies* XVI (3) 1982: 509.
67 Simon I, 270; B.B. Misra, *The Bureaucracy in India: An Historical Analysis of Development up to 1947* (Delhi: Oxford University Press, 1977), 291; Robin J. Moore, *Escape from Empire: The Attlee Government and the Indian Problem* (Oxford: Clarendon Press, 1983), 22–3. Figures for other years can be found in Potter, Manpower, 63; Hauner, India in Axis Strategy, 108. Potter points out that Indians wanting to enter the ICS not only had to pass the exam but also to obtain a character reference from their local District Officer: 'much weeding out took place at this stage.' (David C. Potter, 'The Last of the Indian Civil Service,' *South Asia—Journal of South Asian Studies* II (1–2) 1979: 22.)
68 Simon I, 270, Griffiths, To Guard, 190.
69 See Sujeta Mahajan, 'British Policy, Nationalist Strategy and Popular National Upsurge, 1945–46,' in *Myth and Reality: The Struggle for Freedom in India, 1945–47* ed. Amit Kumar Gupta (New Delhi: Manohar, 1987), 59.
70 Simon I, 266. Ewing adds: 'Clearly then, the I.C.S. was in a sorry state in the early 1920s.' (Ewing, The ICS, 42.)
71 Partha Sarati Gupta, 'Imperial Strategy and the Transfer of Power, 1939–51,' in *Myth and Reality: The Struggle for Freedom in India, 1945–47* ed. Amit Kumar Gupta (New Delhi: Manohar, 1987), 4.
72 N.S. Venguswamy, *Congress in Office* (Bombay: Bharat Publishing Co., 1940), 74 & 78.
73 See Mahajan, British Policy, 60; Burra, ICS and nationalist movement, 410.
74 Cited in Epstein, DOs in Decline, 495.
75 Chandan Mitra, 'Popular Uprising in 1942: The Case of Ballia,' in *The*

Indian Nation in 1942, ed. Gyanendra Pandey(Calcutta: K.P. Bagchi & Company, 1988), 178.

76 See Ewing, Administering India, 47; Mahajan, British Policy, 60; Epstein, DOs in Decline, 509. A British report from a north Bombay district said: '... their present attitude is one of discounting the present for the future, their view being that Congress is bound to return to power.' (Cited in Epstein, DOs in Decline, 512.)

77 Clow to Viceroy 7 October 1942 in Nicholas Mansergh (ed.), *The Transfer of Power 1942-7. Volume 3: Reassertion of Authority, 21 September 1942-12 June 1943* (London: Her Majesty's Stationery Office, 1971—henceforward Transfer of Power III—112.

78 Mahajan, British Policy, 60; Epstein, DOs in Decline, 510.

79 Cited in Epstein, DOs in Decline, 509–510.

80 B.B. Misra, *The Bureaucracy in India: An Historical Analysis of Development up to 1947* (Delhi: Oxford University Press, 1977), 295.

81 Viceroy to Secretary of State 21 February 1942, in Nicholas Mansergh (ed.), *The Transfer of Power 1942-7. Volume 1: The Cripps Mission, January-April 1942* (London: Her Majesty's Stationery Office, 1970)—henceforward Transfer of Power I—216.

82 Bisheshwar Prasad, *Official History of the Indian Armed Forces in the Second World War, 1939-45: Volume Two, The Retreat from Burma, 1941-42* (Calcutta: Orient Longmans, 1959), 382.

83 See Janam Mukherjee, *Hungry Bengal: War, Famine, Riots and the End of Empire* (Noida (India): Harper Collins, 2015), 88.

84 British Library: India Office Records. Home Department War Histories, 33. Mss Eur F161/151/9:1940s.

85 Congress Radio (Parts 1–4). (http://www.gandhimedia.org/cgi-bin/gm/gm.cgi?action=view&link=Audio/Radio_Programs/English&image=AURPEN0010.mp3&img=0&search=congress%20radio&cat=all&tt=mp3&bool=and) Part III.

86 Sanjoy Bhattacharya, 'An Official Policy that went awry: The WW II propaganda campaign against the Indian National Congress,' *International Institute of Asian Studies Newsletter* 13 Summer 1997: www.iias.nl.

87 Renuka Ray, *My Reminiscences: Social Development During the Gandhian Era and After* (New Delhi: Allied, 1982), 89–90.

88 Viceroy to Amery 1 September 1942 in Transfer of Power II, 870.

89 Congress Radio (Parts 1–4). (http://www.gandhimedia.org/cgi-bin/gm/gm.cgi?action=view&link=Audio/Radio_Programs/English&image=AURPEN0010.mp3&img=0&search=congress%20

radio&cat=all&tt=mp3&bool=and) Part IV.
90 Chandra, Writings, 31; Bipan Chandra et al, *India's Struggle for Independence, 1857–1947* (New Delhi: Penguin, 1989), 467. See also Mitra, Ballia, 178.
91 Report by Deputy Inspector-General of Police (CID), Patna 28 December 1942 in Chopra, British Secret Report, 279.
92 Arun Chandra Bhuyan, *The Quit India Movement: The Second World War and Indian Nationalism* (New Delhi: Manas Publications, 1975), 186–7.
93 Intelligence Report, 5 September 1942 in Chopra, British Secret Report, 144.
94 British officials in Delhi concluded that the Congress had a *very* speedy printing press (Francis G. Hutchins, *Spontaneous Revolution: The Quit India Movement* (Delhi: Manohar Book Service, 1971), 270.
95 William Slim, *Defeat into Victory* (London: Cassell and Company Ltd., 1956), 138.
96 *Harijan* also pointed out to the police: 'If you do not resist this occupant of India, you will not find the necessary courage to resist the Japanese.' (*Harijan* IX (31), 16 August 1942.)
97 Police Superintendent, Chapra district, 15 August 1942 in Bhuyan, Quit India Movement, 188.
98 Sir Thomas Stewart to Viceroy, 22 August 1942 in Transfer of Power II, 790.
99 Roy, Military Loyalty, 508.
100 Bhuyan, Quit India Movement, 187–8.
101 Epstein, DOs in Decline, 512–513.
102 Hutchins, Spontaneous Revolution, 277; Bhuyan, Quit India Movement, 187–8.
103 Congress Radio (Parts 1–4). (http://www.gandhimedia.org/cgi-bin/gm/gm.cgi?action=view&link=Audio/Radio_Programs/English&image=AURPEN0010.mp3&img=0&search=congress%20radio&cat=all&tt=mp3&bool=and) Part I.
104 Wavell to Amery, 24 October 1944 in Nicholas Mansergh (ed.), *The Transfer of Power 1942–7. Volume 5: The Simla Conference, 1 September 1944–28 July 1945* (London: Her Majesty's Stationery Office, 1974), 131.
105 Wavell to Amery 23 November 1944 in Transfer of Power V, 229.
106 Described by Amery in a report to Sir Alan Lascelles (Private Secretary to the King), 29 September 1945 in Transfer of Power V, 784.
107 Potter, Manpower, 68; Potter, The Last, 24.

Conclusion

HOWRAH BRIDGE

> He now walked along, taking lengthy brisk strides which resounded triumphantly on the platform. He had won the day. The bridge was ready. There was nothing fancy about it, but it was a sufficiently 'finished' job to advertise the qualities of the Western world in large letters across this Siamese sky.
>
> —Pierre Boulle, The Bridge on the River Kwai.

A bridge dominates the Calcutta skyline today, as it has done since it was built in 1942. In that year, its British makers and perhaps the British in general regarded the Howrah Bridge in the same way as Boulle's Colonel Nicholson regarded his foredoomed project over the River Kwai: a positive example of British know how and expertise—a symbol of which to be proud.[1] The bridge spanned the Hooghly River, connected Calcutta with Howrah and the Howrah Railway Station (completed in 1911) and carried vital railway lines to the north. It replaced a bridge supported by boats, built in 1874, which was regarded at the time as a similar miracle of technology.[2] The Howrah Bridge Act was passed in 1926, opening up the contract for a new bridge to global tender. A German company won the right to construct the bridge in the early 1930s—but this mistake was rectified in 1935 when they lost it. The job was given to the British Braithwaite, Burn & Jessop Construction Company and work began in 1937.[3] The outbreak of war not only increased the urgency of the project for military purposes, it also forced the builders to rely on Indian steel rather than British imports. Twenty-six thousand and five hundred tons of steel were needed for the construction, and each one of them was planned to be brought from Britain. The war made this impossible and in the end 23,500 tons were produced by Tata Steel—a boost for the Indian steel industry. The bridge's military importance gave it a high priority and it was completed on time in four years.[4]

On completion, the bridge was (and remains) 705 metres long and 31 metres wide, with 80 metres high towers. It cost £2,463,887 and it was the last major infrastructural project of the British Raj in India. It did not appear at the time as the work of a power preparing to leave—or of one about to abandon crucial military assets. While the bridge was completed in 1942, it was not opened until February 1943. For a project so huge, so dominating and so important, one might have expected the opening to be marked by a grand occasion, perhaps with the Viceroy and the whole panoply of British rule in attendance. But there was no opening ceremony. On the morning of Wednesday, February 3, 1943, a solitary Calcutta tram trundled along the length of the bridge. And then it was open.

It is said that the opening of the bridge was accompanied by so little ceremony due to fear of a Japanese bombing raid. Perhaps that was the case. It is true, as we know, that Calcutta had been bombed in December and in mid-January. Yet Calcutta had suffered no daylight bombing raids up to this point (and would not until December 1943). And if we cast our minds back to the first months of the war with Japan—a time when invasion was regarded as a real possibility—we will recall the British determination to preserve the outward trappings of imperial style more or less as normal.[5] Why then was the opening of the Howrah Bridge such a parsimonious affair?

The British colonial state in India received a number of blows in the early twentieth century, which in this account I have identified with the counter-hegemonic strategy of the Indian National Congress. The mass movements of the 1920s and 1930s, Congress participation in the Provincial Ministries and the constructive programme in the villages all contributed to the undermining of the state administration, rather than attempting its forcible overthrow. The British response was often repression, but also steps in constitutional reform designed to ease the pressure of the national movement on their embattled state. This course of action brought little relief, for, as Epstein puts it, 'each successive retreat from local or provincial power on the part of the British administration in the quest for new forms of collaboration only served to strengthen the potential hand of the very forces in Indian society which sought its ultimate removal.'[6] As the British—officially or unofficially, consciously or unconsciously—moved out of an area of power, the Congress moved in and proceeded to expand the power, significance and prestige of that area to maximum advantage.

This complex dance may have continued had it not been subject to the violent disruption of Japan's entry into the war. At that point, constitutional issues (for the British) and national freedom (for the Indians) appeared to be swept aside by the imminent danger of the Japanese armed forces. But this was a temporary illusion. On both sides, a possible invasion had to be factored into strategy. Despite this, neither side was prepared to take its eye off the main issue: the freedom of India for Congress, the preservation of Empire for Britain. The Congress, however, was able to evolve a strategy that resisted both the British and the Japanese and defended India—while, through that, building a counter-hegemony on which to establish a new state. The British could only fight for the *status quo*. While Congress stood a chance of mobilizing Indians in the Quit India campaign, the British failed miserably at mobilizing them for their war.

The Quit India campaign, as we know, failed in its immediate objective. But its shadow was long. The Viceroy had written warily to the Secretary of State in September 1942 when it was assumed that the movement was declining:

> ... I would like once again to sound a note of warning against any undue optimism. This business has gone very deep throughout the country, and a good many classes or types have been stirred up which will not too easily settle back to normal.[7]

Sujeta Mahajan describes the position of the colonial state in the aftermath of Quit India as one of 'eroded hegemony'. As a result of the campaign, writes Johannes H. Voigt, 'Britain came to sense fully the basic weakness of the Raj,' while K.K. Chaudhari contends that Indians remained in a state of 'stolid bitterness and restive belligerence against the British.'[8] In some respects, the British were giving way to despair. The new Governor of Bengal (from January 1944), Richard Casey—admittedly under the devastating blows of the Bengal Famine—declared in March 1945, 'the Empire has cause for shame in the fact that, in Bengal at least, after a century and a half of British rule, we can point to no achievement worth the name in any direction.'[9]

This clearly had little in common with the brave talk of 'keeping up appearances' of 1942. After Quit India and the lessening of an immediate threat of invasion, many of the more perceptive British administrators must have realised that the game was up—or, at least, that the nature of the game was changing substantially. Mention has been made in Chapter Four of the relative decline in the commercial aspects of Britain's relationship with India, compared with her strategic ones. India as a profit-making concern was on the wane. The British state could not sustain an unequal economic relationship. On the other hand, Britain's rulers were not prepared to see Britain as anything less than a Great Power in the post-war world—and, for that, her strategic interests (military bases, defence treaties, recruits) were vital.

Britain's new status, stripped back to the bare bones of military power, meant that the hegemony the Empire had used to justify, legitimize and continue its direct rule became less important. Maintaining military assets did not necessarily mean holding the hearts and minds of the Indian people, nor did it mean impressing them with regular demonstrations of military pomp and circumstance.

Back at the Howrah Bridge, the rails were now more important than the rituals. Towards the end of Boulle's book, the bridge, built with British labour at the behest of the Japanese, is ready at the River Kwai. But it would never be the triumphant symbol that Colonel Nicholson envisaged, nor would it be put to the purposes he foresaw. Similarly, in Calcutta, the Howrah Bridge had been built with Indian labour—not forgetting the Indian steel—for the purposes of the British. But in fairly short order it would be taken from them and used for Indian purposes. British colonial hegemony would not survive, nor would it be transformed into a powerful military relationship. The counter-hegemony of the Indian people, built up by the Congress, would not allow it.

Notes

1   Its builder declared: 'With the completion of this bridge, India came of age in bridge construction and bridge building.' (Braithwaite Burn & Jessop Construction Company, 'Rabindra Setu / Howrah Bridge—Kolkata, West Bengal.' www.bbjconst.com/featured-howrah-bridge.html).
2   Ghosh tells us that in 1874: 'The resulting bridge of floating pontoons amazed Calcutta's residents. Songs, dramas and poems celebrating the "miracle" and congratulating the British for achieving it, were published the same year.' (Anindita Ghosh, 'Singing in a New World: Street Songs and Urban Experience in Colonial Calcutta,' *History Workshop Journal*.

76 (1), Autumn 2013: 128.)
3   For the history of the bridge, see Braithwaite Burn and Jessop.
4   Geoffrey Moorhouse, *Calcutta* (Harmondsworth: Penguin Books, 1984), 273.
5   See, for example the Viceroy's remarks on keeping up appearances and the insistence on events such as the Calcutta races in Chapter One.
6   Simon Epstein, 'District Officers in Decline: The Erosion of British Authority in the Bombay Countryside, 1919 to 1947', *Modern Asian Studies* XVI (3) 1982: 494.
7   Viceroy to Amery 1 September 1942 in Nicholas Mansergh (ed.). *The Transfer of Power 1942–7. Volume 2: 'Quit India', 30 April–21 September 1942* (London: Her Majesty's Stationery Office, 1971), 868–9.
8   Sujeta Mahajan, 'British Policy, Nationalist Strategy and Popular National Upsurge, 1945–46', in *Myth and Reality: The Struggle for Freedom in India, 1945–47* ed. Amit Kumar Gupta (New Delhi: Manohar, 1987), 62; Johannes H. Voigt, 'Co-operation or Confrontation? War and Congress Politics 1939–42' in *Congress and the Raj: Facets of the Indian Struggle 1917–47*, ed. D.A. Low (London: Heinemann, 1977), 368; K.K. Chaudhari, *Quit India Revolution: The Ethos of its Central Direction* (Mumbai: Popular Prakashan Pvt. Ltd., 1996), 184.
9   He singled out for criticism 'the pitiful inadequacy of the administration of the province.' Nicholas Mansergh (ed.), *The Transfer of Power 1942–7. Volume 5: The Simla Conference, 1 September 1944–28 July 1945* (London: Her Majesty's Stationery Office, 1974), 638.

FURTHER READING

Christopher Bayly & Tim Harper. *Forgotten Armies: Britain's Asian Empire and the War with Japan*. London: Penguin, 2005
Arun Chandra Bhuyan. *The Quit India Movement: The Second World War and Indian Nationalism*. New Delhi: Manas Publications, 1975.
Bipan Chandra. *The Writings of Bipan Chandra: The Making of Modern India from Marx to Gandhi*. Hyderabad: Orient Black Swan, 2012.
Bipan Chandra and Salil Misra (eds.). *Towards Freedom: Documents on the Movement for Independence in India, 1942*. New Delhi: Oxford University Press, 2016.
M.N. Das. *A Centenary History of the Indian National Congress. Volume Three: 1935-1947*. New Delhi: All-India Congress Committee (I), 1985.
Eugenie Fraser. *A Home by the Hooghly: A Jute Wallah's Wife*. Edinburgh: Mainstream Publishing Company, 1989.
Amit Kumar Gupta (ed.). *Myth and Reality: The Struggle for Freedom in India, 1945-47*. New Delhi: Manohar, 1987.
Francis G. Hutchins. *Spontaneous Revolution: The Quit India Movement*. Delhi: Manohar Book Service, 1971.
Fujiwara Iwaichi. *F. Kikan: Japanese Army Intelligence Operations in Southeast Asia during World War II*. Translated by Akashi Yoji. Hong Kong: Heinemann Asia: 1983
Milan Hauner. *India in Axis Strategy: Germany, Japan and Indian Nationalists in the Second World War*. Stuttgart: Klett-Cotta, 1981.
Bhagwan Josh. *Struggle for Hegemony in India 1920-1947: The Colonial State, the Left and the National Movement. Volume II: 1934-41*. New Delhi: Sage Publications, 1992.
Shashi Joshi. *Struggle for Hegemony in India 1920-1947: The Colonial State, the Left and the National Movement. Volume I: 1920-34*. New Delhi: Sage Publications, 1992.
Indivar Kamtekar. 'The Shiver of 1942.' *Studies in History* XVIII (1) 2002: 82-102.
Yasmin Khan. *India at War: The Subcontinent and the Second World War*. Oxford: Oxford University Press, 2015.
Joyce C. Lebra. *Jungle Alliance: Japan and the Indian National Army*. Singapore: Asia Pacific Press Pte Ltd, 1971.

Wm. Roger Louis. *In the Name of God, Go! Leo Amery and the British Empire in the Age of Churchill*. New York: W.W. Norton & Company, 1992.

Nicholas Mansergh (ed.). *The Transfer of Power 1942-7. Volume 2: 'Quit India', 30 April-21 September 1942*. London: Her Majesty's Stationery Office, 1971.

Nicholas Mansergh (ed.). *The Transfer of Power 1942-7. Volume 3: Reassertion of Authority, 21 September 1942-12 June 1943*. London: Her Majesty's Stationery Office, 1971.

Philip Mason. *A Shaft of Sunlight: Memories of a Varied Life*. London: Andre Deutsch, 1978.

B.B. Misra. *The Bureaucracy in India: An Historical Analysis of Development up to 1947*. Delhi: Oxford University Press, 1977.

Mridula Mukherjee. *Peasants in India's Non-Violent Revolution: Practice and Theory*. New Delhi: Sage Publications, 2004.

Robert Howard Niblett. *The Congress Rebellion in Azamgarh, August & September 1942*. Allahabad: Government of Uttar Pradesh, 1957.

Gyanendra Pandey (ed.). *The Indian Nation in 1942*. Calcutta: K.P. Bagchi & Company, 1988.

Satish Chandra Samanta, Syamadas Bhattacharyya, Ananga Mohan Das & Prahlad Kumar Pramanik. *August Revolution and Two Years' National Government in Midnapore*. Calcutta: Orient Book Company, 1946.

Tanika Sarkar and Sekhar Bandyopadhyay (eds.). *Calcutta: The Stormy Decades*. New Delhi: Social Science Press, 2015.

Roger Simon. *Gramsci's Political Though: An Introduction*. London: Lawrence & Wishart, 2015.

INDEX

Agrarian disputes, 47
Air raids, 5–6, 8–9, 18, 66, 71, 98, 174–75
All India Radio (AIR), 14, 222–29, 232, 234, 239, 241–42, 248
  advent of, 224
  Christmas day special Empire programme, 226
  creating a non-political picture, 225
  extended Transmission hours, 226
  Indian Listener (magazine), 222
  mass broadcasting, idea of, 228
  neutral summing up, 227
  place for political debate, 226
  resistance within, 228
  staff attitude towards war, 228
  'Talks' on various subjects, 226
  under state management, 224
  under the Regulation for the Control of Broadcasting, 227
  war coverage, 228
Allahabad Congress Working Committee, 243
Allies' Asian front, 2
All-India Congress Committee News Bulletin, 93
All-India Congress Committee, 66, 93, 123, 125–26, 129, 132, 141, 145, 147–48, 157, 159, 164, 168, 189–91, 197, 202–3, 207
  twelve-point programme, 197
All-India Satya Council, 208
Amar Kutir, 162–63, 196

Amery, Leo, 6
Amrita Bazar Patrika, 1, 3, 5, 9, 11–13, 15–17, 68, 102–3, 148, 166, 170, 176, 187
Anand, Mulk Raj, 59, 134
Anglo-American forces, 64
Annihilation, strategy of, 30–31
Anti-British feeling, 94, 100, 146, 211, 248, 277
Anti-war propaganda, 93
Anti-zamindar violence, 192
Anushilan Samiti, 92–93
Armed forces, 38, 85, 95, 134, 144, 212, 243, 262–69, 273, 291
  British anxiety, 269
  homesickness, 267
  military discontent, 265
  racial discrimination, 264
  refusal of Sikh troops, 265
  steadfastness of the Indian army, 264
Air Raid Precaution (ARP) groups, 3, 10, 16, 163, 166–68, 172–73, 175, 177, 227
'Artillery attack', 32
Attrition strategy, 30–31
Auchinleck, General, 265
'August Offer' of 1940, 129
Authoritarian regime, 86
Axis broadcasts, 238–46
  'Shanghai calling', 239
  public performances of, 246
Axis propaganda, 88

'Azad Government', 198
Azad Hind Radio, 65, 223, 234–36, 242, 244–45, 248
  broadcast, 244
Azad, Abul Kalam, 105, 126, 131, 145, 166

Barkway, Michael, 230
Bayly, Christopher, 209
BBC, 226, 229–34, 245–46, 248
  'anti-Fascist propaganda', 230, 232
  Eastern service of, 232
  'Hindustani service' of, 231
  medium for British propaganda, 229
  radio strategy, 233
  service's effectiveness, 232
  staff complaints, 231
  truthfulness, 234
Bengal Chamber of Commerce, 8
Bengal Conference of Commissioners, 110
Bengal Congress Committee, 132, 164
Bengal famine, 104, 231, 292
Bengal Government Labour Commissioner, 4
Bengal Home Guards, 175
Bengal Volunteers Group, 92
Berry, Lampton, 106, 145
Bhagiri Sena Sibir, 205
Biswanath Das, 45
'Black Hole', victims of, 65
Bokhari, A.S., 228
Bokhari, Z.A., 232
Bose, Rash Behari, 266
Bose, Subhas Chandra, 61, 64, 125, 223, 230, 235, 239, 242, 245–46, 267
Boulle, Pierre, 289
Boy Scouts, 192
Brander, Laurence, 233
British
  ability of, 85, 261
  air raid, 86
  anti-British feeling, 94, 100, 146, 211, 248, 277
  defensive, 85

denial plans, 102
denial policy, 104–5
dispossession of tenements, 105
economic dislocation, 103
evacuation plan European population, 108
fight, 86-96
flight, 96-110
monopoly on salt, 42
non-consensual war, 85
scorched earth policy, 104-5
stories of misbehaviour, 194
transportation of rice, 105
British hegemony, 20, 84–86, 234, 247, 249
  defence of, 85
  feature of, 84
British War Cabinet, 133–34
Buchanan, W.J., 90
'Burma for the Burmese', propaganda about, 97
Burma Indian Association, 164

Calcutta Racecourse, 86
Capitalist societies, 32
Casey, Richard, 292
Censorship, 46, 70
Chandra, Bipan, 35, 269
Chaplin, 2
Chaudhari, K.K., 292
Chaudhury, Nirad, 228
Chiang Kai-shek, 144
Chittagong, 6, 68, 90, 102, 106–8, 164–65, 237
  air raids, 6, 9
  bombing of, 237, 242
  Burma refugees, 164
  evacuation of, 106–8, 165
  watcher patrols, 90
Chowdhuri, Sachi Mohan, 164
Churchill, Winston, 43, 89, 100, 112, 133, 193, 195
Citizens' Defence Committee, 172
Civic Guards, 163, 167, 175–76
'Civil Defence Committee', 167, 172
Civil Defence Corps, 167
Civil disobedience movement, 40–41, 43, 49–50, 124, 130–31, 190, 225

Civil disorder, fear of, 7
Civil Protection Committee, 166
Class and race discrimination, 99
Clow, Sir Andrew, 274
Coal coolies, 4
Colonial bureaucracy, 41, 270–71
Colonial hegemony, 148, 171, 247, 293
Colonial state, 29, 35–39, 50, 85, 111, 176, 209, 247, 260–61, 269, 279–80, 291–92
Colonialism, 37, 39, 112, 147
Common sense, 246-49
Communal harmony, 159, 175
Communal strife, 95
Communist International, 31–32
Congress
  British concessions for, 129
  Calcutta meeting (1928), 125
  constructive Programme, 124
  counter-hegemonic strategy, 20, 38, 43, 46, 48, 50, 123, 157, 291
  Cripps proposals, rejection of, 134-35
  Delhi meeting (1942), 126-27
  differences within the leadership, 124
  and hegemony, 39–43
  Independence Day pledge, 159
  Lucknow meeting (1936), 125
  Madras session, 125
  panchayat, 47
  political concessions, 134
  Provincial Ministries, 123, 291
  Quit India resolution, 145–46, 148
  salaries of ministers, 46
  strategy towards Britain, 124
  Wardha meeting (1942), 126, 128, 147
Congress Radio, 138, 194–95, 196, 202, 210, 223, 234–38, 249, 268–69, 276–77, 279
  advised its listeners, 277
  British investigation, 237
  finance sources, 235
  first broadcast, 235
  focus on armed forces, 268
  Gandhi's appeal to Indian soldiers, 237
  reports during the Quit India movement, 237–38
  songs and speeches by national leaders, 236
  working station (Bombay), 235
Congress Socialist Party (CSP), 234
Congress Working Committee (CWC), 105, 123, 126–29, 131, 134–35, 141–48, 159, 163, 189
Constitutional reform, 44, 291
Co-Prosperity Sphere, 59, 61, 248, 261
Counter-hegemony, 29–50, 135, 261, 291, 293
  extension of, 44
  extra element, 34
  Gramasci's argument, 34
  mass-based attempts, 50
  ruling class, 31
  See also Hegemony
Coupland, Reginald, 46
Cox's Bazaar, raids, 9
Criminal and civil court, 199
Cripps Mission, 91, 131, 133–35, 141, 143, 18
  failure of, 141, 143, 158
Cripps, Stafford, 47, 58, 89, 100, 133, 135, 227
Cunningham, George, 228

Darling, Malcolm, 231–32
Dash, A.J., 193
Debchaudhury, Sudata, 5
Defeatism, 88, 95, 141, 245
Deo, Shankar Rao, 160
Desai, Mahadev, 138
Desai, Morarji, 45
District War Committees, 176
Dock workers, 9–10
'Doolittle Raid', 59
'Dummy Aeroplanes', 93
Dutt, Asok Kumar, 208

Elwin, Verrier, 226
'Eroded hegemony, 292
European preponderance, pattern of, 271
European war, 65, 67, 71, 126, 128

Evacuation, large-scale, 6

Farmers' boycott, 191
Fascism, 125, 227
Fascism, victory of, 31
Federation of Indian Chambers of Commerce and Industry, 164, 192
Femia, Joseph V., 30
Fielden, Lionel, 225–26, 228, 232
The Fifth Column as a Weapon in War, 88, 96
First World War, 31, 111, 272, 275
Fischer, Louis, 134
Forward Bloc, 65, 73, 204, 267
Fraser, Eugenie, 1, 12
'Free Hindusthan' radio, 245
Fujiwara, Major, 261, 266
Fumimaro, Konoe, 60

Gandhi ashrams, 42
Gandhi Seva Sangh, 49
Gandhi, M.K. 35, 39–43, 49, 100, 110, 123–24, 126, 130–31, 135–45, 147, 149, 161, 174, 188, 190, 206, 222, 234, 237, 269
  advice to soldiers, 269
  call for non-violent resistance, 139
  civil disobedience, 41
  critics of, 41
  -Irwin pact, 43
  moral sympathy for Britain's plight
  philosophical beliefs, 40
  programme of constructive work, 41
  salt campaign, 42–43
German Social Democracy, 29
Goldrush, 2
Gordon, A.D., 131
Gramsci, Antonio, 29–35, 84, 113, 157, 223, 246–47
Great East Asia Co-Prosperity Sphere, 60
Great East Asia war, 59
Greater East Asiatic Nations, 61
Grice, Jane, 69
Guerrilla war, 90, 139, 207–9
Guha, Ranajit, 37

Halder, S.K., 69, 93
Harcourt, Max, 47
Hardiman, David, 209
Harijan, 39, 47, 138, 169, 222, 228, 234, 278
Hegemony
  of colonial state, 74, 96, 212, 244
  crisis of, 84, 113
  leadership and persuasion, 30
  struggle for, 31
Herbert, Lady Mary, 2, 13
Herbert, Sir John, 3
Hindu Mahasabha, 170
HMS *Prince of Wales* and HMS *Repulse*, 67
Home Guards, 134, 163, 175–76
Hong Kong, Japanese attack, 6
Hope, Arthur, 18
Hostility, 94, 96, 109, 125, 272
Howrah Bridge, 289–93
  British Braithwaite, 290
  Burn & Jessop Construction Company, 290
  military importance, 290
  urgency of project, 290
Howrah Bridge Act, 289
Hutchings, Robert, 98

Ibbotson, A.W., 172
Illustrated Record of the Greater East Asia War, 63
Imperial Conference, 60
Imperial Rule Assistance Political Association, 59-60
Imperial Tobacco Company, 1
Imperial troops, 70
Indian Broadcasting Company, 223–24
Indian Civil Service (ICS), 90, 231, 270, 276, 279
Indian Evacuees' Relief Committees, 164
Indian Independence Army, 59
Indian Independence League (IIL), 64, 266–67
The Indian Listener (magazine of All-India Radio), 222, 239
The Indian Nation, 68

Indian National Army (INA), 64, 244, 249, 259–61, 266, 269
Indian National Congress, 20, 29
Indian State Broadcasting Service, 224
Indian Tea Association, 108
Industrial establishments, raids on, 8
'Instructions for Civil Resisters', 189
Insurgency, paradigm of, 34
Intelligence Service, 6
Iqbal, Muhammad, 235

'Janarksha Bahinis', 170
Japan Broadcasting Corporation (Nippon Hoso Kyokai—NHK), 240
Japan
  bombing raids on Ceylon, 7
  fear of invasion, 12
  imperial vision, 60
  military success, 11, 60
  military triumph, 62
  Pearl Harbour attack, 11, 13
  scale and method of attack,, 72
  war economy, 62
  'strategic positions', 72
Jatiya Sarkar, 205–7
Jinnah, Muhammad Ali, 68
Joint Planning Staff (JPS), 70, 73
Joshi, Bhagwan, 158
Joshi, Shashi, 36–37, 39, 41

Kamtekar, Indivar, 267
Kaur, Rajkumari Amrit, 231
Kautsky, Karl, 29–30, 32–33
Khadi and other village industries, 40
Khadi, constructive programme of, 159
Khan, Aga, 13
Khan, Shah Nawaz, 259
Kripalani, J.B., 164

Labour attendance, 10
Labour shortages, 4
'Land Disposal Plan', 62
Laski, Harold, 133
Linlithgow, Lord, 6, 13, 69, 91, 93, 112, 195, 237
Lohia, Ram Manohar, 197
Lohia, Ram Mohan, 234–36. *See also*

Congress Radio
Lokamanya, 67
Lover, Her Cardboard, 2

Mahajan, Sujeta, 35, 292
Malaya, Japanese attacked, 6
Martial races, 263
Martyn, P.D., 86, 94, 110
Mashruwala, Kishorelal, 169
Mason, Philip, 69
Mass meetings, tolerance of, 37
Maxwell, Sir Reginald, 193
Mehta, Usha, 234–35
Methods of rule, 30, 132
Militarism, 125, 207
Military interests, 112
Mirabehn, 110, 141, 161, 174, 190
Montagu-Chelmsford reforms, 272
Mookerjee, Shyama Prasad, 12, 176
Municipal Volunteers Corps, 167
Muslim League, 68, 164, 167, 170, 172
Mutiny, 93, 243, 269

Naidu, Sarojini, 226
Narayan, Jayaprakash, 207–8
National Defence Council, 129
The National Herald, 17
National Volunteer Corps, 162
National War Front, 91–93, 110
Nazism, 125, 136, 227
Nehru, Jawahar Lal, 44–46, 48, 66, 91, 95, 106, 124–26, 128, 130, 134, 139–46, 158–61, 163, 171, 174, 226–27, 231, 244
'Nehruvian centre', 127
New Statesman, 232
News Chronicle, 138
Niblett, Robert H., 187, 196
Nipon Club, 14
Nippon Hoso Kyokai, 240
Noakhali, raids at , 9
Non-co-operation, 136, 139–41, 146, 162, 190, 273
'Non-martial races', 263
Non-violent approach, 139
Non-violent resistance, 139, 141, 195, 244

Noon, Feroz Khan, 267
Nyanya mandals, 200

Official evacuation measures, 16
Operation 21, 66
Opportunism, 48
Orr, J.W., 192
Orwell, George, 230, 232

'Pakistan', concessions to, 140
Pandey, Baldev, 199
Pardon My Sarong, 2
Patel, Vallabhbhai, 142
Pati, Biswamoy, 94, 200
Pattern bombing, 5-6
Patwardhan, Achyat, 234
Pearl Harbour, attack on, 11, 13
Peasant agitation, 47
People's Volunteer Brigade, 167–68, 170
Peoples Army, 163
Philippines, Japanese attacked, 6
Police, mass resignation of, 279
Political dictatorships, 30
Political prisoners, 46
Political reforms, 36
Prasad, Rajendra, 141–42
Prati Sarkar (parallel government), 200
'Pre-evacuation' measures, 16
Preferred policy of the Government of India, 13
Prince of Wales, 67
Princely States, 44
Printer, Nariman Abarbad, 234. *See also* Congress Radio
Prison Notebooks, 84, 246
Provincial government, 5, 16, 44–45, 47, 69, 110, 124, 246, 262, 270
'Psychological transformation', 37, 40
Puckle, Frederick, 88, 227, 230
The Punjab, 95

Quit India campaign
alternative governments, 197-203
Amar Kutir, 163
balance sheet, 209-12
in Bengal, 199
Bhagiri Sena Sibir (Sisters' Army Camp), 205
in Bihar, 199
in Bombay province, 200
British reaction, 171-77
commencement of, 157
design, 159
end of, 211-12
freedom brigade, 208
initial stages, 196
insurrectionism, 206-9
leadership of, 207
mass attacks, 196
mass demonstrations, 204
mass militancy, 196
Midnapore, 203-6
in Orissa, 200-1
parallel government, 202
Prati Sarkar (parallel government), 199–200, 207
progress in rural areas, 198
radical programmes, 203
relief work for cyclone victims, 205
Santi Sena [Peace Corps], 201
Tamluk War Council, 205
through Azad Hind Radio, 243
Vidyut Bahinis (Lightning Armies), 205
volunteers, 162-71
weak Muslim participation, 210
weaknesses, 210

Racial discrimination, 61, 99, 108, 132, 161, 264, 269
Racial divide, 99
Radio licences, suspension of, 226
Rajagopalachari, 126–27, 128, 134, 140–42, 144
Randhawa, Katyun, 4
Rangoon, 69, 97–99, 100, 108, 132, 240
air raids on, 98
Committee for Evacuation, 98
fall of, 16, 69
heavy air raids, 97
municipal services, 97
Rashtriya Yuvak Sangh, 137
Ray, Renuka, 276

Refugees, 4, 95, 101, 132, 164, 193
Rendall, R.A., 230
Repression, 36, 47, 84, 93, 130, 192–93, 198, 205–7, 211, 291
Right of conquest, 37
Rotary Club, 107
Roy, M.N., 68, 111
Royal Calcutta Turf Club, 86, 87

Sahgal, Prem, 259
Salt campaign, 42–43. *See also* Civil disobedience movement
Samanta, Satish Chandra, 201, 203
Sampurnanand, 144-45
Santi Sena, 201
Sanyal, Hiteshranjan, 197
Sarat (Bose's brother), 73
Satyagraha centres, 42
Satyagraha movement, 131, 203, 163
Scavengers' Union, 5
'Scorched earth' policy, 101
Searchlight, 68
Second World War, 47, 50, 123, 225
Sevagram, 130
Shanti sena, 160
Shen, Wang Pun, 59
Simon Commission, 263–64, 270–73
Singapore Turf Club, 260
Singapore, fall of, 68, 85
Singh, Gurubaksh, 259
Singh, Mohan, 259, 261
Singh, Pritam, 266
Sircar, Joydeep, 3
Slave mentality, 37
Slim, General William, 12, 69, 72, 195, 278
Smith, George, 16
Social Democratic proletariat, 32
Sovereignty and self-rule, declaration of, 42
Special Congress Worker for Burma refugees, 164
State bureaucracy, 269-80
The Statesman, 3, 7, 13, 67
Storry, Richard, 62
The Straits Times, 99
Strategic opportunism, 62
Student Defence Corps, 167

Sunday Standard, 232

Taylor, Robert, 2
Times of India, 223
Tojo, General Hideki, 58–59, 61, 63–64
Tokyo conference, 64
Tressell, Robert, 29
Trikandas, Purshottam, 234
Twynam, Sir Henry, 89

United Provinces, 7, 91, 100, 163, 170, 174, 191–92, 197, 199, 201, 203, 241, 245, 269, 278
Untouchability, removal of, 159
Uprising of 1857, 262

Venguswamy, N.S., 274
Vidyut Bahini, 205–6
Villager swaraj, 169
Voigt, Johannes H., 292
Voluntary organisations, 163, 173, 175–76

'Wait and see' approach, 145
War and Revolution, 111
War Cabinet, 112, 133–34, 148
War Committees, 175
War Council, 201, 205
War Front, 93, 95
War Fund, 67
'War of attrition', 32
War of position, 31–35, 37, 39
'Watcher patrols' along the Chittagong, 90
Wavell, General Sir Archibald, 13, 72
Western imperialism, 60–61
Wilfred Burchett, 5, 59
Women's Army Corps, 70
Women's Auxiliary Corps, 2
Woodcock, George, 232-33
Wren, George, 264

Yosake, Matsuoka, 60

Zahir, Mohammed, 265
Zivin, Joselyn A., 91–92, 225, 239, 248